Virginia Wales Johnson

Joseph the Jew

The Story of an old House

Virginia Wales Johnson

Joseph the Jew
The Story of an old House

ISBN/EAN: 9783337133436

Printed in Europe, USA, Canada, Australia, Japan

Cover: Foto ©ninafisch / pixelio.de

More available books at **www.hansebooks.com**

JOSEPH THE JEW.

The Story of an Old House.

"There is a divinity that shapes our ends,
Rough-hew them as we will."

NEW YORK:

HARPER & BROTHERS, PUBLISHERS,

FRANKLIN SQUARE.

1874.

Dedicated

TO

THE GENERAL WHO TOOK THE CITY,

PRESIDENT GRANT.

CONTENTS.

JOSEPH THE JEW.

CHAPTER I.

THE FAMILY SECRET.

"SAMUEL must go," said Uncle Abraham Rost, finishing his portion of rice-gröd, with a relish unimpaired by the fact that his sister Martha had carefully prepared the favorite dish for his supper these thirty years. For the advent of Abraham Rost was hailed as a great event in the household.

"But he leaves Rachel, in that case," returned the father, thoughtfully.

A grave, wrinkled, care-worn man was the father, stooping in gait, yet with a certain dignity of manner. A safe man, the merchants knew, and when he moved one of his pieces in the great game of life, with a thin, firm hand, it was after due deliberation, and the move was never withdrawn.

"Tut! tut!" scoffed Abraham. "I tell thee, I left wife and little ones, early and late, for bread. I crossed the steppes in winter; I never failed yet to be at Nijni-Novgorod every fair; and I traveled in my sledge from house to house in the Baltic provinces, when our need was bitter, after the persecution of our chosen race."

"I know," assented the father, half absently.

"Samuel is a man—not like the other chicken-hearted youngsters," observed Abraham. Out of the gloom peered a face. It was young and soft in outline, but it was terribly eager and wrathful in expression. Uncle Abraham might well look to himself with such a watcher.

The household had retired for the night. Twelve o'clock was the hour chosen by Abraham Rost to discuss important matters with his brother, for he was a very owl for wakefulness.

"The time has come, and we have waited long," pursued the older man, in a half musing strain. "I have saved thaler by thaler; my fortune has been built up of single little coins, and the diamonds that have ceased to delight our eyes by their flashing splendor have brought a safer return in solid gold—eh, brother? Hist! what was that?"

"I heard no sound," said the father, calmly. Uncle Abraham rose from his seat in the radiance of the swinging silver lamp, suspended by chains from the ceiling, and groped about the room. On one side of the low, dark chamber was a wooden stairway, with heavily-carved balustrade, which led to a small door high in the wall. The old man, still suspicious that his keen ear had not deceived him when he fancied he heard a stealthy, suppressed sound, ascended the steps and tried the door.

It was fastened on the other side.

Re-assured, he resumed his arm-chair, and had no sooner done so than the little door flew noiselessly open, and the eager young face appeared among the shadows of the balcony again.

Abraham laid on the table two morocco belts lined with money, a small pouch of coins, and a red Circassian bag, richly embroidered, from which he drew a yellow paper, crumpled and faded. He read aloud:

"Never cease to search for the treasure I lost, my sons. The workmanship was so perfect that it may have possibly been preserved in its original form, if it be not too much taste to expect of a blood-thirsty robber. I had been in the far East, seeking rare gems for our house, when this necklace was sent unexpectedly to reward my toil. How I loved it! How rapturously I gloated over it in secret, until, in the long days at sea, I lost myself in reveries over the future disposition to be made of my treasure. Sometimes I climbed the rigging to be quite alone, and let the sunshine play over the stones, which shot forth rays of splendor, or I leaned over the bulwark in the calm moonlight, holding it in my hand, with the waves breaking in long furrows of changing lights against the prow, pale rose and pure green scintillations, comparing the jewels of the sea below with those of the earth in my grasp. I had heard that the Roman Catholics of Havana, on the island of Cuba, would give great sums for such jewels to adorn the Virgins of their cathedrals. If these failed to give me my price, I would then return home, sure of a market among the princes of Europe. Eagerly I looked for the chain of islands, lying in tropical beauty, surrounded by the sea.

"Before we reached them, an accursed pirate swept down upon us, with guns flashing in every port-hole, boarded us, and rifled us of our possessions. I might well utter the prayer of David the King, 'Lord, deliver me from mine enemies.' I shall see that dog of a Christian, as he stood over me, with my dying eyes. The hatred bred of wrong is unquenchable. He was an English buccaneer, such as then infested the region. The setting sun, shining dully through the smoke, which hung like a pall over us, illumined his form with a blood-red glow; his face was dark with evil passions, and his cold, cruel gray eye chilled the beholder with apprehension. Any deed possible for man to do might readily be ascribed to him, and still the cruel gray eye would search for more. Cowering on the deck, in momentary expectation of death, I yet had time to reflect that if he were not a pirate, he would be something else. What? I searched my bewildered brain, and even in such a tumult the answer was unhesitating—'A madman.'

"He spurned me with his foot.

"'Jews are made of riches; search him,' he commanded.

"'Then my treasure was torn from me. The captain was a silent spectator. The two commanders were both young men; they stood opposite, and measured each other from head to foot. The captain's look expressed plainly wonder, pity, and contempt for the conqueror, which stung more deeply than the wildest ravings of despair. Dissimulation is safest under such circumstances. I dared not raise my eyes from the deck, for fear the pirate should read the helpless rage and defiance seething within me.

"'As we are of the same race, I will let you go,' said the pirate, carelessly.

"'I am ashamed of my race,' replied the captain, firm and low.

"A sudden pallor crept over the other's dark face—or was it only the dipping of the sun beneath the wave? There was a sharp report, a flash, and the captain fell. But it was one of the buccaneering crew that did the deed. My curses have followed the pirate night and day. Find him or his descendants, oh my children, and recover the inheritance of which you have been robbed. I discovered his name—Frederick William Goffe.

"(Signed)   SOLOMON ROST."

Uncle Abraham refolded and replaced the paper with glowing eyes. Even the father's pale face flushed with a kindling enthusiasm.

"Ah! had Providence decreed, we should have found the necklace long ere this; had we not been hampered by troubles, and Manasseh's death out yonder. The young one must undertake it. I tell thee, Samuel is the man. We will unfold our plans when he returns, but the children must know nothing of the secret; it might spread, through such idle babblers, to avaricious brethren. The Wentzels over the way would fly in pursuit. The Lord saw fit to afflict me with girls: had He granted me a son for mine old age, I would have trained him to fulfill his grandfather's command." The sorrow of Abraham Rost's life was that he had no sons.

This great city of the far North, standing in the icy stillness of lingering Arctic winter, and wrapped in a soft snow mantle, had no more curious picture of home life to reveal, that night, than the common living-room of Solomon Rost, the diamond broker's home, presented. The single lofty window, with double sashes excluding the bitter cold, was concealed by a curtain of heavy red cloth; the furniture was plain, with an instinct to avoid display, taught by cruel oppression. A solitary star of light—the silver lamp—gleamed in the centre of the room, framing the two gray heads bowed together in a mellow radiance. Shrouded in a twilight gloom, the great porcelain stove loomed up in one corner, and opposite the wooden stairway wound upward into obscurity, each step farther from the light, even as the young face was destined to recede.

Intense attention marked the attitude of the listener; an increasing confidence on the part of the brothers, as they warmed over a theme, a mystery which had served as the romance of their lives. "So! my grandfather left this secret, and my uncle Manasseh died of yellow fever in the West Indies, searching for a clue," said the young man, drawing a deep breath, and raising himself erect when the others had finally separated for the night.

He passed swiftly through the little door, and came face to face with a woman.

CHAPTER II.

RACHEL.

"WHAT are you doing here?" the girl asked, with both authority and suspicion.

"And you?" questioned the young man, with a perceptible sneer curling his haughty lip—a sneer that gradually changed to an expression of incredulous amazement as he gazed at her.

The girl's wrapping, a gorgeous cloak of Eastern fabric, with silk wrought upon velvet to resemble jewels, and a heavy border of gold fringe, slipped aside, revealing her dress. She bit her lip with vexation. The dropping of the mantle was no intentional feminine artifice; it did not matter what Joseph thought of her.

A delicate lily of snowy purity, upspringing in the forest's deepest recess, could not have afforded a more vivid contrast than did the girl figure to the dark corridor. She was enveloped in gauzy raiment, one frost-work of costly lace. Lustrous pearls were wound in chains about the slender throat, and depended on either side of the oval face, while a coronet of massive braided hair crowned her head, and eyes of wonderful depth and brilliancy proudly confronted the young man.

"Samuel's bride," muttered Joseph, with whitening lips.

"Yes, Samuel's bride," said Rachel, calmly. "I have put on my dress, like any other girl, and am going to the great chamber to see myself in the mirrors. I have stolen Aunt Martha's keys for the purpose."

And then, being a girl conscious of her own beauty, she bent her head gracefully, expressing the "am I not worth looking at?" which she scorned to speak. Joseph's features grew dark with bitter hatred and despair.

"Every thing for Samuel! Life, love, honor, riches! Why were the rest of us born?"

Rachel recoiled, shocked and startled.

"He is your brother; surely you will do him no harm"—anxiously.

"No: I am not a Cain," said Joseph, still looking at her with the unwilling fascination of a man who both loved and hated her. "Well, are you going to tell of me? I have been listening to the father's conversation."

"You are safe with me," returned Rachel, haughtily, and swept away to insert the ponderous key into the door of the sacred great chamber.

This state apartment had once been fitted for the reception of a prince of the Hebrew race, a great banker and statesman, who was the confidential friend of emperors, and who wore more noble orders on his breast than royalty itself. Rachel stood on the threshold of the lofty room, and held her lamp above her head. Venetian mirrors, framed in silver, lined the walls; the floor was polished wood, in mosaic patterns, with a Persian carpet laid in the centre; amber satin curtains shrouded the bed and windows; the chairs and sofas were solid ebony and amber satin, relieved by graceful festoons of lace. A chandelier of pure cut crystal held wax-tapers, half consumed. Indian vases wafted still a lingering aromatic perfume.

There were pictures in that dim light. Andrea del Sarto was reproduced in Cæsar receiving tribute of birds and wild animals, instead of the Pietà. Leonardo da Vinci, by a copy of the Leda, instead of the Last Supper. Raffaelo, even, by his heathen philosophies, rather than the tender Madonna and Child. Nowhere was Christ to be seen.

At the end of the room a satin curtain was looped back, forming the portal to an alcove. The velvet divan, the wine jar, the pipe with long stem and jeweled mouth-piece, the leather pouch of Latakia denoted its purpose. Beside the divan a tiny table of ebony supported, on a bronze salver, a pitcher shaped like a bird, exquisitely tinted purple and amber, with ribbed glass handle, and two shallow cups with iridized fluted rims, and richly incrusted sides. A second alcove beyond was a marble bath.

The silence and desertion of the great chamber was dispelled by a charming, fleeting vision. In every mirror grew a luminous form out of the mist of bridal veil. Rachel, beholding her image, yielded to the irresistible impulse of self-admiration, and, placing her lamp on a table, posed in beautiful attitudes, her draperies now flung back, with arms wreathed above her head, and again wrapping herself close in ghostly white folds.

She was interrupted in these girlish freaks by the sudden appearance of Aunt Martha in night-cap and dressing-gown, who speedily relocked the great chamber, and bore away the culprit. She was amazed at Rachel's audacity. Besides, the wedding-dress worn before the time was, in her estimation, an ill omen.

Aunt Martha was watchful guardian through all the silent hours of night. Not a mouse gnawed behind the wainscot but she heard it, and was on the alert for robbers. The Rost family had been diamond brokers for generations, the sons being instructed in the business at an early age, and succeeding the fathers regularly. The father was the actual head of the house ; but Uncle Abraham, whose restless nature tended to greater activity, traversed Europe in search of fine stones. Every instinct of their lives prevented them from adopting the mode of living of many families in their midst, occupying a floor in some large building. The Rosts must live entirely to themselves, not because their ways were evil, but secretive. The house was plain and old ; the office in one portion, and the family having possession of the rest.

Every night a strong box was brought to the father's bed-chamber, so heavy that three clerks lifted it, and because of the box Aunt Martha listened for robbers. She importuned the father to have an iron door with filagree openings set to his chamber, secured by a bar ; she made him burn a lamp, and at any hour of the night she might have been seen gliding to the iron door, to see if the father slept and the box was safe.

Not for worlds would the Rosts have had it known in the city that their house boasted an apartment like the great chamber. To be sure, the days of heavy tribulation were past ; yet the safest course with the descendants of rulers who had extorted the uttermost farthing from Jews, was to avoid a display of wealth.

"We do our best in our humble way," Aunt Martha would remark, with an hypocrisy which fear had taught her. Had one of her neighbors, Christian or Israelite, inquired what the great chamber contained, she would have unhesitatingly replied, "Rubbish! It was a lumber-room."

In the mean while Joseph had gone to his own room, and stood beside the couch of the other occupant. A faint white gleam stole in the casement from the snow-covered street and roofs, tinging with an unearthly pallor the sleeper's face, which was as spiritually sweet as the face bent over it was morose. These two were twin brothers, and the mother had died in giving them birth.

The sleeping Benjamin was as faultless as the perfection of delicately chiseled features and a blameless life could render him. The waking Joseph had already lines of premature manhood, which would possibly bring sharp contests and sorrows, and as yet had none of manhood's philosophy ; lines which Benjamin's smooth brow would never know, for he was blind. All that was tender and generous in the Rost nature was lavished on him. His existence was made one of music in flower-scented nooks, of caressing words and unrebuked caprices, of summer excursions to the palace, of intoxicating delight at the theatre, where Holberg moved to laughter, and Olenschläger inspired awe. If there were selfishness and sin in the world, he had not discovered it, for the father jealously guarded the bloom of his innocence, and was ever watchful to ward off disease that might dull the transparent skin, or taint the soul.

Habitually the family laid aside their grosser selves when they entered the presence of Benjamin ; while so startling was his serene beauty, that involuntary praise followed his steps in the streets. Unconsciously, Joseph's whole youth had been a sacrifice to his brother. He had served as eyes and ears, a rougher, firmer bulwark of strength, to protect his tender helplessness.

Joseph had a separate life, the one of education in school and college, which was to fit him to do battle with the world ; Benjamin had no separate life from Joseph. The harmonies that flowed through Solomon Rost's mansion were interwoven by the twins. Deftly Joseph's bow sped over the vibrating chords of his precious Cremona violin, while Benjamin's white fingers glided over the piano keys.

To Joseph age seemed possible, in the fretting wear and tear of daily routine ; Benjamin was imperishable youth in its most ethereal-ized type.

The following day was the feast of Pesach. The preparation for and observance of religious services were always strictly discharged by the diamond brokers. There had never been a backslider from the faith of their fathers among the race.

For three days before Pesach, glass utensils were immersed in water, copper and iron vessels purified by fire, and the whole house cleansed. The appointed fasts had been kept, and the second day — Enf Pesach — sacredly observed, because on that day the Lord slew the first-born of Egypt, and Israel was spared. The previous night Solomon Rost had passed through every room with a wooden bowl and quill, to detect stray morsels of food. Aunt Martha took care that he should find some scraps in his progress, as that was expected. At dark the family assembled around the table, where the Paschal Lamb was served with unleavened bread and bitter herbs.

The father presided in a white linen robe. This robe was the epitome of Hebrew manhood. Presented to the bridegroom by the bride, it was ever after kept to be worn at the Passover, at Yokmkipur, feast of reconciliation, and when he was laid in his coffin.

The father's face was always sad when he appeared thus arrayed: the hands had long since crumbled to dust that wrought the precious garment.

On his right hand sat Uncle Abraham, and on the left Benjamin, whose Oriental imagination clothed religion with all the splendors of worship belonging to Solomon's Temple. He saw the priests and the cherubim, the ark of the covenant, the ivory throne. Uncle Abraham was especially to be revered, because he had journeyed to Jerusalem to pray for the restoration of his people in the wailing-place of the Jews. Aunt Martha wore her white hair brushed back in a massive roll, like the Russian ladies, a black velvet gown, and a broad collaret of yellow gold. Rachel, in a gay silk skirt, muslin stomacher, embroidered with silver, and purple velvet jacket, was so quiet and self-possessed that she could not have been recognized as the radiant figure of the previous night.

She watched Joseph furtively from her place by the chair of her betrothed, the absent Samuel.

The young man was pale and taciturn.

The doors of all the rooms were opened wide by a servant, for the entrance of the Holy Spirit, and then Solomon Rost read from the book of the captivity in Egypt.

A profound silence ensued.

Benjamin listened with parted lips, as if for the rustle of wings.

Suddenly a figure appeared with uncovered head. Rachel uttered an exclamation of joy. Joseph turned white, and glared at the intruder.

Swathed in furs until he seemed a movable mountain of wraps, cap of sea-otter, gloves of yellow fox, Samuel Rost, fresh from his Lapland journey, stood in the door-way.

CHAPTER III.

JOSEPH'S FLIGHT.

"WHERE is Joseph?" complained Benjamin. Several hours had elapsed since Samuel's return, and the harmony of the meal had been further disturbed by Uncle Abraham—superstitious in the extreme—discovering a pin in his meat.

"Unclean!" muttered the strong man, dropping his knife in dismay.

"The priest's seal was set upon it," maintained Aunt Martha, whose housewifely dignity was assailed.

But Uncle Abraham did not recover from the shock, which he persisted in regarding as a misfortune.

"It never happened before at such a season," he said, gloomily; and at his words a strange chill of apprehension stole over the family group. Then it was that the blind brother asked for Joseph, whose absence was noticed for the first time. A servant was dispatched in search of him.

Old Gottlieb returned and beckoned Aunt Martha away, silently. She returned with a troubled mien, which she vainly endeavored to render composed.

"What is it, woman?" asked Uncle Abraham, harshly.

Benjamin lifted his head like a startled fawn.

In vain Uncle Abraham sought to clumsily laugh away his sharp question, which had produced more alarm even than Aunt Martha's startled countenance. In vain they soothed Benjamin, and tried to lead him away. He refused to move.

"You are deceiving me," he cried, turning from one to the other; "I too will hear the truth." Then the thunder-bolt crashed down. Joseph had gone away!

In his room Aunt Martha discovered a letter, which the father opened:

"I go without the father's blessing. Forgive me. Time will prove if Samuel is the only man of our race. I know the family secret; I have taken the papers and money. It is useless to send Samuel after me; I shall maintain the advantage of being first. Let him remain at home for Rachel's sake. If I am successful, I will return. If not, forget me. The Lord be with Benjamin!   JOSEPH."

As a river, born in high mountain cradles, and flowing quietly through sequestered valleys, suddenly sweeps into rushing current and foaming cataract, rending a channel through ravines, so Joseph's manhood had come. As a volcano jets living flame where flowers have bloomed, so the repressed fire of the younger son's jealous hatred of Samuel, chafing in subterranean channels long, burst forth, amazing the family with its fury.

The father had intended to be just in rearing his sons, lavishing all the care on their education in which the superior class of his people delight, but he had made the fatal error of treating Joseph still as a youth for Benjamin's sake. Unintentionally he had slighted the masculine fibre in his second son, wishing to keep him at home for companionship to the darkened life. Samuel might assume the double burden of responsibility and success which his bold, ambitious nature craved.

Now Joseph's right had asserted itself, and the father discovered it all too late.

"The dolt! The young fool!" stormed Uncle Abraham. "He has ruined our enterprise by his presumption. Overtake him! Make him repent of his madness."

"Nay, father, Joseph is no fool," said Rachel.

"Of what has the young whelp robbed me?" questioned Samuel.

"He has gone to the New World in thy place," groaned Uncle Abraham.

"Who calls Joseph a fool?" cried Aunt Martha, shrilly. "Give the lad a chance and he will equal Samuel any day."

When the twins lay in one cradle, two little round heads exactly alike, the Rabbi placed a gold piece and the horn on them, to avert the Evil Eye; and his blessing for Joseph was: 'He shall be strong like Judah, and have the riches of Asher.'"

Benjamin stretched forth his hands with a groping, fluttering movement, and his soft, sightless eyes wore a mournful expression as he murmured, in Hebrew, "Why hast thou forsaken me, oh my brother?"

Then the father and Uncle Abraham rent their clothes and bowed their heads.

Rachel alone was happy. Joseph had gone for her sake, and she was grateful. Now Samuel was spared to her. She nestled close to her betrothed, admiring his robust form, his handsome face, and curling auburn beard.

"Thou art safe!" she whispered.

Samuel's black brows met in a sharp frown; his thoughts were not of Rachel. If he could have reached the fugitive, he would have smitten him down. He thrust her aside.

"Why do we stay moping here? He has only the start of three hours. The ports are not yet open."

Uncle Abraham exclaimed, "Right, lad! Bring out the sledge."

The father spoke for the first time, slowly and distinctly.

"Samuel may follow to the Small Belt; and if he has reached the other side, Joseph shall go in peace."

Filial reverence was exacted by the father before all other considerations; Samuel bit his lip savagely.

The sledge and horse were gone.

A curse rose from Samuel's heart at the delay. Another vehicle was procured, and he drove away into the silent night. Rachel stood at the window, watching his departure; he had passed her without a glance. Joseph had his revenge, if he desired it, for the dark cloud of discontent even now rested on her lips. She was bound to Samuel by one of the long betrothals of the North, and he would always regard her as the obstacle which prevented him from going to the New World. If reality would dissipate glory, Samuel's imagination for life must picture the dream in glowing colors.

"I wish that I might never wear the brid-

al dress. What prize am I, compared to gold!"

Aunt Martha, who sat weeping after the excitement, smiled sadly. In her day she had loved a Christian, and refused to wed. Benjamin folded Joseph's letter on his breast, where it was found when he died.

In the mean while Joseph had matured and executed a plan, which first took root when he overheard the family discussion, and Samuel proposed as emissary.

By nature and circumstance both crafty and secretive, he evinced no interest until Samuel returned. The moment had arrived; he acted with prompt decision. He wrote his letter; found, in a desk in Uncle Abraham's chamber, the money, belts, papers, and pouch of coin; slipped his violin into a shagreen bag; and, wrapped in a fur cloak, stole from the house. It was the work of a few moments to harness the horse to the sledge, and with one searching, farewell glance to disappear.

At that hour the city was brilliant with life and gayety, yet the presence of lingering winter gave to the metropolis a solemn covering of white snow, suggestive of the ice-cliffs linking distant shores in crystal fetters, of frozen seas, and the vast fields of desolation bounded by the midnight sun. The Oster Gade was illuminated from end to end, the light from spacious windows shedding rosy gleams on flitting forms and cold streets. From the two broad, airy market-places—the Amargatorf and the Kongens Nytorf—wide streets diverged, throbbing arteries of the city's warm life; but winter had laid an iron grasp on the shipping, holding masts and hulls in rigid suspense of motion.

A sob rose in the fugitive's throat as he looked back on the beloved home spread out before his gaze, low and flat, with the palace looming up above the domes and spires. How he loved the naked beech-trees, the chain of islets, the childhood memories of good Bishop Absalom! How he wished he had embraced Benjamin; won a smile from Rachel before he fled! above all, received the father's blessing!

Goaded rather than softened by these reflections, the young man turned away, setting his face steadily forward. What if he should be overtaken through lingering to indulge in sentimental fancies?

Samuel's mocking laughter seemed to follow him, urging greater speed.

The mysterious influences of spring were everywhere silently at work, rilling through the earth's rigid frost mask. The snow was no longer a firm pavement, and Joseph's sledge grated in many spots over the ground. This made his progress often painful and slow. The fever rose in his veins; he glanced frequently over his shoulder to see if he was pursued; he spurred on his flagging steed. Reaching the water at last, he paused at bay. Was he to be thwarted, checked, and turned back now? Spring-time was at work on the water, no longer with gentle fairies that tinkled and purled as on the earth, but with the labor of Titans, sapping the ice with mighty currents, smiting the winter fetters in crashing battle, gathering hills of huge green blocks, and leaving an unbroken plane of the crystal surface between, rolling in continuous ripples above the swell.

Unsafe to cross in sledge, impassable by boat, Joseph Rost scanned the barrier far and wide. No hope. But just at the climax of his agony he glanced back, and saw Samuel approaching at furious speed. Joseph looked once, twice, then urged his reluctant steed out on the trembling strait.

"Stop, fool!" shouted Samuel, reining up.

Joseph cracked his whip; rapid motion was the only safety. The horse flew; the ice cracked with startling concussions; the groaning, submarine thunder warned of danger; water gushed up in the track behind.

The horse flew, but the whole space was in motion; the ramparts heaved; the glittering pinnacles toppled forward; a yawning blue chasm grew and grew above.

They were on a slender, brittle ice-bridge; they were on a twirling island; they were on a transparent raft—then the horse slipped, the sledge disappeared, but the man, on a single cake, was nearing the opposite shore, and the free waves were singing their song of release to a new year.

Thus stood the two brothers on opposite shores.

"Curse thy ungrateful child," prayed Uncle Abraham. But the father uttered no curse, yet he gave no blessing.

Thus Joseph Rost crossed the line of the future.

CHAPTER IV.

THE FAIRY ISLES.

THE steamship approached land. She swept in grandly from the far horizon of distance, churning the wide, tranquil sea into foam, threaded her way among the tortuous windings of the coral channel safely, and dropped anchor in port.

Among the motley crowd on her deck a young man stood silently but rapidly scanning the shore.

He beheld a chain of tiny islands, linked together by sharp-fanged reefs, and anchored, as it were, on the broad bosom of the ocean; born of volcanic throes, built up from submarine depths in many an arch and column by the busy coral polyps, and fringed by all the beauties of the tropics. A miniature world, isolated, and unlike any other portion of the earth's surface, swept by the tempest's wrath, sunny and smiling in the bland caresses of the south wind, with the ships coming and going, messenger birds of the distant great continents.

The stranger on the steamer's deck had beheld the low rim of cloud grow to a level shore, with a line of white, firm road winding along above the breakers' crested margin, where the surf masses rolled, and houses were visible beyond, framed in stunted palmetto groves.

Now they had paused in a harbor before a town. The harbor was inclosed by gently undulating hills, and the clear, pellucid water mirrored the tapering masts and graceful hull of a vessel here—shaded from turquoise blue to vivid emerald and rose, as it rippled over some sandy beach, and revealed in its pure depths the delicate sea-weed forests, brainstones, and purple fans, waving slowly in the current, where fish, in gorgeous mail of silver and gold, darted about in quivering flashes of light. The town was narrow, crooked, and quaint. Rising from the harbor's brink, and

sloping up an acclivity sufficiently steep to render the ill-paved streets precipitous, and to place the houses one above the other, it presented a confused mass of stone wall and roof, whitewashed to dazzling brilliancy, most painful to the eye beneath that hot sun. The summit of the hill was finally crowned by a fort, signal station, and soldiers' barracks.

The passengers landed on the low quay, and made their way to the open square beyond; and, in so doing, added their own individuality to the curious mixture of nationalities there collected.

It was Sunday; yet, owing to a common cause of excitement, the square presented any thing but a Protestant sobriety of appearance.

Troops of the line, clad in scarlet, passed constantly, with stiff, military bearing; groups of engineers and artillerymen, resplendent in blue and gold, lounged about verandas; and jolly Jack Tars lurched along, carrying their shoes and a bottle slung over one shoulder, each wearing a big rose in his button-hole —emblem of a day on shore. Eager, sallow-hued Americans conversed with placid, blonde Englishmen; a Frenchman gesticulated to a grave Spaniard; gangs of low-browed, swarthy men, gathered from the worst elements of all races under heaven, awaited orders or smoked in idleness. These last were the crews of vessels.

Truly, the birds of prey had gathered from afar on the Fairy Isles.

Everywhere strolled merry, careless negroes, some in rags, some in gaudy finery, children of the plenty of the hour, unvexed by the cares which drew sharp lines in the white faces about them.

Tucker (lineal descendant of old Dan, possibly) lay on his back in the sun, basking among the lizards, eating bananas, his black, beady eyes twinkling over the newly-arrived strangers.

Susan, in her striped organdie muslin, brass ear-rings, and yellow turban, cared not that the week would bring its inevitable burden of soiled linen, to be laid on rocks and pounded with stones (Susan's mode of cleansing), as long as she could flaunt her present splendor.

Old Mahala, with an eye to the main chance, had driven her sturdy little donkey into town early, and stood beside the small wagon heaped high with amber-tinted Lisbon lemons, clusters of Loquot plums among their own cool, green leaves, and great globes of shaddocks. Flags fluttered from many houses in a fitful breeze that made the colors of France salute Austria across the way; those of Belgium and Italy droop one instant, and the next fling abroad, as if in mutual defiance, the starred banner of the United States and the white emblem of the then Confederacy. The young man gazed long and earnestly at a red standard with painful emotions, and uncovered his head reverently to the ensign of King Christian. Few persons had noticed him; men's thoughts were engrossed by the one anxiety of the day; but as he stood before the flag, a small, bent figure turned, glanced at him, with a sudden recognition leaping out of the greenish gray eyes.

Moving slowly back toward the quay, the young man won a ready knowledge of the cause of this general condition of expectancy by the ease with which his tongue glided from one language to another. This gift is possessed, to a remarkable degree, by Northern nations.

"The *Swan* is overdue, and we are watching for her," said a captain, in reply to a question.

"I am watching for her also," returned the young man, smiling.

He was grave and reticent, but he made his way. The captain stroked his sandy mustache, and eyed the other a moment, then nodded encouragingly.

"Going to run in, eh? Well, the *Swan's* the best craft afloat, and the men are a plucky lot. I don't mind saying that, although my tub down yonder has never been caught yet."

The crowd in the square had waxed impatient, gloomy, or reckless, according to their several natures. Where was the *Swan*, already famous for her success?

Probably many of them had staked their all on this one vessel. They had cast their dice on a perilous throw in this, the gambling game of the nineteenth century, par excellence, and would be encouraged to further hazard if she won.

Groups had gathered on house-tops with telescopes; individuals climbed elevated spots for a first glimpse; all eyes were fixed on the signal-station pole.

Suddenly the ball ran up the pole, dipped, and remained stationary. Then a distant murmur echoed along the hills, and gathered to a jubilant shout as it rolled through the town. Reaction from doubt and despair was the maddest ecstasy. Men gave way to extravagant rejoicings; they wrung the hands of known foes; they embraced; they wept.

The *Swan* was safe, and they were rich!

Infected insensibly by the general enthusiasm, and the entire novelty of the scene, the young man watched the *Swan* approach.

A low, slender-built vessel, wearing her gay pennons streaming much as a coquette does holiday ribbons, she glided through the water like a snake, until within range of the shouts of welcome which greeted her from the shore.

"One would imagine they owned the islands," said a harsh, nasal voice in Danish.

The young man wheeled round, and surveyed the small, bent figure with amazement.

"Reuben Wentzel!"

"Joseph Rost!"

CHAPTER V.

AT THE POOL.

THE two men were well matched. If Reuben Wentzel, by virtue of his superior age and experience, fancied that he was to obtain an advantage over his young countryman, he was mistaken. The close visor of Joseph's cold, proud features had been raised for an instant, revealing surprise and annoyance; afterward it fitted down with impenetrable reserve.

A meeting with prying, peering Reuben, at this juncture, was unfortunate. The Wentzels were vastly inferior in social position to the Rost family, and that, too, in a race where the distinctions between rich and poor are rigidly maintained.

Joseph's earliest instinct of childhood may have been contemptuous superiority for the cringing, servile Wentzels over the way, who were sometimes employed by the diamond brokers in a menial capacity, and invited to sit at feasts below the salt.

As for Reuben, he was on the *qui vive* of curiosity to know what had sent young Rost to this quarter of the globe. On the other hand, young Rost intended to take particularly good care that his newly-found acquaintance should not discover the actual object of his mission.

"It is pleasant to meet one from fatherland out here," observed Reuben, smoothly, when a somewhat constrained silence had followed the first rapid greeting.

"If the person is a welcome friend," returned Joseph. He had not yet been able to decide what course to pursue with Wentzel, the rencontre had been so sudden; but his first impulse was to erect such a barrier of haughtiness, founded on his own higher rank, that Wentzel would leave him alone for the future.

Perhaps Uncle Abraham and the father would have crossed weapons with Reuben instead, tried the subtler art of deceit in exact measure for measure, yet Joseph, the novice, felt a conviction that it would require a consummate actor to deceive Reuben's ferret eye.

Observe, we are not describing an Anglo-Saxon youth, bluff and honest, but the son of a people whose aims and operations have, from necessity, followed circuitous avenues of thought for ages.

Reuben chuckled as if vastly amused by the other's curtness.

"We are all equals in America, remember. My faith! A different lesson from Denmark. Who would have thought of seeing young Rost, the college student, out here? Is Benjamin with you?"

"Herr Benjamin Rost is at home."

"Ah, yes. There's money to be made, lad, when a country is at war. Did the uncle think of that?"

His familiar tone galled the young man, but he kept his temper under control, well knowing that Reuben's aim might be to throw him off his guard and reveal more than was wise, in a hasty burst of wrath.

"I have an enterprise in South Carolina; share it with me," said Wentzel, earnestly, laying his hand on Joseph's sleeve.

Joseph shook off the touch disdainfully, and replied, coldly:

"I am less likely to share your projects than you are to divide mine. You are old enough to learn the lesson I was taught from the cradle."

"And what may the lesson have been, my pretty boy," interrupted Reuben, with an ugly sneer.

"If a Hebrew does not often trust a Christian, still less frequently does he trust one of his own kind," said Joseph, slowly and distinctly.

"As you please," retorted Reuben, shrugging his shoulders. "If you are not too *old* to learn, I will quote to you the Spanish proverb: 'Hast thou one friend, it is not enough. Hast thou one enemy, it is too many.'"

Joseph laughed scornfully, and turned away. The face of his late companion grew dark with anger, not entirely because the young man's insolence had stung him—insolence in every form had too frequently been his portion—but because his hatred of the more prosperous Rost family was kindled by the sight of one of them. What venture had they out here? Was he to be foiled by a mere stripling? Already he hungered to solve the secret of Joseph's mission and share the spoils, yet his very greediness rendered him precipitate. As a natural result, he watched Joseph day and night.

And Joseph? Waiting for the blockader to be ready for her voyage, he spent long days rambling through avenues where the oleanders extended for miles in twin rows of rosy bloom; or he sought gently-curved dells, cups lined with green moss velvet, dewy and cool, where the rocks rose steep, draped exquisitely by nature with delicate fern fronds, plumes and tufts of starry flowers, vines clinging with emerald-tinted, transparent fingers to the face of the stone; while air-plants twined their clustering blossoms, and spread waxy, thick leaves, icy-cold to the touch, as a parapet.

At times his gaze rested on country houses, with low, sloping verandas and detached slave-quarters, deserted long ago, set in a tangled wilderness of palms, orange and papaw trees, golden-fruited, dank, stained, and dark, where sluggish centipedes crept, and huge tarantulas lurked in the gloom for prey.

At times he explored the dim recesses of coral caves, with arch-fretted dome depending glittering stalactites, where the sea stole in limpid ripples out of the sunlight, and the purple-rayed anemones expanded silky tentacles to the tide.

Again, he flung himself on the strand, slipped the tiny, perfect rice-shells through his fingers, watching idly the sea-birds wheel in rapid flight, and the cedar smoke curl from the chimneys, fragrant as incense.

All about him stirred the mysterious impulses of a world of which he took no heed. Lo! from the door of his pearl mansion, with whorled roof and cunning device of architectural design, stepped a fairy crab on that wide plain of the unknown—Joseph's hand. The young man looked curiously at this atom of the crustacea, in lustrous armor arrayed, and the little crab looked at him, until, terrified by the vastness of the subject, it skurried back into the shell. "This thing is too wonderful for me. I must ask the lobster what it means," reflected the crab. The man tossed the shell carelessly away, and sat with moody brows.

A sea-egg rolled along the brink of the water, a crimson ball of bristling spines—far too insignificant for Joseph to notice, absorbed in his own affairs; but soon the sea-egg, with the aid of wee pickaxe and shovel, would hollow out for itself a cave in the cliff, where it might rest secure, and the dancing waves would bring food to the very door. Could Joseph achieve more in his day, than to drill a habitation in the living granite of his universe?

In the great deep around, countless flower-heads crowned the submerged reefs, the masons and builders of the ocean laboring quietly, united by a common life, working for a single purpose, then perishing when their destiny was fulfilled. Would the young man on the shore raise firm battlements and castles of right to oppose the restless main, or would he join the army of waves trooping onward to crumble such fair foundations?

A coral-builder instead of a wasting billow, Joseph Rost, although ignorant of it yourself.

Constantly he carried the thought of Reuben's watchfulness with him, and turned it over in his mind. Although it troubled, it did not actually alarm him. Instinctively he was bracing himself for the struggle, in whatever form it might come; and when once he had left these islands he need be no longer annoyed by close proximity with his enemy.

People are very apt to underrate the power of enemies to work their injury in this world. They are contented to go their way peaceably; why may not the mischief-makers? But the mischief-makers are not satisfied, prompted by malice or envy; and so harm is done, by total inaction on one side and excessive activity on the other. If it requires two to make a quarrel, it is also possible for one to drag the other into final altercation, and rejoice in the achievement. It is also possible for men and women to hate intensely those they have never seen, from preference and precedence accorded them. Reuben might hate Joseph for being a Rost; but Joseph, who had always tasted the sweets of that lot, and never the bitter dregs pertaining to a Wentzel, would not be likely to fathom the depth of the emotion. Thus, on the

Fairy Isles were pent up some of the basest, most selfish passions of the human heart.

Joseph wished nothing of Wentzel, felt no interest in his success or failure, despised his vulgar exterior, and most emphatically intended that he should not meddle with his own business.

Wentzel, on the contrary, determined to possess Joseph's secret, if not by fair means, by foul; for he was proud of his cunning. To say that he was disappointed by the young man's reception of him, thousands of miles from home, and under circumstances which would render a familiar face welcome, would be true; yet he was only piqued by a first failure to redoubled exertion.

There was fatal leisure for plotting and reflecting — those tropical days on the Fairy Isles.

At last the time for sailing approached; the *Swan* would start next morning. Joseph roused himself from apathy; for his external indolence seemed apathy, whatever his mental activity might be.

Before the sun has run its course, and sunk again beyond the horizon, as it was then doing, painting water and sky with crimson glories, he would be far on his way. The mirage of sunset held strange cloud-phantoms suspended in rose mist for a moment, and vanished in the clear expanse of evening sky. Then the moon sailed up the heavens, large, soft, and mellow, shedding a wealth of silvery radiance over the broad track of waters. Tremulous rays of moonbeams quivered through the masses of foliage; the roofs of the town glittered like marble in the pale light.

Here and there a mountain cabbage-palm reared a slender column and feathery crown; the mahogany-tree spread black and motionless above the broad space of road; every spike of the Spanish bayonets, bristling over the garden wall, gleamed; and from the garden floated the mingled perfume of jasmine, allspice, and orange blossoms.

A holy calm seemed to brood over the place on snowy pinions. The sad plash of the pulsing tide, the sharp tap of a drum, the careless mirth of negro laughter, occasionally smote the ear, succeeded by restful silence.

Two men met suddenly on a lonely height.

"Still interested in me?" questioned Joseph, mockingly. "I assure you it is useless."

Reuben nearly lost his temper.

"Young one! I am a better friend than foe," he warned, shaking one yellow forefinger. "Let me help you, and I am your servant for-

ever; cast me off and I will work you deadly injury."

"Do not threaten *me*, Reuben Wentzel," said Joseph, sternly, all his manhood on the mettle. He walked on.

Reuben resembled a fox as much as it is possible for a human being to look like an animal. A rusty, red fringe of hair encircled his sharp face, rising above the forehead in a thick brush, in the manner of Reynard's fur. A narrow head, high cheek-bones, long, thin nose, with eyebrows meeting and describing an upward curve toward the temples, and small eyes, set close together, completed the similarity. To see Reuben softly tracing the steps of men, or cogitating in his burrow, reminded one forcibly that his own brothers of the animal kingdom trotted through sheltered paths of the Black Forest, and doubled back cleverly on the hunters, obliterating their traces in the snow by means of their own plumy tails. Yet he had never been specially successful. His very greed of gain was against him; and the world claims, in its transactions, a larger return of honest equivalent than Reuben was likely to give.

The road turned abruptly, and descended to the shore. The ocean had here hollowed out a sheltered cove, where the water now spread like a crystal shield, with a sparkling ripple flashing and breaking along the sand. On one side the ocean lapsed, on the other was a deep pool, fed by subterranean rills, and protected by a railing around the margin. The spot was entirely secluded.

Half of the road lay in ink-black shadow flung by the overhanging hill, while opposite stretched the dazzling splendor of the moonlit sea, every crest flecked by changing, flickering reflections. A negro hut, perched above, afforded shelter to the owner of the pool.

Joseph leaned over the railing, and gazed into the shadowy depths with a strange fascination. Dusky shapes flitted far below, growing out of obscurity, and melting into it again.

"Tush! A Wentzel is far too prudent to do me an injury," he deliberated, dropping a pebble into the water, and watching the wide rings circle from it.

Instantly the dusky forms below became animated, and rose to the surface. They were large fish, with gorgeous scales, protruding eyes that stared cruelly in search of prey, and mouths which gaped, revealing broad, scarlet throats, as if stained with the blood of victims. Was it the moonbeams resting on the pool, or did a pallid phosphorescence mark their sinuou-

movements? In this pen the fish were fed and fattened for the table of epicures.

Joseph's arms were suddenly pinioned to his side, and the upper portion of his body thrust far over the frail railing, which creaked beneath his weight. The fish glared up at him in expectant suspense; he gazed back at them in horrible agony. It was as if voracious, cannibal death waited to devour reluctant, animated life. Terror paralyzed him. Dull sounds rung in his ears, perhaps his own knell. A white film floated between him and the pool, out of which gazed earnestly the shadowy faces of Rachel and Benjamin. Oh, the leaden agony of suspense! The more fearful dread of fulfillment!

"Well, have you seen enough?" said the man behind, with a grating laugh. "I am tempted to drop you. I told you I was a better friend than foe. Make me a friend."

Joseph had remained passive in his grasp, with remarkable presence of mind, fearing that any struggle would break the railing, and precipitate both into the pool. Of a lithe and agile build, he now concentrated all his energies into one unexpected, backward spring, which made his captor reel, and twisting around, seized the other, raised him from the ground, with nerves strung to steel by intense excitement, and threw him to a distance, where he fell stunned and senseless.

The moon shone down upon strange scenes that night—the struggle of armies, the plotting of monarchs, souls born, souls departing; yet, surely, there were few more startling than the silent strife between these two men on the quiet shore of the peaceful islands. "It was but a jest," muttered Reuben, rising slowly, and looking vacantly around.

He was alone.

CHAPTER VI.

RUNNING THE BLOCKADE.

A SLENDER, graceful craft, built for stealthy treachery her enemies affirmed, for lawful speed her friends protested. In color, a part of the leaden, twilight waters and dim horizon; in progress, noiseless, ever ready to turn in her own length of water, the *Swan* was the choicest stake of the gamblers.

Her crew was a curious assortment of men, at once reckless and anxious, bound together by a common interest in danger, yet each moving in a separate atmosphere of suspicion and mystery. Not an officer failed to take some private venture in quinine or liquor, and indulged in pleasurable anticipations, during the voyage, of fabulous prices paid in a war-smitten land.

At the last moment the captain came off in a gig, laden with honors by his friends ashore; for the Fairy Isles were enlisted heart and soul in the cause, although much was said about occupying neutral ground.

Then the *Swan* steamed away, and the Fairy Isles faded from palm-crowned beach to a cloud line, where a star flashed and waned against the clear sky, as the light-house turret shed a warning beacon over the sea.

Oddly enough, Joseph Rost and Reuben Wentzel were fellow-passengers; the latter submissively conciliatory, the former more affable than formerly.

In fear of being summoned before the authorities, Reuben sought Joseph after the struggle at the pool. Joseph betrayed little resentment, and accepted Reuben's statement that he was in jest.

"Of course a man of your prudence would not be rash enough to get into trouble. Never repeat it. I warn you. There! We will forget it."

"You are generous," said Reuben, doubtfully.

On board the *Swan* all were strangers, all bent on gain, running to one goal, and fearing to be outstripped by a more successful competitor.

The taciturn captain moved among them, ever ready to detect treachery and punish it; the *Swan* in her race for life could by no means afford to harbor traitors.

The captain was a squarely-built, muscular man, with a tinge of Welsh blood in his proud face, black-bearded, the shaven mouth revealing thin lips, which closed like a spring, and parted very slightly to give egress to his few words. He wore a havelock, the dazzling white linen affording a striking relief to the bronze face, and a superb intaglio ring on the third finger. Passengers on the *Swan* knew as little about the captain as he did about them. Rumor dealt with his rank, and raised him to a baronetcy. Names? He rejoiced in half a dozen, all of which suited him equally well.

Two other men on board attracted Joseph's attention. One was a tall, erect veteran, scarred in many battles, and turning toward a war from the ends of the earth, if need be, as naturally as birds of prey gather to the feast. This soldier had witnessed all the campaigns of his day, had braved the Crimean snows, served under Garibaldi, and with equal ardor aided Austria; his keen glance, now, was directed to the New World.

The other was a small, limp man, wrapped in a faded cloak, who lounged listlessly against the bulwark, and appeared to see nothing. Joseph could not determine whether he wore a wig or not, but certain it was that the insignificant little man beheld more than was apparent.

The *Swan* slid over the tranquil waters, threaded daintily the sullen billows of that dark, blue ribbon, the Gulf Stream, and saw, on the right hand or the left, no danger. The sun ran its course twice, and the captain paced the deck, one monotonous round, smoking cheroots incessantly, while his eagle glance swept the horizon. Others might droop with the unnatural strain of fatigue and suspense, but the captain never did. Each successive morning found him at his post, composed and wakeful, sipping café noir, a palor growing in his swarthy face.

The third day dawned, murky, hot, foggy, and the *Swan* altered her previous rate of speed. She drifted irresolutely on the surging waves, toy of the elements apparently, and part of the shifting mists.

"We could not have more favorable weather," the captain observed.

Toward evening the vessel ceased to sport with wind and waves; every thing denoted a change. It was as if the bow—each man a muscle fibre—was bent to the work, and the arrow fitted to win the mark. Hovering on the verge of obscurity eager eyes could discern a blur of stationary light in the fog. The seal of silence stamped the whole crew, yet it was a stillness electric with purpose. Figures moved about, as if shod with velvet, and obeyed gestures; smoke-stacks were lowered; the very machinery of motion ran in oiled grooves.

"Steer for the admiral's light," commanded the captain, scarcely above a whisper, but every soul heard.

Joseph turned to look at him. Awaiting with the zest of intense enjoyment the issue of his dangerous enterprise, the veins beat in his olive cheek, his hand clenched over the telescope he held, and a defiant exultation expanded his whole person. Peril was to him an exhilarating tonic. He had played hide-and-seek with violent death all his life, and was contented to so poise the balance until the end. Reuben Wentzel sank down on the deck, clasped his hands, and groaned aloud.

A terrible light flashed in the captain's eye: without uttering a word, he lifted the Jew and dropped him down the companion way. Then he motioned contemptuously to Joseph Rost to follow. Stung by the look, the young man braced himself, and responded by a glance equally bitter. The captain bowed and resumed his place.

A phantom ship, breathless, lifeless, the *Swan* crept on. She advanced nearer the admiral's light-ship—her very audacity her chance of safety—glided like a spectre almost beneath the stately bows of the man-of-war, and slid on beyond. She had run the gauntlet! "Safe,"

was the word framed by voiceless lips. Already visions of Champagne suppers and reckless rejoicing in port were indulged in. Only the captain's features were haggard with expectation. A wide, white fog wall shut down before and behind them, blank and impenetrable. Suddenly a dark spot appeared and loomed above them: it was the broadside of a ship. An involuntary exclamation of dismay welled up to Joseph's lips; the captain was at his side in an instant, with a gesture of silencing menace. A shudder palpitated through the *Swan;* she trembled at her own peril; then swinging around, causing scarcely a ripple, she glided away, making all speed for the open sea. But a note of alarm had roused the ship to immediate pursuit.

Dawn found the *Swan* flying over the billows, with a black object and a trail of smoke following steadily in her wake. Evening found pursued and pursuer occupying the same relative position. The captain kept his sleepless vigil, cigar in mouth, with the occasional cup of coffee, his chief nourishment—every nerve was strung to the highest pitch of excitement, every eye and ear strained for unusual sight or sound. What if another black speck appeared in an opposite direction, and joined in pursuit? What if a shot came hurtling over the sea, and crashed through the *Swan*'s unprotected side? The crew looked worn and gloomy. Below, Reuben Wentzel might be heard invoking the aid of all the prophets in his distress.

The faded little man approached the captain. "If you wish to blow up the craft, I can do it. Would you rather surrender?"

"We need do neither," said the captain, coldly.

At midnight noonday was longed for in sight the enemy, at noonday the shelter of darkness again. There she was, neither gaining nor losing.

Forty-eight hours, weary, heavy laden with danger, replete with the shock of surprises, lagged on.

"The barometer is falling," said the first officer, when night gathered in of the third day. The captain, bleached to a ghost by harassing fatigue, straightened himself, and said, cheerfully,

"Now for our chance, men!"

When darkness settled on the face of the waters, the *Swan* deliberately altered her course.

"Out of sight!" exclaimed the commanding officer of the pursuing *Pewiterwce*, lowering his glass. "We should have overhauled her, but for our heavy armament."

The *Pewiterwee* gave chase hopefully, if doubtfully. It was no easy matter to track the *Swan* on the high seas.

Dull clouds spread over the heavens, rising in darker masses from the horizon. There was an ominous hush of suspense, a pause, broken only by the heaving of the ocean; then the clouds rose in form of an arch, spanning the sky, and the rush of the storm swept near, with blinding glare of lightning, crash of thunder, and a mighty tumult. No easy matter, indeed, to track the *Swan*, with the tossing surges rearing their feathery crests, and the mist sheeting her like a bridal-veil.

"Man is a worse enemy than the storm," quoth the grim captain.

Lo! the prize was lost; for the *Swan* had doubled back, passed the *Pewiterwee* in the night, eluded by a hair-breadth the notice of a war-vessel, and stolen into port. The helm slipped from the captain's fingers; after the nerve-tension came total collapse. At that moment was revealed what his iron will had compelled the physical frame to endure; the strong man fainted.

Said Joseph Rost to Reuben Wentzel, with a manner both friendly and hesitating,

"We have reached our haven. Let us be fellow-laborers."

Reuben, sallow from fright and illness, had yet life interest enough left to scan his companion. Joseph leaned against the rail idly surveying the town, as if unaware of the scrutiny.

"What do you wish?"

"Listen! There will be rare opportunities to get diamonds for a song."

"Leave a Rost alone for thinking of that," interpolated Reuben, with a grin.

"Assuredly; and leave a Rost alone for discovering the best places in advance."

"Humph!" said Reuben, still on his guard.

Joseph had never once looked full at the other during the conversation, but continued to survey the town.

"Herr Wentzel, are you to be trusted?"

"Yes," replied Reuben, unblushingly.

Joseph frowned as scornfully as Samuel could have done.

"Truly, I have reason to trust you!"

"I tell thee"—began Reuben, hastily.

"Bah! No doubt I am foolish to talk about my own affairs; yet I need a confederate. I am so young, and we are countrymen. Surely we should work together rather than thwart each other."

"I will not fail you. Moreover, my experience may serve. What is the business?"

"Two families will have rare stones to sell. What if I send you to one, and find the other myself?"

"Yes," assented Reuben.

Joseph spread a pocket-map on the bulwark, and traced a route up to the State of Virginia, and a line to a town in Kentucky. Then he referred to a data in his memorandum-book, and wrote a name and place on a card, which he gave to Reuben.

"Meet me here in two months, and write me to the Burkville post-office—cautiously."

Reuben was silent a moment. "Suppose I do not find the family there?"

"It is their homestead. If they are fugitives, trace them; they will be all the more anxious to part with their jewels."

Reuben again reflected, nursing his chin in one palm.

"What good will I gain for my trouble?"

"If you do not see, Herr Reuben, no one can teach you. You hesitate? Don't play me false, after what I have communicated. Abandon the matter, only do not meddle afterward."

Joseph tore up the card, scattered the fragments into the water, and walked away. Reuben continued to hold his chin, and think in silence. Next morning he said:

"I will go." And he went. Joseph Rost's mental adieu was—"I fear I shall never have the pleasure of seeing you again."

CHAPTER VII.

THE OLD HOUSE.

A CITY, older than three centuries, stands a crumbling relic on the shores of a New World, and lives only in the remote past.

A warrior, imaginative and romantic; nay, more! dreading the sure approach of age, which would sap the strength of his stalwart limbs, sailed over the seas in search of the crystal waters of regeneration. Ah! fountain of youth! Was Ponce de Leon the only mortal who sighed for immortality?

Thus the first wave of European invasion swept up to the unknown shore, which received its name—Pascua Florida—in honor of the day, Palm-Sunday. Blooming the paradise, yet made terrible by lurking foes. Bronze faces peered from sheltering thickets, and the unerring arrow hissed after the foreigner as he sought roots; or stealthy canoes darted through the still waters of creeks, when hunger sent the explorer to gather oysters.

Instead of the fountain of youth, the warrior met death from a poison barb—gained his immortality, after all.

Then the second wave broke over the strand: a band of peaceful French Huguenots, seeking an asylum where the ghostly reverberations of St. Bartholomew bells might never reach them.

Then the third wave stormed the land.

Crafty Philip of Spain must exterminate the Protestant band; and so his mail-clad Adelantado stepped ashore, from the galleons anchored in the harbor, bearing the royal standard, and followed by a brilliant train of cavaliers. The Adelantado kissed the Cross piously, then drew his sword in the cause of religion, and the land flowed with Huguenot blood. Under the saint's especial patronage, whose name the town still bears, fortifications were erected. For sixty years the conquered Indians, whose ancestors roamed the savannas in freedom, toiled under cruel task-masters, dragging huge masses of stone to construct rampart, glacis, and ditch. Unconsciously these sons of the soil built not only frowning battlements and massive archways, but a volume in stone that, as future generations turned leaf by leaf, revealed in dark chambers and walled-up vaults, skeleton-strewn, the hideous character of their oppressors.

Heretics must be warned off by moat and wall of solid masonry, quoth the Adelantado.

As it happened, wave the fourth brought an incorrigible heretic, Sir Francis Drake, who swooped down like an eagle on the labor of years.

Then the fifth wave curled up, obliterating Saxon rule; restoring the old dispensation, gloomy, sombre, superstitious, and in that darkness the city must evermore remain. No active life stirs the sluggish pulses. In youth the city's garment was deeply stained in blood; in age danger sends no thrill through the palsied frame.

On the day of which we write, a young man passed through the narrow, sleepy streets in the direction of the fortified castle beyond. On either side the houses were built of coquina rock, flat-roofed, with wooden galleries and balconies, while over the high garden-walls glimpses of fig and pomegranate trees were visible.

At the castle the stranger paused, not so much to notice the venerable churches where old bells hung which had tolled the Catholic Spaniards to prayer, as to look cautiously about him. He had the appearance of a person dreading his own shadow.

It was Joseph Rost, in no very happy state of mind. A week before he had seen Reuben Wentzel, without being perceived in return, and had turned his steps to this remote region in order to avoid pursuit.

On board the blockade runner, he had intentionally deceived that crafty Jew, and rejoiced in the achievement.

Reuben could not have found any such family homestead as he mentioned. Now, if they met, it must be war to the knife between them. The thorn in Joseph's side was this unexpected spy, but his thoughts never descended to the black depths necessary to contemplate removing Reuben as an obstacle from his path. He was not a great diplomatist, or he would have felt no such scruples. He enjoyed outwitting Wentzel; and in sending him to the very heart of the war, a State swept and desolated successively by contending armies, the chances were against his return.

And here was Reuben back safe!

Nothing could have been more unfortunate. Better to have defied him utterly from the first, to have crushed the nettle firmly, which wounded by a lighter touch, than to have been tempted into this fatal course of pacification.

A dark present—a dark future—to return home unsuccessful?

The thought roused Joseph to uncontrollable anger; he had never received the discipline of patience. In his battle with the world, he was only too likely to be worsted. In this irritable mood the young man wholly underrated his own ability, and exaggerated difficulties. Better this lack of self-confidence, than an inflated faith in himself.

The quiet life of the city ebbed and flowed at his feet; low marshes and wooded shores extended to the line of glittering blue Atlantic in the distance. Joseph was a stranger. Nobody noticed him in those strange times, when disguises were frequent. The old city would scarcely have elevated its hoary eyebrows in surprise if as complete a transformation had occurred under its venerable nose as the harlequin in the pantomime.

Before many hours had elapsed, Joseph had formed his resolution.

It would require a keener scent than that of Reuben Wentzel to follow his steps. Afterward he could resume his own business. Not the slightest thread had yet been discovered to the clue of Grandfather Rost's heir-loom. It would require more than a month of surface study in a large country to discover the buccaneer's descendants, if they were actually in the Southern States at all. But he was not discouraged on this score. He possessed all the curious submissive patience of his people, united with a tenacity of purpose, a persistent adherence to one fixed aim amidst adverse

buffetings, if need be, that would achieve the end. Call it obstinacy, call it bravery. It is the great central motive power which, once kindled in men's bosoms, moves the machinery of a world. The wilderness received him a lonely wanderer. No anxious eyes followed him. He was friendless and alone.

Above sparkled a sky of clearest blue, below extended ridges of pine barrens, savannas starred with wild-flowers, and shaded tracts of hummock-land, catalpa and cotton trees, mingled with the waxy fruit of the candleberry-myrtle by the way; and as the traveler advanced, thickets of live-oak, cedar, and palmetto, all interlaced with long, briery vines and rank grass, became more frequent. Occasionally an Indian mound rose above the monotonous level of the surrounding country. Occasionally he had glimpses of swamps—shadowy, vague, dim—where lurked poisonous reptiles, and the wild fowl gathered fearlessly with discordant clamor, the blue heron, scarlet ibis, imperial eagle, and fleets of cormorants on the surface.

He confided in no person; but simply allowed his horse to journey on, as the animal would, provided a small pocket-compass was followed.

The second evening brought him to a dilapidated cabin, the only habitation he had seen for miles. A man was seated on a log before the door, smoking a cob-pipe. The malarious atmosphere of river-banks, rich with oozing mud and rank vegetation, had colored the man's life and appearance in dull yellow and brown tints. His slouching, ungainly figure, hollowed and pinched by poison breathed from infancy, seemed to utter a feeble protest against fate, which inertia counteracted. In garments a mere shade removed from his own complexion, there the man sat, a part of the landscape. No beau of Regent Street, or the boulevards, ever wore a costume more completely in harmony with his person and surroundings, than were the butter-nut coat, shrunken trowsers, gray hat, frayed and worn almost beyond semblance, of this early settler.

He neither moved nor spoke as Joseph dismounted.

"Can I sleep here to-night?"

Perfect English, spoken with a slight foreign accent.

"Wal, I dunno—ask her," indicating some mysterious power within, by a gesture of the pipe.

The floor of the cabin was earth, and fowls straggled in and out at pleasure. An untidy, hard-featured woman sat mending some rags by the light of a tallow-dip. Beside her stood a jar of snuff, into which she occasionally inserted a stick, and then thrust it into her mouth. The power of thought seemed to have deserted both, save for a sense of enjoyment in smoking and dipping.

Joseph repeated his question.

"I reckon so," replied the woman.

"And food?" suggested Joseph.

"Sakes alive, man! don't be in such a hurry. Go tend yer horse fust, an' I'll be ready soon's the boys come."

With a half smile, Joseph led his horse to a crazy shed.

The man continued to gaze into space, smoking stolidly.

Two boys now appeared, one carrying a rusty fowling-piece, the other a wild-turkey, and shrilly demanded their supper. The father arose slowly, yawned, lifted the turkey critically, and came to table unkempt and unwashed. With this homespun family Joseph partook of bacon and eggs, bread marbled with saleratus, corncake, and molasses. Afterward he was permitted to sleep on a straw sack in one corner, stifled by the fumes of burning corn-cobs, placed in a pan of coals to drive away insects.

Next morning he resumed his journey. The woman looked after him, turning the money he had given in her hand.

"Some thief, I reckon," was her comment.

The horse rambled on.

More wild and lonely grew the country, and it was almost with a sensation of surprise at any life that Joseph paused before a little hut on the verge of the woods to parley with the inmates. The hut was less dilapidated than the cabin where he had spent the previous night, and an old negro was chopping wood near by. He removed his tattered straw-hat courteously in response to Joseph's salutation, and bade a grimacing grandson take care of the gentleman's horse. Joseph soon obtained the knowledge he required. He could ascend the river above, with old Jake acting as boatman and guide, leaving his horse at the hut.

Once on the current of the stream, they floated past gloomy cypress swamps, past broad, level savannas, where bird and insect seemed brilliant, wandering flowers, rainbow-tinted, then curved into shadow again. The dreamy, listless progress lulled to repose, the soft enervation of the climate stole on the senses unawares. It might have been that days, instead of mere hours, were slipping unheeded by, even as the drops fell one by one from the glistening oar-blades back into the river. Trout flashed through the waters, cat-fish moved above the mud bottom, where alligators lurked; then a space of delicately-ribbed white sand appeared, draped by the waving sedge-ribbons and threads of aquatic mosses.

Suddenly Joseph asked himself the practical question: Where was he going? Was he to bury himself forever in such a wilderness to evade Reuben Wentzel?

"House up yer," said the sable boatman, paddling inshore, mindful of the claims of hunger.

There stood the house, half revealed through the matted shrubbery. Joseph's heart leaped as he looked at it. Did it appeal to his imagination only, or was there something more?

The river here widened to a broad stream, the ripples breaking musically on the pebbly beach. The forest rose dark and unbroken in the background, and the house was further sheltered from the river by a grove of oak and pine trees, so that the young man's first scrutiny only discovered toppling chimneys and projecting roof. The wind whistled through the sere grass, and murmured overhead with a melancholy sound. Joseph climbed the bank, in his eagerness to explore the spot, before the negro had beached the boat. He forced his way through the grove into a tangled wilderness of garden, choked with rank weeds, but blooming with the splendor of tropical flowers. A solid wall of verdure impeded his progress here; fallen urns and a broken fountain, moss-stained from long contact with the earth, lay beyond; he thrust aside the green veil of a parasite, and stood before the house. There it was, wrapped in a brooding silence in the bright day, presenting a fair front to the world, even in decay, yet with something sinister about it that would have arrested the eye, if located on the busiest thoroughfare traversed daily by the traffic of busy humanity. If ever a house had a story to tell, this one must have. It was built of time-stained stone, with an arched portico, supported on pillars, sheltering the sunken entrance-door, and with narrow casements seeming to stare blankly, like eyes robbed of life.

The stranger's interest was not attracted at first by these details, nor the irregular balconies and dormer-windows flanking the roof. A niche beneath the eaves held a marble figure of the Virgin Mary, still beautiful in classical drapery, and forming a startling contrast to the surrounding dilapidation. A natural ladder of twisted vines led up to the niche, as if frequently used. An old mansion, deserted, with decay sapping the very foundations, and wrinkling its front with many a seam and discoloration, yet wearing a marble saint on its brow!

A thrill shot through Joseph's veins.

"Who lived here?" he asked.

"Nobody dis forty year, massa," replied Jake, rubbing his white wool respectfully. "De ole gemman, he hung hisself, dey *do* say."

"Why?"

"Lord knows, honey! 'Spect his conscience hurt him. Nobody suspicions round yer what he did or didn't do."

"Did his family live here with him?" inquired Joseph, looking at the rude carvings of the balconies.

"Bress you, no. *He* nebber lib here 'tall. He jest come and go, like a sperrit. My ole mammy, she say he was de debbil. Scared dis chile mos' to def once, comin' sudden, when he hadn't been seen for tree year. Bernardo stay here all de time. Him mighty close, nebber say no word about ole massa."

Jake shook the door. He had no sooner done so, than a figure glided around the side of the house and confronted them—a woman clad in a cotton gown, old and wrinkled, yet tall, supple, strong, with lank gray hair hanging loosely about her shoulders. No need to ask her nationality. The brown face, piercing eyes, and prominent cheek-bones proclaimed her a descendant of the powerful Indian race who once burned aromatic shrubs as incense, on high mountain altars, to their god, the sun, and worshiped the springs; who cultivated the soil peacefully at home, while their women wove mats from gay feathers, and spun simple garments from hemp or mulberry bark, but who sallied forth bravely to war abroad.

She leaned on her stick and looked at them, latent hope, suspicion, and defiance in her eye, partially neutralized by the Indian impassiveness of expression. Jake at once made peaceful overtures, and explained that the gentleman wished to stop on the river for a few days.

"Where does he come from?" demanded the Indian.

Now the negro had not the most remote idea where Joseph Rost belonged, nor did he possess that active curiosity which would have led his white brother further north to have riddled the Jew with a small shot of questions. He pointed in a northern direction—"Up yonder."

The effect on the woman was startling. Her features grew keen and sharp, as she whispered, "Did Bernardo send you?"

Surprise prevented Joseph from speaking.

"Bernardo been gone forty year. Must be dead, I reckon," chimed in Jake.

The strange creature's eyes blazed wrathfully a moment, then the fire flickered out; she shrank, aged, drooped hopelessly.

"He said he would return," she muttered; adding, with indescribable weariness, "I die too—me tired."

Then she disappeared.

Jake soon forced an entrance into the deserted house. A musty odor assailed the intruders. Mold everywhere on walls and ceiling, a fungi-tapestry in each crack and fissure of the windows and fire-place. The door opened into a large hall, which occupied the central part of the building, and was ornamented with heavy axe-work and curious joinery. Massive cypress beams supported the ceiling, a wide hearth yawned black and void, and two richly-carved arm-chairs flanked the hearth, with faded tatters of velvet clinging to them, and rows of gilt-headed nails. This hall had evidently been used as a chief living-room; for a hammock had rotted from its fastenings and fallen in one corner, a mahogany writing-table was ink-stained, and held rusted writing-implements.

As the sunlight poured in a warm, golden flood into the darkened place, former occupants were disturbed. A web hung across the door, a castle of spun silk which caught the sun-rays in varying shades of blue and pink, and in the centre rested the spider-ogre in magnificent livery, velvet down upon his back, horny limbs, scarlet-tipped, and banded, as if with the blood of victims. Within the threshold the coiled folds of a snake stirred in pallid and dark shadings, a flattened head upreared, a forked tongue protruded with warning hiss, then glided away to obscurity.

On the chimney-piece lay a leather cigar-case. Joseph lifted it, and the clasps fell apart. There was a name on the plate inside, tarnished, but still legible. Joseph went to the door and studied the plate. His heart stood still: the name was Frederick William Goffe.

"For over all there hung a cloud of fear,
   A sense of mystery the spirit daunted,
And said as plain as whisper in the ear,
   The place is haunted!"

CHAPTER VIII.

DISCOVERY.

JAKE plodded about, making things comfortable for the night, after his fashion, and a very good one it was. A fire blazed on the broad hearth, shedding a cheerful warmth abroad, while a thousand airy sparks danced up the black chimney from the glowing bed of coals. Joseph stood motionless in the doorway facing the river. The negro came and went, now borrowing from the Indian's humble larder, singing and soliloquizing, now bringing forth his own stores, a frying-pan and provisions, for Jake thought a deal of creature-comforts.

"Supper ready, massa," he finally said, from the now glowing hearth, where savory odors steamed, accompanied by mysterious, hissing, bubbling sounds.

The young man did not respond, but stood as if carved out of stone.

Jake stared, chuckled a negro, oily laugh, and tasted a bit of crisp bacon surreptitiously. "Ain't yer gwine to eat yer supper, honey?"

Joseph turned quietly, as if some spell was broken, thrust the case into his pocket, and came forward.

The meal was primitive, and taken on the floor, the chairs being far too rickety to trust with their weight. Jake withdrew respectfully to the farther corner of the hearth, much amazed at Joseph's entire rejection of the bacon.

"Who was Bernardo?" inquired the young man, abruptly.

"He be Yankee; ask so many questions," thought Jake, deeply interested in his supper; but he answered,

"Bernardo ole gemmen's servant. He hang hisself, and Bernardo go 'way next day. Never seen no mo'."

"A Spaniard or Italian?" suggested Joseph.

"Some sort o' furriner, massa; dat is, he be Minorcan. Mightly select, sah, dem Minor-cans; lib and marry by demselves always. Lord! what's dat?"

A sound rolled and reverberated through the upper story of the house, causing Jake to clutch his plate nervously, and become rigid with terror. Joseph cocked his pistol and listened intently. The noise gradually died away.

"We will see what it is."

"Oh! no, massa, not in de dark," implored Jake, growing ashy gray with fear.

"To-morrow, then," assented Joseph.

He insisted, however, on exploring the lower floor, and, taking a pine torch, led the way.

The hall formed a square room in the centre of the house, with a door on each side. These doors they tried successively, and found them fastened within. In the rear means of egress were easy. At the end of a paved passage, they found themselves in a sort of court, formed by three sides of the building, with a stone flight of steps leading to the second story, and a gallery extending the length of the house.

Day had long since waned. A light burned in the ruined fragment of a detached kitchen, where the Indian woman lived, and through the aperture, once a window, she was plainly visible. A highly-colored picture of some martyr hung on the wall, wreathed in artificial flowers, such as are used to adorn altars; before it stood a large ivory crucifix, mounted in silver, and two candles in massive candlesticks. The Indian knelt in rapt devotion, slipping a rosary of pink coral through her fingers. The faith of her ancestors had been replaced in her breast by a passionate Catholicism. She would have killed any one who robbed her of her treasures, and she made candles from waxy fruits in the forests, to adorn her altar. In all that did not pertain to her religion her attitude was expectant : she watched for one who never came.

Joseph Rost ascended the steps, and peered along the weird gallery, Jake following, timorously protesting, yet afraid to remain behind.

"We shall sleep better if we look," said Joseph, and so the flaring torch made the rounds. Everywhere were traces of desolation and neglect. Numerous small rooms opened on the gallery, vacant and unfurnished. Bats darted in noiseless flight about them, skimming like shadows in the twilight of the long gallery.

"'Spect it was a bird, or sufin," said Jake, re-assured as they descended the steps.

The Indian had extinguished her candle; the darkness was becoming palpable; and a low, sad sound smote the ear, like the blending of the wind-rustling foliage and the half-articulate moan of creatures in the swamps. Twilight lurked in the forest's leafy depths, wove a dark mantle from tree to tree, moved stealthily among the trailing garden-vines, seemed to screen gliding terrors of the wood in deeper hollows of obscurity. The light lingered softly on the river's surface in violet and gold, paling to gray, and was at last folded in the universal night.

An overwhelming homesickness crept over the young man. He seemed to be no longer in the same world with those he loved. They decided to spend the night in the hall. Joseph, wrapped in his cloak, on one side of the fire, and Jake, indifferent to covering as long as his head was nearly in the coals, on the other. While making these preparations, Joseph noticed the clock for the first time. It was

3

an old time-piece, fitted in the wall above the chimney, and the pendulum had stopped on the stroke of one. Around the margin were letters printed in India ink—"A good clock, if regularly wound up, and never moved."

The negro heaped on fresh fuel, stretched himself luxuriously on the floor, and was soon fast asleep. The Jew's brain was more active.

In fleeing from Reuben Wentzel, he had discovered a clue to his own secret. How much of a one? A name, simply. Who was the old gentleman? Who was Bernardo? Above all other considerations, why were the two doors locked?

Long he lay revolving these matters in his mind, gazing wakefully at the shadows in the dim corners of the large apartment, at the patch of ruddy crimson on the ceiling reflected by the fire, counting the strokes of the death-watch, which ticked monotonously in the crumbling wall, and listening to the regular snore of the negro, a human, cheerful note in that lonely spot. Finally, almost unexpectedly, weariness mastered his excited senses, and he sank into a dreamless sleep.

He awoke with a violent start. A cold perspiration bedewed his forehead; a great horror and awe, indefinable, but terrible, oppressed him. Stirred by a current of dread, the hair of his flesh stood up, while an icy touch grasped his heart. The negro had not awakened. The fire was a castle of fiery splendor, with fantastic peaks and flaming arches. Yes, and the clock *was* going.

There was some one in the room!

CHAPTER IX.

PEGGY'S FORTUNE.

A YEAR before Joseph Rost left his home, a very small house on the cliffs of the shore of another continent displayed a light only in the kitchen window one evening. Beyond a wide stretch of beach the town sloped down to a harbor, and the inmates of this house were obliged to cross the sands to reach it. On this particular evening the little house had a lonely and friendless look, away off there by itself, near the closed gates of a large property, yet not a porter's lodge, with the rain dashing against the windows in chill gusts, and the sea murmuring below.

Within doors not a sound broke the stillness except the ticking of the kitchen clock. Beside the table, where the lamp was placed, sat a gaunt, hard-featured old woman, with her iron-gray hair screwed up into an uncompromising little knot at the back of her head, and a half-knitted stocking lying in her lap. She was entirely forgetful of her neglected work and the storm outside. On the table she had spread a pack of cards, arranged in a half circle, after the fashion of fortune-tellers; but at this moment she seemed to have drifted away from contemplating them, and sat gazing stonily at the opposite wall. The expression of her face changed as rapidly as shadows ripple over the surface of a pond—eager anxiety, dreamy triumph, sharp pain, succeeding each other, while her eyes appeared contracted, as of one with an introverted vision. Clearly she was in a psychological condition, verging on clairvoyance.

A slender girl appeared on the threshold, yawned as if from a period of cramping inaction, and looked at the woman with saucy amusement. Then a second girl, smaller and darker, joined the first one, and they exchanged significant glances.

"Peggy sees a ghost," whispered the taller sister, tripping across the kitchen.

"We'll not go on like this always. There's a change coming—a great change. Ethel won't stay moping here forever."

The sisters were startled. Often had they seen their old Peggy poring over the cards, but never like this. *The voice seemed that of another person.*

The smaller girl stepped quickly to her side, and placed one firm little hand on her shoulder, inquiring,

"Peggy dear, what is the matter? Are you dreaming?"

The woman gasped, or sobbed, several times, blinked, and resumed her knitting as if by a strong effort of will.

"I was not asleep, children. I calculate I saw a leetle ways beyond this kitchen, though."

The small girl compressed her lips in a peculiar way of her own when displeased. The other one asked, carelessly,

"How is the Queen of Hearts to-night?"

Peggy smiled, and resumed her natural manner.

"The Queen of Hearts has happiness, and plenty of money in the end, but there's trouble between. Olive may laugh. Of course it's mighty smart for young folks to laugh at their elders. I never drew three aces together in all my born days that a surprise didn't come before twenty-four hours."

"I am glad I come out all right in the end, like the story-books," said Ethel, moodily gazing at the lamp, and rumpling the masses of her golden hair.

Peggy and the quiet little sister Olive regarded her wistfully. Ethel had been a problem from her birth. The noblest developments of the human soul are not always made in the wide arena of God's world; for in this humble country-kitchen these two women, sister and servant, would have yielded the best portion of their lives to make that of Ethel happy.

"The Queen of Clubs has something on the road, too," pursued Peggy, tracing her way around the magic circle with one long, bony forefinger and a disengaged knitting-needle.

"How does she end?" asked the little sister, demurely.

"I do not see the end," returned Peggy, soberly, pushing the cards hastily into a heap.

For years the family in the cottage had been divided thus: Mrs. Hearn, Queen of Diamonds; Olive, Queen of Clubs; Ethel, Queen of Hearts; and Nicholas Hearn, Knave of Hearts. Peggy allowed herself no place at all in this book of fate.

These girls had spent the evening, as they did many of their young lives, sitting in a hushed room, afraid to disturb the slumbering mother by the rustle of a book-leaf, and dreading the moan of pain which would bring her back to consciousness again.

"The Queen of Hearts will give a party when she is a great lady," said Ethel, resting her elbows on the table in a comfortable, if ungraceful, attitude. "There shall be an awfully grand dinner first—such as the mighty ones around here give, and we have the pleasure of sniffing at a respectful distance—and a ball afterward. Peggy shall come with the best of them. I think I shall wear pink velvet and diamonds. Perhaps Cinderella in her glass slippers will be an honored guest. One is as probable as the other—heigh-ho!"

"You may have all that, and not the mother," said Olive, tenderly.

The latter possessed one of those divine gifts of suggestiveness of blessings enjoyed, when comparison seems about to create unhappiness.

"God knows I don't want it without her," retorted Ethel, quickly, tears rushing to her eyes.

"The young birds leave the nest; it's natur'," said Peggy, dryly.

Ethel roamed to the window, pressed her face to the panes, and looked out into the dark, stormy night. Was her future to be as dark as that?

Something of Peggy's superstition infected her charge. As Ethel Hearn looked out, a curious circumstance occurred. A face formed out of the obscurity on the other side of the pane. She started back with a faint scream. The face disappeared, and a knock on the door succeeded.

The stranger beheld a girl of amazing beauty; her face framed in a shimmer of soft hair, her cheek slightly flushed with excitement at some vague expectation, and her eyes glowing like luminous stars. The world is full of such surprises; glimpses of a loveliness whose fame would last a century hidden beneath a sunbonnet. He looked at her attentively, as any one, man or woman, must have done; but he was a gentleman, and did not prolong the scrutiny to a stare.

"Pardon my intrusion; but can you tell me why the Raines's place is deserted?"

The little sister first recovered from the surprise incident to receiving a visitor at that hour and season of the year. Peggy, the avowed guardian of the household, who scoffed at "noises," and openly defied vagrants, stood dumb.

"The Raines family have been absent in Europe for years, I believe. The servants may have gone to the town to-night," said Olive.

"They are careless to leave the place," rejoined the gentleman, abruptly. "Do that class keep late hours in the town, may I ask? If so, I suppose I may have the pleasure of sitting on the door-step until they return."

"I am sorry you should be inconvenienced. Our parlor is at your disposal, sir."

"Thanks. Perhaps I may be able to effect a burglarious entrance into my own dominions, if you will lend me a lantern."

Evidently past the romance of youth, or a chat with the inmates of the cottage, a possible glimpse of the beauty again might have been considered more enlivening than forcing an entrance into a dark house. But having outlived that delightful period, the stranger thought far more, with wet clothes and muddy boots, of a good cigar and glass of wine in his own house, than all the pretty girls in Christendom.

Peggy stood rigidly by the door, lamp in hand, her eyes following every movement of the gentleman like a basilisk. It therefore devolved on Olive to kindle the lantern for him. A fretful groan was heard in an upper chamber. How suggestive it was! How quickly it explained the shadow on the little house!

"Dear me! Have you illness here?" asked Mr. Raines, with real concern.

"My mother is always ill," said Olive, with a quiver in her voice.

"I am sorry. Can nothing be done? Have you the best medical advice?" What a good face it was! sharp-featured and plain enough, but firm and self-reliant.

"The best the town affords."

Then he departed, and as he plodded along through the darkness he soliloquized :

" I wonder where they came from! I don't remember seeing them before. How the old woman glowered! Considered me a wolf among her lambs, I suppose. She is quite right to guard them."

When he had gone, Ethel emerged, showing, from her proximity, that she had lent ear to the conversation.

" You mean thing! to leave me in the lurch," said Olive, with playful severity.

" Caught in the kitchen!" snapped Ethel.

" Peggy, if ever I was ashamed of you, it was to-night," continued the little sister. " Did you never see a gentleman before, that you must stand and gape at him in that fashion ?"

" I've seen *him* before," said Peggy, with peculiar emphasis.

" When ?"

" An hour ago. I didn't think he'd come so soon. I should hev knowed him this side of the grave. There was a cloud yonder, beyond the light, and his face grew and grew out of it, until it was as plain as yourn. He's come for our Ethel."

" Then he may go away again," cried Ethel, tossing her graceful head with all the arrogance of youth. " I shall not marry a small, stumpy creature with gray hair and a long nose, thank you. No, not for all the diamonds in creation."

" Very well, I dare say he does not mind ; he has not asked you yet," said the little sister, calmly.

Ethel's defiance collapsed. To be sure, he had walked off when he might have remained, and talked with her.

" Now, Peggy, you must be well scolded. What did you eat for your dinner ?"

" Lord ! I dunno. A bite of what you had, I s'pose."

" Let me tell you it must be indigestion, or you never could have such nightmare visions. If you go on like this, I will steal your snuff-box, and throw it away. There !"

It was droll to see this wise little woman scold her great Peggy, and afterward pack her off to bed, whither she prepared to go quite meekly. Ethel stood trifling with a chain about her throat.

" Where did you get that, child ?" asked Peggy, making a pretense of trimming the candle in order to secure her snuff-box on the shelf, against possible raids.

" I didn't mean to show it. I should like to know what could remain concealed in this house. I found it in the mother's desk to-night."

She drew forth a gold cord with a pendant attached. This pendant was a beryl of oval shape, framed in dull yellow gold, and having these Persian characters exquisitely engraved on the stone :

CHAPTER X.

BERNARDO.

"CAN I find shelter here?"

"If you wish to enter, you will, I suppose. We are only women."

"Madame, for that reason I would not intrude. But observe, this is the. last point of safety, and in crossing the hill I shall probably meet my death in a shower of minie-balls."

"Enter then, by all means," said the lady, solemnly, resuming her work, a bit of cambric, which might be crimsoned with her own blood before completion.

It was surely the most primitive habitation to which a stranger was ever invited—a burrow in the side of the hill. A central tunnel ran from the entrance to the rear of the cave, where two passages branched on either side, thus affording sleeping accommodation, and additional protection from the steady rain of shot and shell that fell all day. The place was damp and unwholesome; from time to time little rills of soft earth crumbled from the ceiling and walls warningly, and moisture trickled along the floor. Beetles trotted in crevices, and a slimy worm, rightful possessor of this dim subterranean world, slid and twined into view occasionally.

The young man who had sought refuge there stood just within the entrance; the lady opposite keeping a sunny-haired child farther back; while an older woman crouched in the darkest corner, silently wringing her hands. Suddenly she darted forward and accosted the young man.

"What are you doing here with women? Why are you not helping to sweep away our enemies? A deserter! sickened by the scent of powder. A spy!" She looked at him with flashing eyes, and accompanied her scornful words by a gesture, as if she would have spurned him.

The younger lady made no comment; yet in her more gentle face might have been read contempt also.

"What would you have me do?" asked the young man, mildly. "It is not a war of my making. I have not a friend on either side."

"Then why are you here?" demanded the old woman, imperiously, looking at the smoke filling the lower atmosphere, with hatred and vengeance depicted on her weary face.

"I am here for you to tell me if Bernardo died in this city thirty-nine years ago?"

If a shell had exploded in the cave, the effect could not have been more wonderful. Her gaze wandered, her features contracted; she put her hand to her forehead and recoiled a step. The younger woman laid down her work and stepped forward to her side.

"Thou hearest, Maddalena?"

"Truly, my great-uncle, Bernardo, died then," said the young woman, crossing herself rapidly.

"He was his own master," added the old woman, recovering herself. "If he lived years away from us, he was a good brother all the same. What is it to thee?" the passionate Minorcan blood beginning to rise in the withered cheek.

Joseph Rost bit his lip to repress the exultation he felt at this information. He was saved the necessity of a reply. The blithe little child, unconscious of danger, and tired of the restraints of the gloomy prison, had availed herself of the absorption of the others to creep along the passage and dance out into the sunshine. A bubbling laugh of perfect glee warned them of her escape. There stood the little figure, white-robed, flossy curls wind-blown, poised airily on one tiny foot, innocently facing death—death everywhere.

The city was besieged. Great iron balls screamed through the air as if tossed by giants, and the earth reverberated with the concussion of heavy explosions; but the town received the storm in sullen silence, and would not yield.

The mother stood a moment petrified, then uttering a piercing shriek, rushed out.

"Stay, I will go," cried Joseph, forcing her back.

In the mean while the child danced on, casting mischievous glances backward, and only flying faster when she saw Joseph start in pursuit.

"Me go home; tired of dat ole hole;" the childish voice sounded sweet and clear in the lull of the bombardment.

Life was very precious to the Jew at that moment; he was on the eve of success. War kindled no glow of excitement, but rather curdled the blood in his chilled veins. He looked to the right and the left, gasped once, and dashed on. A rushing sound filled the air, succeeded by a roar, a shock, and Joseph was thrown violently on his face. Staggering to his feet unharmed, he saw the child running back, calling piteously for her mother. He caught her in his arms, and crept behind a rock just as a second shock made the earth tremble. Then he flew back to the cave with his precious burden. The child laughed as she was restored to the trembling mother.

This event changed the current of hostility toward the stranger into fervid, impetuous gratitude; he had risked his own life for the child. The young mother wept and kissed his hands; the old aunt embraced him; then she held up her crucifix for Joseph to salute, swearing that he meant no harm in his questions about Bernardo. But here the curious conflict of races jarred unexpectedly. To the terrified women, indeed to all the contending hosts battling for possession of the town, the Cross was an emblem of salvation. Joseph Rost put it aside.

"I am an Israelite. My faith differs from yours. I will swear that I meant no harm to Bernardo's family."

"You have saved the child, you shall hear. We are Minorcans, but we have never seen our home beyond the seas. Our fathers were cruelly deceived by Sir Nicholas Turnbull, who founded our colony. We never mingled with Spaniards or English; we were one family. Now it is different. My niece here is married to an American. Bernardo was a sailor from choice. Once there came a ship, and he ran away to it. After that he was true as steel to his master, and made many voyages."

"The master was a pirate," said Joseph.

"Madre de dios! since you know so much, there is little need of my knowledge," she said, her mobile features gathering wrath again.

Then she stalked back to her dark recess, where her brilliant eyes gleamed in the obscurity. A negro boy came running over the hill, and paused at the entrance breathlessly.

"Massa George safe dis mornin'. We git up pretty soon. Golly! de cow gone. She feedin' in de hollow, an' a ball come take her clean off her legs. No milk for little missy no mo'. De sojers cut her up with swords in no time 'tall. Mighty hungry down yonder keepin' guard."

Exposure to the vicinity of deadly missiles had made the boy reckless. Indeed, groups of negroes gathered around in a circle at night, listening to the recital of narrow escapes, the ludicrous incidents of the previous day, with the keenest sense of humor. Each day the boy coolly built a fire on a ledge in the ravine below, and cooked the family dinner, such as it was, for the place was becoming straitened for provisions. The enemy's aim was nearly sure to fly over the ravine, but in passing from this improvised kitchen to the cave, he ran the gauntlet.

"Dis chile got sufin," he grinned, displaying a portion of the slaughtered cow triumphantly. The faces of the besieged brightened in anticipation of an unusual feast.

The boy stood on the brink of the ravine one instant; the next, that ominous hissing sound cut the air from a new quarter: he threw up his arms in silent agony and disappeared.

Then followed a rattling, grinding, rumbling noise; the top of the hill broke off and slid down, a mass of loose sand and stones covering the mouth of the cave. They were buried alive.

CHAPTER XI.

HOW THE CITY WAS TAKEN.

THE city was located on a commanding height, and was built street above street, broken by neglected, sandy spaces, and frequent ravines. Toward the east, bluffs surmounted it, which commanded the river north and south.

"I can laugh my enemies to scorn. The mighty river—a stem yellow and turbid, down among the sedges of the coast, is a flower, unfolding petal within petal of beauty as it approaches me—winds in a silvery current at my feet, and is my friend and protector. Will not the waters overflow? Will not the deadly swamps breathe pestilence to invaders, suffocate them in quicksands, poison them with reptiles lurking in obscurity? I am safe; I can defy a continent." Thus reasoned the city, fringing her garments with rifle-pits, and donning her armor of defense.

Her conquerors reasoned otherwise.

She was the one impregnable fortress on the stream. She was the magazine for the riches flowing from the veins of rice and cotton producing States. Thousands of troops diverged from her over the land. She *must* be taken. In justice to the city must it be said that she left no measure untaken to verify her boast. The air rang with the hammers of foundries; stately trees fell to serve for breastworks; hospitals warned of an approaching necessity; the banks were drilled for marksmen to sweep the decks of passing vessels; the bluff bristled with cannon. Then the commander bade the women and children go forth.

"Never!" shrieked the women, with hysterical patriotism, and sent up their flannel petticoats to the commander to be used in the ammunition, an offering on the altar of country. Old Maddalena was foremost. Patriotism was intensified into enthusiasm by her Southern temperament.

One day a gun-boat came around the bend of the river, fluttering a white signal.

No surrender! was the defiance hurled back at the peaceful messenger from the fortified heights.

There sat the city, wearing her tiara of bristling bayonets, with the river at her feet. Hours elapsed, and, when the sunset crimsoned the river's face, a fleet was visible coming down stream. What did it mean? Simply this: a vessel appeared below, and glided toward the town. She might have been a wreck, for any sign of life she gave; not a soul was visible on her deck. In a channel half a mile wide, past a bank lined with rifles below and guns above, she made her way silently, boldly. An electric flash crackled along the shore, balls of flame broke on her iron sides, columns of spray spouted from the seething waters, yet she kept steadily on. The shot might burst on her deserted deck, rattle against her steel ribs; she would reach the point above, and, with one grand broadside poured into the batteries, disappear behind the trees. Afterward the cannonade commenced—the heart of sultry summer, when life fainted in the pulseless atmosphere, with fiery cloudless sky above, and brazen, molten river below.

By day, the crash of shells exploding in the very streets, and the bitter retort of shore-batteries beneath the sweltering sun. By night, the fog creeping along white and chill, and, in the silence of exhausted nature, the melancholy chirp of birds distinctly audible; while the city was mute, and the bombarding fleet lay at anchor on the motionless current.

In the mean while a Thing was floating down the sluggish River of Death above. It was neither steamship nor raft, yet partook of the nature of both. Huge logs of timber, sufficiently green to resist fire, were linked together in an unwieldly mass; iron plates sheathed it, funnels breathed black smoke. A bogy—a terror in the darkness, an anomaly in the light. The fleet formed a chain to grapple with it. Forthwith the Thing stretched forth one massive paw, and a vessel sank. With engines crippled, but by sheer force of size and strength, the monster rent a passage through, and was anchored beneath the city's guns. Oh the terrible glow of, cloudless sky and reflecting waves! Oh for a breath of pure air, keen with frost and hail!

At length the fleet withdrew slowly, and the city's heart beat high with triumph. Was she saved? Or was she only allowed a respite in which to heal her wounds and strengthen her position?

There was need to gird herself for the tempest gathering!

It was during this period of inaction that Joseph Rost left the old house, which had curiously enough served him the double purpose of concealment and discovery, and made his way across the country. Once drawn into a region which had become a net-work of rival armies, his safest course would have seemed to have sought refuge in the fortress city, whose position was well-nigh inaccessible. But Joseph Rost had another motive. The old house had revealed a clue. The barred doors had, in spite of the Indian's jealous vigilance, admitted him, in part, to their shadowy secrets. He came to the fortress city to learn if Bernardo was dead; for not a doubt remained in his mind that the Minorcan servant had possessed himself of the master's wealth and departed with the booty. He dared not reflect on the extent of the robbery. Might not the heirloom have disappeared wholly, even if in the buccaneer's possession at the date of his death? In the warmest flood of noonday a shudder crept over him at the .remembrance of the night spent before the fire. Holding the one frail thread he had discovered, it drew him straight to the abode of Bernardo's relatives, whither he had gone forty years before.

The Indian woman patiently, dumbly waited. The Jew sifted, thought, moved rapidly; but when he reached the city he found himself besieged. He would have ample leisure to trace Bernardo before he again escaped from it.

A daring, impetuous general had approached the line of bluffs without awaiting re-enforcements; had waded through marsh and winding bayou with desperate valor, and thrown his troops straight on the hidden foe. The hill-side burst into a storm of flame from deep-mouthed cannon, and the line of attack rolled back torn, bleeding, dying. Again the city waved her banner victoriously. She would be the citadel around which clustered the growth of a new Government.

This happened four months before Joseph Rost arrived; but with his advent another man was approaching, far more important than our Jew. The river was the city's guardian. Grandly it emerged from the distance, and, sweeping onward, gathered the tribute of many small streams, like the monarch it was — not only gathered their tribute, but swayed so absolute a rule, that in wayward temper of despotism it surged back into them, overflowing the face of the country, making it a dreary waste of bog, lake, and fen. The general surveyed the scene, and thousands of workmen scooped a trench which should divert the river from its channel, leaving the city stranded—an inland town.

A pause of intense anxiety!

Would the river indeed turn into the new channel? The ripple of a wave, the rude breath of a wind, might decide the question. Then the majestic stream crumbled a frail dike, flooded the half-finished work, and rushed on in scorn at the pigmy efforts of man to curb its turbulent current. Undaunted by failure, the general next proceeded to create a rival river, as it were. Might not two lakes be connected, and form a chain with small rivers, by clearing shallows, felling trees for a distance of one hundred and fifty miles, and a new stream be formed parallel with the old? Now a steamer paddled down the open route, where never steamer ventured before. Would the river favor the enterprise, and flow through this fresh outlet? Alas! no. True to its allegiance with the fortress city, it withheld its waters and passed on. Then the general tried the same plan with a lake on the other side of the great unconquerable giant, hoping to form a connection with the winding, sluggish bayous, thus reaching the city in the rear. Again steamers cautiously paddled where the light Indian canoe had never attempted to penetrate the labyrinth, guarded by the low, sweeping branches of sycamore and cypress, shielded by blackened roots, interwoven with knotted coils of fibrous vines, defended by a battery to face which, whirled by the eddies of dangerous currents, was certain death.

With a persistence which nothing could thwart, the general formed a third plan.

Gun-boats boldly pushed their way through a

maze of creeks, to gain a position behind the fortifications. The venture was fraught with peril. Cutting their way through sombre forests, where enemies perpetually hovered to dispute the advance, their course impeded by the crash of falling trees, their retreat threatened in the same way, the waters ebbing ever more shallow beneath the keel, at length the invaders had to turn back to escape capture in an unknown wilderness.

Joseph Rost, arrived in the city, was subjected to some narrow scrutiny, which could not elicit any suspicious circumstance, and sought shelter for the night in a humble tavern. Sleep visited the inhabitants; the horrors of siege were forgotten. At midnight dark masses of shadow floated down the river. Did lynx-eyed sentinels see nothing? Yes. Simultaneously the guns awoke the echoes, and shivered the calm silence of night. Joseph Rost sprang from his bed and rushed into the street. Scarcely had he escaped when a ball sped through the tavern, and the wooden frame collapsed like a house of cards. Frightened groups of people ran hither and thither helplessly; the fire from the boats was raking the very spot where they stood.

"What has happened?" asked Joseph.

The needful answer came. A light of intense splendor flashed on one of the hills above, illuminating the scene. The beacon-fire threw a lurid glow over the city roofs, revealed the gunners stooping low behind their ramparts, and rested on the river in a wide effulgence. There were the war vessels coming down in a line, sheltering with their iron mail three fleet transports. Night was turned to day. They could not escape the careful aim of eight miles of guns.

A murmur went up from the town.

In the midst of the excitement, Joseph Rost saw an old woman fall on her knees and murmur a prayer in Spanish. It was Maddalena. He did not lose sight of her again.

Down rushed the boats. The first transport received a death-blow, wavered, drifted disabled, and was towed beyond danger by the sheltering gun-boat. The next flushed rosy red; the cotton protecting her boilers had caught fire. Transfigured into a ship of flame she seemed; then, the brief glory of conflagration past, shriveled to the water's edge. Then the rest swept triumphantly on. Next morning the city questioned the measure in vain. The commander haughtily repelled advice, and a chill doubt for the first time thrilled through every heart.

Joseph Rost speedily learned that the old woman was a Minorean, and had resided there for many years.

Rumor flew on every breeze. What would be the point of attack? From up the river, surely. Hark! Even the crack of artillery already promised it. Still rumor flew, the city hesitated, and the delay was her ruin. At any time the commander might issue proudly forth, and join his forces with veteran soldiers mustered miles away to rout the enemy. What if the foe marched so rapidly that this junction was prevented. That is what he did.

The storm of war was battering at the city's stronghold before she realized it. From the highways, bordered by hedges of roses and cane, where the houses and sugar-mills gleamed, deserted, among the avenues of shrubbery— from the morass, and bayou, and forest, came the winding train of army, bugle peals awakening the echoes of victory.

CHAPTER XII.

IN THE CAVE.

WHEN the accident occurred, the besieged were speechless for a few seconds in that oppressive darkness. Horror paralyzed them. The child first recovered sufficiently to sob quietly. This roused the mother, who crawled to the entrance and began to push at the obstruction with two feeble hands. Old Maddalena was silent. Joseph seemed passive from a very confusion of thought. How should he escape? —first thought; then he followed another still darker in its selfishness. He crept through the darkness, and touched Maddalena on the shoulder.

"Tell me what I wish to know about Bernardo before I attempt our release."

After a sullen pause,

"What do you wish to know?"

"Did he bring gold to you?"

"Yes."

"Jewels?"

"Yes."

Joseph caught his breath; he forgot that he was buried in a cave. It was the ruling passion strong in death.

"He did not give them to me; they are gone," said the old woman, quickly.

Joseph laid a hand on her shoulder.

"Must I remind you that I have saved the child once? Must I tell you that I am going to try to unearth us now? You saw the gems, at least, and I wish them enumerated."

By this time the young woman had ceased her helpless groping at the entrance, and caught the drift of the conversation.

"Holy St. Francis!" she cried; "shall we perish while you talk? How long can we breathe in this hole? When will the roof fall and crush us? Tell him quickly—any thing."

Thus adjured, old Maddalena, who never supposed that Bernardo's riches were lawfully gotten, and feared that Joseph had some claim on them, said reluctantly,

"A ruby necklace; an emerald and pearl cross; a diamond ring."

"*Any thing more?*"

"Nothing."

Joseph turned without a word, and began to attack the mass of rubbish blindly and recklessly. It seemed as if he could not wait to overcome the obstacles in the way before pursuing his search. He did not heed the boom of guns, the dead and dying about him. One motive alone impelled the young man. Oh, if he had never left the old house until he had torn it down piecemeal! He hurled himself against the débris, but it might well have served as resisting fate. Finally he recoiled, spent and breathless. They were buried away from sun and air, with human beings moving above them.

"If I had a spade or a crowbar!" he groaned, wiping the perspiration from his brow.

The women were ready with an expedient— a broomstick. Inserting this into the mass, he discovered, after penetrating a few inches, a large rock filling the mouth of the cave. Joseph pushed against it with his shoulder; it did not yield. Then he felt around the edges with the broomstick; there was a space at one side corresponding with a jagged edge of the stone. The young man worked patiently at this opening; it was their one hope; through it they might breathe, if the broom reached far enough; for he could not push his own body into any aperture because of the rocky ledge.

With intense anxiety the women watched his progress. The stick met with no obstacle in the soft earth. After a time he drew it back cautiously; there was a noiseless dropping of soil above, obliterating the end of the slender tunnel; but, oh joy! a ray of light darted into the cave like a friendly messenger of hope, followed by a current of pure air. Each of the women in turn placed their mouths at the opening, eager for air; after, the child; then subsided into dull endurance of their captivity. Joseph did not dare to make the opening larger, fearing to shatter the precious rift.

Thus the displacement of a few soil-particles preserved the lives of four persons, and a further dislodgment of a handful of earth would occasion death. Joseph shouted. No reply. So faint a cry from the depths of the hill was not likely to attract attention.

"By-and-by we shall not be able to appeal," said old Maddalena, with grim suggestiveness.

In turns they occupied the opening and implored aid. At last the light beyond the hole faded; it was night. No thought of hunger had visited them yet. Now the child wailed for food. Old Maddalena remembered a taper, and a feeble yellow ray flickered in the dismal place. Another horror confronted them—there was no water! A cup of cold coffee quenched the child's thirst; for the rest, privation.

With desperation Joseph recommenced his cries at the opening. The enemy's fire had ceased, and the towns-people were no longer confined to their burrows like wild animals.

To think of the morrow brought a shudder of sickening apprehension; they dared only to live in the agonizing possibility of the present. With the two women there was a measure of relief, after frantic ravings, in tears and prayers. The child fell asleep. For Joseph Rost there was no such refuge. His eyelids began to swell; lights danced and whirled when he closed them; his tongue was parched in his throat. He was obliged to exert the most strenuous self-control to turn his thoughts back from contemplating the horrors of suffocation. He was forced to bite his lips to keep from shrieking aloud and going mad. Was it imagination, or did the atmosphere, robbed of all vitality, grow dense with a grave-like chill? Were they panting for breath under an oppression which threatened every moment to check respiration? Old Maddalena flung herself on the ground and beat her head passionately against it. Then she lay very still.

"Help, help!" called Joseph, in hoarse, despairing tones.

A faint echo responded: "Where are you?" "Here, buried in the cave."

Snatching up the expiring taper, the young man held it to the crack; the gleam was visible through the accumulated rubbish. The voice promised assistance. Then they waited, minutes, hours, days, it seemed, the young woman and Joseph looking at each other speechlessly, with every nerve strained to listen. Old Maddalena and the child were indifferent; both were sinking into stupor. A distant sound greeted their keenly-strung senses, then followed in quick succession strokes of spades. The mother laughed deliriously. Joseph looked at the roof apprehensively, for at any time the friendly efforts without might convert the cave into their tomb.

Lanterns flashed over a group of negroes and whites, thrilled with ready sympathy, and in the midst was the bent form of a little man with greenish-gray eyes, who had first discovered the catastrophe.

Cautiously the débris was scooped away, consisting of crushed flowers, torn branches, and shattered rock. The unwieldy stone blocking the entrance at last yielded to the united efforts of Joseph within and those outside. First the senseless forms of a woman and child were unearthed; next emerged the young mother, who had borne her sufferings patiently, but now flung wide her arms in a rapture of freedom, and, oddly enough, with sudden fierceness cursed the enemies who had brought these afflictions. Joseph Rost followed, and met Reuben Wentzel. They stared at each other like ghosts.

"You here!" exclaimed Reuben.

"We have endured the same siege, it seems," returned Joseph.

He had leaped one barrier, and here was another.

The first duties were to restore Maddalena and the child, repair the cave for the missiles of another day, and accept food. Joseph took a cup from the officious Reuben's hand, and overturned it in the grass afterward. The released family stretched themselves on the slope to enjoy the freedom night usually gave.

"I will see you to-morrow," said Reuben, significantly.

"Very well," replied Joseph.

CHAPTER XIII.

DAWN.

DAY came in pale, tremulous pencilings of light on the horizon, in cold glimmerings radiating the valleys, and the women searched for Joseph Rost, who had disappeared. Old Maddalena feared suicide or an accident, and was more than half disposed to resent the continued absence of their protector of the cave, so curiously are people brought together in war. But Joseph Rost never returned.

He had not committed suicide, yet he had taken a step scarcely less rash. He seemed so near the fulfillment of his project, that it was easier to evade Reuben Wentzel once more than to contend with him. Reuben was not sufficiently reckless to shoot him in cold blood, Joseph reasoned, but in that storm of bullets might not a chance one bring him low? Better to risk fleeing to the enemy's lines. Better to risk finding a way through them, than to stay in the city like a penned sheep.

Joseph escaped in this wise: a log drifted down the stream, hugging the shore so close that the words of the sentinels could be heard, and guided by a man swimming. He reached a low protected spot safely, drew the log ashore, and untied from it a bundle of clothes, in which he dressed himself.

The dawn glowed, flushed, brightened into the promise of perfect day. Never had the future looked so hopeful. To return home respected and honored for his success! To be equal with Samuel! To see Benjamin again —perhaps find Rachel unwedded.

The tempest broke with tenfold fury that day. On one side stubborn despair; on the other cool, persistent bravery. Gone was the early dewy freshness of morning, quenched in the fiery breath of battle, which rolled a heavy, sulphurous cloud up the hill-side, with gleams of color, and flashes of light shimmering through.

Joseph Rost was swept away like a feather. Retreat or advance were alike impossible. The tumult came unexpectedly. Quickly climbing a tree to avoid being trampled by the charging regiments, he scanned the scene.

A baleful smoke canopy obscured the blue heavens, and hung low over ranks of dead, mown down, over crippled chargers, over pain in every shape possible to strong men smitten low. Down rained the blighting fire of shells and balls; a perpetual whistling sound hissed past Joseph's ears, as he crouched close to the tree. Who was victor in the tangled heaps surging to and fro? There was a rushing noise heard above the roar of cannon; it reached even the dulled ear of the wounded. What was it? a wind—a rising storm? The smoke rolled back up the hill toward the masked batteries on the summit. The rushing noise was the advance of the pursuing column, sweeping over all obstacles, charging under a galling fire, broken, reeling, reunited, and pressing on. What had happened?

Only a tree fallen, snapped in twain, into the hollow, carrying with it Joseph Rost, mortally wounded.

He lay helpless and alone. His couch was tender green verdure, with delicate waxy flowers starring the turf, just as if beyond the curving rim there was no carnage and strife. Joseph, passive and faint, wondered if he was to be obliterated by an inundation of blood, or left in peace. He longed for human aid, then dreaded the form in which it might come. He had deserted the city in her need, and she was avenged. The shot had come from the battery above. The wounded man had no idea of the lapse of time; he only realized that all had grown quiet about him; the battle was ebbing away in indistinct mutterings. Gradually he was lifted and floated far away by the transition incident to a mental condition which made no change startling or improbable. The struggle of fierce passions merged into peace. He saw the tabernacle shrouded in a heavy silk curtain. Large candles burned on the reading-desk, where lay the book of the Law, and before the desk stood Benjamin, clad in a woolen mantle richly embroidered with crimson and gold. The delicate, beautiful face was upturned, and shone with unearthly radiance; he touched the book reverently with the corners of his Thalis, and his voice fell like the melody of harps on Joseph's ear:

"Blessed be Thou, oh Lord! Ruler of the world, who hast blessed us above all other people, and hast given to us the Law."

Then the tabernacle crumbled, and Benjamin, rising from glory to glory, was lost in the immensity of heavenly distance.

A sharp thrill ran through Joseph's veins; the throbbing in his side was there again; the remnant of life surged to his brain. A man was kneeling beside him with a canteen of water.

Joseph Rost and Nelson Thorne looked into each other's eyes.

The stranger wore an officer's uniform, torn and blood-stained. He was young and handsome, with a terrible gravity in the tense lines about the mouth. Joseph sipped the water held to his parched lips gratefully, eagerly gazing at his companion the while. The black Hebrew eyes searched the honest Saxon blue ones, which had been sleepy and tender, but were now steady, clear—a trifle hard. The officer asked no questions; it was too late. He had discovered a perishing creature, and held a draught to the dying lips. That was all.

"Take the book from my breast," whispered Joseph. The officer obeyed.

Joseph sighed, and closed his eyes.

"I am a stranger — a foreigner — on business."

Suddenly he looked around and paused. A wild light of anger, doubt, and agony broke over the dying face. Creeping along the edge of the hollow was pursuing Reuben Wentzel, goaded on by eager hatred, driven back by mortal terror. Joseph raised himself on his elbow, and cried, "Hunted to the death! Keep the book, it belongs to me alone. Never, never let him touch it! He's a thief, a spy. The poor Wentzels." (Inexpressible contempt, even at the end.) "I trust you," and, falling back, expired.

Joseph the Jew was like the old Italian artist, who wrought a crystal bowl with a life's labor, and then accidentally broke it.

Reuben Wentzel knelt, and repeated a Kadesch for the dead.

CHAPTER XIV.

JOSEPH'S POCKET-BOOK.

THE officer would have buried the book in Joseph Rost's grave had he not feared disinterment by Reuben Wentzel, whom he was disposed to regard in the light of a jackal. Indeed, the hungry keenness of Herr Wentzel's face was against his chances of success with a candid mind.

The dead youth's clothing was carefully searched for some clue to his identity, a search rewarded only by the name of Rost. Returning to camp, the officer seated himself on a tree stump and drew forth his meerschaum. What should he do? Open the dead man's book? How else could he discover his home? A man was brought to him by the sergeant: Reuben Wentzel prepared to make a final struggle for the possession of Joseph's secret.

"Doubtless you are an honest gentleman, and will do what is right. The book belongs to me, and my dead brother," he began.

"Was the dead man your brother?" demanded the officer, sharply.

Reuben shot one sidelong glance at him, and replied, unhesitatingly,

"Yes."

The officer puffed a cloud of smoke from his pipe before he said, with military brevity,

"False. Your name is Wentzel, his was Rost. You may go. I shall keep the pocket-book."

Reuben grew pale, and twisted his beard.

"What if I demand it?"

"When you show me that you have a right to claim it I will listen to you. Sergeant, take him back."

Left alone, the young man unfolded the leather book, with Joseph's last words ringing in his ear—"I trust you."

Touched by the confidence, he soliloquized,

"Poor fellow! I will prove myself trustworthy."

The pocket-book had the name of Joseph Rost inscribed on the fly-leaf; but, with a curious degree of caution, it would seem, was without city or country.

"Joseph Rost, citizen of the world," observed the officer, turning another leaf.

A fresh puzzle. The book was full of notes —mere memoranda jottings, which would be suggestive to the writer alone—in five languages: here two lines of English, there a dozen in Danish, here a paragraph in Spanish, there a page of French or German. In a pocket were the papers of Grandfather Rost and the directions for Samuel's journey, written in Danish, and therefore unintelligible to the officer. In addition, there was a letter folded in an envelope, but not directed. The officer felt that on the clear translation of this letter depended the discovery of the dead man's relatives. Acting on his first impulse, he inclosed the package to one of his professors at college in the North, requesting a legible interpretation. Had he been at all aware of the value of the papers to himself, he would scarcely have risked allowing them to pass out of his possession.

Before the answer came, the fortress city had struck her flag and yielded to her conquerors, and with her fell the fabric of rebellion. The officer's regiment was still quartered outside the town when the reply arrived. The letter read:

"I can now send home tidings of my success. I have been here five months, and am about to grasp the prize. Could Samuel have done better? I have met Reuben Wentzel here, whom we all despise. The rencontre was unfortunate. I deceived him as to my real object. He tracked me again, and would have inevitably discovered the secret by watching me had I not eluded him. To do this I struck into the wilderness of savannas and everglades, where I decided to stay at the most retired house I could find for a time. Under the guidance of a negro, I discovered an old mansion on the river's bank, ten days' journey on horseback from the city on the coast. The place had been deserted for forty years, yet a cigar-case on the chimney-piece had a name on it—'Frederick William Goffe.' This, then, must have belonged to the buccaneer mentioned by my grandfather, as having robbed him of the necklace. I determined to search the place thoroughly for further information, and then prepared for the night's repose.

"In vain I had reasoned with myself that the deserted house was only dreary and ghostly from long disuse. There was something significant in its very desertion. The negro slept beside the fire, and I soon followed his example. I was aroused by a deadly fear such as I had never experienced before. The place was infused with a new atmosphere. With that I discovered a change; the door behind me was wide open, and through it stepped an old man. He walked slowly to the hearth, without apparently noticing the negro or myself. There was nothing terrible in his appearance, as he stood gazing thoughtfully at the fire; the chilling fear he inspired was, that I knew he did not belong to this world. He was tall and angular, he wore a curious olive-green coat of a past generation, and a silk scarf was knotted in the most peculiar fashion around his neck, with the ends trailing on the ground behind him. He drew through his hands, half absently, a glittering object. Surely if I had not been paralyzed I should have sprung to my feet; it was my grandfather's necklace.

"Flashing before my eyes with a thousand rainbow reflections, quivering in broken stars, in limpid ripples of light, as he threaded it through his fingers or laid it caressingly against the dark relief of his sleeve, was the heir-loom of which the Englishman had robbed us. Had I not been held in icy dumbness of suspense, I must have leaped up and claimed it. A doubt held me back: What power do the dead possess? Was it actually the chain?

"The old man turned his head suddenly, and appeared to listen intently. I feared that the negro's heavy breathing had disturbed him. No.

"He glanced sharply in the direction of the opposite door, hastily thrust the chain into his bosom, and then the fire went out in total darkness, as if quenched by water. After that I slept, or swooned. I only know I was unconscious. Next morning the negro awoke, merry and active, after an uninterrupted slumber. I kept silence as to the events of the night, and began to reflect on the best mode of penetrating the closed rooms. This would have been easy, but for the vigilance of the Indian woman. Evidently she had fastened the rooms after Bernardo's departure, and would permit no one to enter. I did not wish to betray an interest in the house to either of my companions.

"The first day I contrived to send the negro down the river to his home for supplies of food, and especially lights. The Indian woman refused to give me one of the candles used to burn before her altar. During Jake's absence I hoped to gratify my curiosity. In vain! The Indian woman seated herself on the floor in the hall, folded her hands, and held me inactive with her glittering eye. I affected an interest in the birds and flowers; I caught fish in the river's sparkling tide; she never left her post. This much I accomplished, I decided not to enter the rooms by the doors, as she would soon detect it, but to penetrate by one of the windows instead. I studied one casement in rambling through the garden wilderness, and observed that the shutter hung loose.

"The negro returned at nightfall, loaded with provisions, and the woman, her weird brain filled with fancies, talked long and earnestly with Jake. He laughed and shook his head, told her there was a great war, and I was hiding from my enemies. Partly satisfied, she withdrew. I allowed several days to elapse before I made my first attempt.

"By that time we had settled into a routine of life; the negro cooked, hunted, and fished; I strolled about indifferently, and slept much, or appeared to sleep. At last my opportunity came. Usually, the negro coiled himself up before the fire when supper was over, for I took care that he should take no naps during the day. I then lighted one of the tapers and read or wrote in my memorandum-book for hours, in order to be up the latest. Often I fancied that the Indian's eyes were scrutinizing my movements through some crack. My heart beat quickly as I closed my book, when my watch assured me it was eleven o'clock. I put two candles into my pocket, extinguished the light, removed my shoes, and stole out of the hall. The night was horribly thick and impenetrable, even the masses of foliage were but another fold of the darkness. To lift down the shutter and try the window-sash was the work of an instant. It yielded with a grating sound.

I listened breathlessly to learn if it had disturbed the sleepers. The next moment I was in the room. Necessity alone would ever have made me venture there at night. Noiseless, filmy shapes seemed to brush past me while I was lighting my candle.

"A room dead these forty years, with bare ceiling, discolored walls, and not one article of furniture to break the monotony of its four sides. The Indian woman must have fastened the boards across the door leading into the hall, and climbed out of the window afterward. Certainly there was no other means of egress. With cunning she had fastened this door to match the secrecy of the opposite one.

"A glance convinced me that the place was vacant, although I inspected it carefully before climbing out of the window once more. Cautiously I made my way to the other end of the house. Reasoning that this door was also fastened on the inside, and that the Indian had then escaped through one of the windows, I removed the shutters of three successively, and ascertained that a rusty bolt secured each sash within. I could have broken the glass, but that would have made a noise. I did not exactly fear the woman, but I had no knowledge whereby to gauge the depths of a savage's anger, and I preferred to outwit her. There must be a door, either in the floor or the ceiling. Giddy with excitement, I forced my way into the cellar, where my candle threw feeble rays on heavy beams, crumbling earth, and several huge casks moldering away from their iron hoops. The cellar was full of lurking terrors; I saw the old man mocking me; I saw the Indian fiercely watching from the archway; there was a head leering at me from the cask. A stone stairway led to the room above.

"I ascended nervously, received a blow from some unseen source, and reeled back into total darkness, for my candle had slipped from my grasp, and rolled on the ground. I lay silent, expecting an assault, but no sound disturbed the dreadful stillness. Finally, I groped after the missing taper, found and relighted it. Then I discovered what the obstacle actually was; the woman had placed a log on a projection. I slipped past, and found the door, which was fastened with a cord twisted so ingeniously about a hook, that I lost patience while unfastening it. At last I pushed the door open, and entered.

"The floor was covered with a straw matting, used in these hot countries, and a rug was spread before the cane-seated lounge. The matting had become shreds, the curtains had

fallen from their hangings in the lapse of years. Time's tooth had been busy with the embroidery of the arm-chair, the warped and honeycombed wood-work. With a shudder I glanced around for the old man. The place bore evidence of haste and disorder. It was as if some person had searched the effects of another, careless of consequences.

"This is the servant's work. He rifled his master's desks after the latter committed suicide, I instantly decided. Heavens! Was the shade I had beheld that of the man who hung himself? In one corner stood two large vases of solid silver, but of rude workmanship, an ivory idol, in a shrine exquisitely carved, and some massive pieces of plate, which appeared to be placed together ready for removal. Although there were traces of the chamber having served as a sleeping apartment, yet it had more the appearance of a strong-room. The fastening of the door leading to the hall had been formidable; a solid bar of iron crossed the once stout oak panels. My attention was chiefly absorbed by two objects. One was a metal plate containing a pile of ashes, with several bits of charred paper in the midst. Documents had been destroyed, either by master or man. The other was a box with brass clamps inserted in the wall, with a fallen portrait lying on the floor below. Raising the picture, I found that it cleverly concealed the aperture, when hung in its proper place on the wall. With a sudden thrill I recognized on the faded canvas the harsh features of the old man. The portrait was roughly executed, and was possibly the work of some amateur. With trembling fingers I raised the lid of the box, loosely adjusted, after the rifling touch of Bernardo had carelessly prepared the way for me, or whoever came next. It was empty. In vain I tapped the sides for secret inclosures, there was absolutely nothing left but a single gold coin of old Spanish date to reward my diligence. The coin taught me something. The box was used to hold treasure, probably money.

"I next proceeded to examine the table. Every scrap of paper had been burned; the quill pens were perfect, but the inkstand had been converted into a spider mansion. However, a half leaf of a letter had fluttered beneath the table, which I appropriated. Having now remained as long as I dared, I closed the door, adjusted the cord, and made my way back to the hall.

"Next morning I was awakened by the scrutinizing gaze of the Indian fastened on me.

"'Sleep much,'" she muttered, doubtfully.

"I availed myself of the first opportunity to draw forth the paper and study it. As much as the latter half of a letter — therefore without date or address—can teach, I learned. It was the very shadow of a letter, with filmy characters traced on it, some lines dim beyond recognition of their meaning, with here and there a word gleaming out. The language was Spanish. I gleaned that the recipient was urged to go at once to a distant city on the great river, as the writer was very ill. The signature was —'Thy sister, Maddalena.'

"For hours I pondered over this slight clue. To whom did the letter belong? I concluded it must be Bernardo's property, for this reason: If his master was the buccaneer, he was English; therefore *his* sister could scarcely have addressed him in Spanish with the name of 'Maddalena.' The servant, on the contrary, was a Minorcan, had left suddenly after his master's death, had promised the Indian to return, but had never done so. The plate left in the room would have brought him back, although he probably carried off all available booty. No doubt he had also taken the necklace; and to ever find it, I must trace the Minorcan family. Once more I searched the

4

room, but found nothing. I believe the Indian had no suspicion of my clandestine visits.

"I left the place, recovered my horse, and went across the country to the distant city. I am writing now from that city, which is being furiously bombarded; but I seem to have a charmed life. I can not now describe the siege.

"I have found the Minorcans. Bernardo died here. He did not bring the necklace. I believe it is still concealed in the house. He was ignorant of its existence, or he left it safely hidden until his return. I am going back now to seek for it. Had I only known before what I now do, I should have escaped the accursed conflict of these armies, whose victory or defeat are alike a matter of indifference to me. I write this information in event of any misfortune befalling me. I shall post this letter by one of the blockade-runners of the coast."

Here the letter ended abruptly.

The officer turned over Grandfather Rost's papers, and the directions for Samuel.

"What are you reading?" asked Nicholas Hearn, jocosely, as he passed.

"A romance," quietly replied Nelson Thorne.

CHAPTER XV.

NELSON THORNE.

WHEN Joseph Rost was being educated in the north of Europe, the young officer, seated on the tree-stump reading his papers, had received his training for life in a far different school.

Possessed of unfailing sweetness of temper and an indolent disposition, the boyhood of Nelson Thorne refused to yield to the restless impulses of activity about him. His teachers termed him a dunce, his fellow-pupils lazy-bones. His father was simply amazed at the healthy animal, who possessed so little of his own ambition and industry.

Experience Thorne was a stern man, of strong passions and curbing will. About him lingered a far-distant reputation of extraordinary gayety in early youth, succeeded by a reform to staid, severe middle age, as complete as the Catholic devotee's laying aside of earthly vanities for cell or hermit's cave; in either case, a frequent phase of human nature after idle frivolity, and apt to run to the same extreme. Of this gay youth there came to the son not even the romance; he only knew the father of a dark, roomy house at the corner of two narrow streets in the city of his birth. At the back of the house was a small garden and one walnut-tree, drooping its branches over the kitchen-shed. This tree was associated with his earliest remembrances, because of an attempt to climb, frustrated by a firm grasp on the ascending little legs.

A still more remote memory lingered, like a star glittering in darkest night, somewhere back in the very realm of babyhood; a graceful form had flitted among the roses of that tiny garden, and had rested in silent repose afterward, with the roses drooping in fragrant clusters about the chamber where Experience Thorne was praying wildly to be taken also, kneeling, in agony, beside the voiceless clay of his idol.

The little son stood at the door, peering wonderingly in at the strange scene. Over the chimney-piece hung the portraits of a blooming girl in a short-waisted gown, with her hair confined by a high Spanish comb, and gloves drawn over the elbows. The little son, forgetting to taste the ginger-cake the sobbing cook had just given him below stairs, stared at the portrait, and the waxen face beneath. The girl's eyes in the picture sparkled with hope, which life in her home on the bleak hill-side beside the frozen river might never quench, and here the hope was quenched in death to Experience Thorne. The rounded bloom of the cheek was gone; the light feet had not been able to outstrip the pursuing enemy of all her race of blithe sisters—consumption.

After that the mother was gone; only the picture remained. A stolid man came to the house every night, and went away again, with a lantern, and supper of cold meat, bread, and cheese in a napkin. There was nothing terrible in this man's aspect; he was a steady, matter-of-fact English laborer; but the little son grew to have a shuddering interest in him somehow associated with the dead mother. Perhaps he gathered crumbs of mysterious talk from the servants' allusions to grave-yards, and attached them all to this stranger.

Sometimes he came in heavy rain-storms, with the moisture dripping from his oil-skin coat; but, whatever the weather, he invariably carried away the lantern and his supper. More curious still, the lantern was back in its place in the morning, hanging on a peg in the kitchen hall. Often the little son climbed on a chair to investigate, but the lantern had no tales to tell.

At last the laborer disappeared, the lantern rusted on the peg, and the little son forgot a matter which was still fresh in the bereaved heart of Experience Thorne: this man had watched beside his wife's tomb.

From that date the father perceptibly changed, grew stern in his religion, and, meeting with a reverse of fortune soon after, applied himself diligently to business. Only in one phase of character did he evince enthusiasm, and was easily swayed by the influences of progress about him. A race foremost in the enterprises of the century, with the fresh ardor of a new nation, we Americans often leap at the fruit before it is ripe for plucking, and sometimes grasp leaves instead of any fruit at all.

Experience Thorne possessed an iron constitution, and he proceeded to test the metal of it in various ways. Four o'clock of a winter morning found him reading a book of devotions aloud by the light of a solitary candle. At five he was trudging through the snow-covered streets, skirting wide parks, ermine-draped, peering into his office to see if the clerks had done their duty overnight, and inspecting the markets.

If the drowsy little son was not standing behind his chair at the breakfast-table on the stroke of six, he knew only too well what to expect.

Experience Thorne became a Grahamite, and fed his family conscientiously on bran. He employed the little son in reading aloud pamphlets on his favorite hobby; he weighed the food he ate with scales, and counted narrowly the sips of water imbibed by the little son at a meal. A favorite theory was, that one article of nourishment sufficed for a repast, but facts conquered one unwilling little disciple.

A supper long to be remembered was that at which Experience Thorne and his son partook gravely of a feast of Brazil-nuts in the dark oak-wainscoted dining-room. The doctor was summoned before morning. The nuts were packed off up garret; and as one experiment succeeded another, the result of failure being thus swept out of sight, the Thorne garret became a museum of wonders, a banquet of delicacies to the children of the neighborhood. The master was proud, even in his foibles, and never again alluded to discarded theories. He clothed poor lecturers; his parlors became the rendezvous of eager, cadaverous men, who came and went with much apparent bustle. The little son hated these visitors with all the intense, unreasoning animosity of childhood, and resented the bland pats on the head he received from their cold fingers.

The temper of Experience Thorne's household suffered severely under these trials, although he was unconscious of it. Was it not sufficient to depress the spirit of Bridget M'Grath, cook, to be kept on slops of Indian meal (indignantly rejected by old Ireland in time of famine), without even a taste of meat or wheat bread allowed? Then to be called into the parlor to show the approving gentlemen how she throve on the diet! And the blessed, motherless child, that went prowling about the empty cupboards for a bit of something to his mind! Sure, it was many a surreptitious beefsteak he discussed with Mrs. M'Grath. Hence the rosy appearance of the victims. Hence the hypocrisy practiced under Experience Thorne's very nose.

If during the week the son was subjected to much discipline, he experienced no pleasure in looking forward to the Sabbath at the close. The Puritans seldom understood teaching children the religion of love in Jesus Christ. He might lay the foundation of a future firm and noble manhood, but during the transition of tender youth he scattered no flowers. Nelson's boyhood consisted of a series of spiritual buffetings, as it were. If he was good, he would be saved for awful glories which frightened him. If he was wicked, he would be doomed to torments which terrified him still more. The process of being either good or bad was not made at all clear to his comprehension, for the simple reason that he asked no questions, so glad was he to escape from the subject to foot-ball and hop-scotch.

At the age of eight years the case stood thus: He was not to steal or tell falsehoods, of course. But what else was expected of him? He was told that a change of heart was necessary, and to the boy's mind the expression had only a literal significance. Many a time he listened to the throbs of the great organ of life, wondering what was to happen. Once, when he bade his father good-night, the latter said, with impressive earnestness,   *

"My son, you can be a Christian before you reach the top stair. Remember how much I wish it."

Up the staircase, shrouded in shadows, went the little figure, carrying a lamp, oppressed by an indefinable dread, yet listening to the strokes of his heart step by step, slowly, wonderingly, pausing on each one to discover if he was still the same boy, until the landing was gained.

"Guess I never shall be any thing but a bad boy!" he exclaimed, making a petulant rush into his chamber. Afterward he laughed merrily; childhood re-asserted sway over healthy nerves.

Years afterward he saw the Saviour in the

glories of a painted window, through which the light flowed in wide effulgence down into the twilight dimness of a church.

He had not been slain by a thunder-bolt of wrath on the stairway, and so might live after his own fancy. A sensitive child would have suffered the pain of self-reproach more keenly; but Nelson was not a very sensitive child. He became only more indolent and carelessly good-humored.

Sunday was then a moral strait-jacket, a season of wearisome exhortations, alternating with rebellious thoughts of what he would do when a grown man.

There stood the old minister in the pulpit, with wiry hair bristling upward from his forehead, and a funny nose, at which Nelson stared from his father's pew three times a day. The preacher's words might be eloquent to older ears, his eyes beaming with zealous intelligence; the boy seldom noticed either. If a fly ventured into meeting, there was food for speculation whether it would continue to buzz and bump stupidly against the glass pane, or escape before the sermon was over, as Nelson would like to have done.

In the adjoining pew sat an old lady, whose appearance inspired awe in the lad's heart. Her silk gown seemed to creak with richness, and her brown curls were so primly smooth that Nelson could not but wonder if they were laid away in a bureau drawer all the week, to keep so nice, 'as indeed they were. He never dared to gaze openly at the old lady, but made these discoveries in a series of sly glances during prayers. Imagine his astonishment when she stealthily pulled his sleeve and popped a large peppermint-drop into his hand. The influence of that peppermint-drop was incalculable. Nelson placed it on his tongue; a balmy fragrance was diffused, which caused Experience Thorne to sniff suspiciously, and glance at his son, who maintained an immovable demeanor. The little man's thoughts were busy. Here in an arid desert was unexpected peppermint, and the kindly impulse to give it to a strange boy. His heart warmed, glowed when he thought of the old lady in the false front. Previously he had misjudged her by the supposition that she was a stiff spinster, a term of indefinable disgrace among his schoolmates; now he firmly believed her to be grandmother.

The very next day he expended his hoard of pennies in the purchase of a nosegay, learned the old lady's address from the sexton, and took it to her. The recipient did not know which to consider the most beautiful—the flowers, or the lad's flushed, happy face.

The peppermint became an established institution, in the second prayer.

If there was much prose, there was also one gem of romance, a beautiful young lady. The boy's sharp young eyes examined the plumes of her hat, the pattern of her ear-drops; above all, the soft outline of her face and silken masses of golden hair. Often did Nelson become so pleasantly absorbed in sketching the husband she would marry, how she must look without her hat, that he aroused with a start, to the consciousness that the minister had ceased speaking, and pulled down his spectacles from his forehead the bridge of his nose, preparatory to giving out the hymn.

Nelson fell into deep disgrace. Some trivial matter brought to his father's mind the subject of card-playing, and, with that horror of an infatuation which he recalled only with shame and disgust, he strove to imbue his son with a like principle. The son was innocent and ignorant. Forthwith he questioned his schoolmates concerning this ensnaring delusion, and the result was, a big boy permitted him to witness a game of high-low-jack. The big boy played with the skill and coolness of a veteran. From admiring inaction, Nelson became a timid participant. In a week he would have wearied of the sport, had there not been that zest of clandestine danger about it. Then the big boy dared Nelson to play at home, and the latter, writhing under the taunt, waxed sufficiently bold to invite three friends to a game in the pantry, with Bridget M'Grath's sanction, on a holiday.

The pantry possessed many advantages; there was a sugar-barrel to serve as a table, and the various avenues of escape were easy, in case of alarm. Mrs. M'Grath even agreed to rattle the poker, and sing the "Banks of Killarney" louder than usual, as a danger signal. The M'Grath creed was indulgent.

"Let the darlints enjoy theirselves. Faith! it's a little drop they'll be getting out of life, anyways."

The fun was exhilarating; the game progressed famously; Nelson was actually beating the big boy, when a shadow fell athwart the sugar-barrel table. Experience Thorne was gazing down at the youthful gamesters from the street above. The big boy ignominiously fled. Experience Thorne swept the cards into the kitchen fire, and it was understood at school that he did not spare the rod on that occasion.

A second dishonor followed swiftly on the first one. Nelson daily took his way to a large school, with sachel slung over one shoulder, joined by mates on the way. Nelson was far from being a brilliant scholar. In vain did his father wait for him to win some prize for diligent application or talent. The son was far more likely to be nibbling an apple furtively, or drawing a caricature of the master under his desk-lid than conning his lesson. Experience Thorne vented sarcasm and reproach; the boy was hurt, and made good resolutions, which evaporated before the next hard task. "Unstable as water, thou shalt not excel," was a sentence which he read on the wall opposite his bed, when he opened his eyes one morning. He could readily surmise whose hand had framed it there, and for life the sentence haunted him uncomfortably, although at the time it bore no fruit.

Destiny was commencing her work on this heedless lad, one bright September day, when he strolled along to school, as usual.

Destiny brought Sam Howson around the corner with such precipitation that he rebounded from our hero into the gutter, spilling the treasures of his luncheon-bag. He was up again, with the agility of a cat.

"Guess what has happened to Tommy?" he demanded, breathlessly.

"He's not dead?" queried Nelson.

"No: worse than that, mother says. He's gone to the insane asylum, clean cracked," replied Sam, tasting his crisp turn-over, to judge if the fall had at all impaired its flavor.

The two boys walked on soberly. Tommy, a slender, delicate child, had been the precocious scholar of the class, the pride of the master's heart, who never wearied of displaying what Tommy could do at blackboard or recitation. Of course Tommy was the knight who carried off the prizes in the tournament of unfolding minds. How about unfolding bodies? In the act of receiving the well-earned reward of his industry fragile little Tommy fell, and was seen no more in the busy walks of life.

Presently the boys were joined by the big boy, who was profoundly respected by both in their hearts. The big boy had a certain lofty patronage of manner, which became him well, enjoyed a liberal supply of pocket-money, and was supposed to have seen much of the world. The trio approached a building which had always been to Nelson's imagination a temple of wonders. It had a faded appearance by day, and the spacious entrance was redolent of stale tobacco-smoke, but a flag fluttered bravely from the roof. At the door lounged a young man, with a profusion of cheap jewelry flowing over a gay waistcoat, a cane, his hat worn very much on one side, and his hair oiled. He winked in a friendly way at the three boys as they passed. "Do you go to the Comet often?" inquired the big boy.

Nelson was obliged to confess that he had never been to "the Comet," or any other theatre in his life.

Experience Thorne considered the theatre as the epitome of all evil, and his son had been early fortified against its wiles, indeed before he could well understand the warning. Moreover, he had been strictly forbidden ever to enter a place of amusement.

"Never been to a theatre!" scoffed the big boy. "You *must* be precious green!"

Nelson reddened to the roots of his hair; but as the scorner took himself off to recognize an acquaintance at that painful moment, a reply was unnecessary. There was balm, also, in Gilead. Sam Howson was in a like predicament.

"I wonder if it is nice. What do they act?"

"Lots of fun to see—eh?"

Suddenly the two boys halted and looked at each other. Black eyes twinkled: "Let's go and see for ourselves." Gray eyes flashed back, "Now! instead of going to school." The smart young man had strolled away; they entered the passage, crossed a vestibule, and were suddenly ingulfed in darkness. Half an hour later Nelson was lying at the foot of a crooked stairway with a dislocated ankle, and Sam Howson was groping blindly after assistance.

The young explorers had entered a vast place which seemed like a cavern. Faint rays of daylight gleamed through the closed windows, here and there showing shadowy outlines of gallery, and a dome spanning the obscurity far overhead. Every object was strange and mysterious to the children, who peopled the cavern with a race entirely dissimilar to themselves. Unaccountable sounds rumbled through the building, now under their feet, now overhead, succeeded by unearthly silence. The busy street they had so recently quitted seemed miles away.

A dusky curtain flew up, revealing a second abyss of darkness, lighted sparsely with flaring gas-jets. There was a hum of voices, and a great many people to be seen rushing wildly about, talking and gesticulating. Evidently there was a serious quarrel. Spell-bound, the boys watched a deadly strife, in which one man defended himself with desperate valor against a dozen ruffians, tripping them up like nine-pins as they approached. Most puzzling were the comments of a person who leaned against a pasteboard castle with a book in his hand.

"Try that once more, Jenkins. You die too easy."

Forthwith up popped the first assassin and attacked the solitary man again. So palpable a sham made Sam Howson cynical.

"It's only make-believe," he whispered.

Then a lady wearing a shabby bonnet and shawl sang a song hoarsely about being a queen, and then the curtain swept down once more.

No great harm was done had the boys then departed; but the spell of curiosity was on them, and they made their way to the orches-tra, climbed to the stage, and penetrated to the world behind the scenes. They clamber-ed over carpenters' tools, narrowly escaped fall-ing through a trap, and finally toppled down a screen with a dull reverberating noise. In his haste to escape after this disaster, Nelson plunged headlong down the crooked stair-way.

"Where are you?" quavered Sammy How-son, his courage failing in this emergency.

"Down here; and oh, Sam! my leg is bro-ken, I know."

"P'raps we are caught in a cage, and can never get out," suggested Sam, in great ex-citement.

At this moment a spark of light approached, shed from a taper in the hand of a pallid man, clad in a flannel dressing-gown. This man was talking to himself in a way that froze the blood in Sam's veins as he listened.

"If sooth I say, I must report they were
As cannon overcharg'd with double cracks;
So they doubly redoubled strokes upon the foe:
Except they meant to bathe in recking wounds,

Or memorize another Golgotha,
I can not tell:
But I am faint, my gashes cry for help."

"Please, sir, Nelson is down there," faltered Sam, plucking timidly at the flannel dressing-gown.

The stranger drew himself up, surveyed the very small boy haughtily, and waved his hand majestically:

"So well thy words become thee as thy wounds;
They smack of honor both:—Go, get him surgeons."

Sam was on the point of ducking behind a canvas rock which the candle revealed, and leaving Nelson to his fate, when the latter cried, pettishly,

"Do help me up!"

"Eh? What the deuce is this?" said the stranger, in natural tones, putting down his pa-pers, and lifting the boy carefully.

Soon they were surrounded by the assassins, director, and even the hoarse lady, who kindly laid Nelson's head on her shoulder in a moth-erly way, calling him "poor dear" repeatedly. Sam Howson was questioned as to the cause of their appearance on the stage, but was re-markably reticent in his replies.

It happened that as Experience Thorne was passing "The Comet," he beheld a procession issuing forth, consisting of the assassins in a body, bearing along his son, with a woman in a shabby bonnet holding his hand. Sam How-son followed, furtively-wiping his eyes on his jacket-cuff.

The result of this escapade was that Nelson was sent away to school, and afterward to col-lege. Here he made the acquaintance of Nicholas Hearn in a curious way. He had the honor of losing one of his cherished whis-kers, and having an eye endangered by an ex-plosion of gases at the hands of Nicholas.

CHAPTER XVI.

ST. CHRYSOSTOM.

IT was small, musty, and damp, but these qualifications only imparted a flavor of age in a land where all things are new. Erected by a former Mrs. Raines, St. Chrysostom was the result of piety, as well as an imitation of the churches on English estates for the tenantry, only here there was no tenantry.

Little St. Chrysostom, ivy-grown and gray, was held dear by all succeeding members of the family, and that was sufficient reason to make it the fashion of the town, for the Raineses had owned this property quite from the date of the colonies.

There were tablets on the walls lauding the virtues of departed Raineses, royalists and patriots; a memorial window to the good lady-founder; and beside the chancel an alcove, where the glowing warmth of a rosette casement fell on a marble group, angel alighting, with snowy wings outspread, beside the children who will awaken when "the sea shall give up her dead."

Not for any consideration could St. Chrysostom be modernized. The clergyman ascended a spiral stairway to the pulpit, perched above the clerk's desk; the pews were square boxes, into which the occupant vanished. This seclusion was grateful to the true worshiper, but displeasing to the gay summer frequenters of the shore, who lived on the excitement of assuming fresh toilets, and languished with envy over a neighbor's French bonnet. Yet the quaint little church was thronged of a summer Sunday, because it was the proper thing to do.

Unusual preparations were being made to celebrate Easter. The Raines family had returned, after years of absence in Europe. Mrs. Raines had made her advent acceptable by presenting a new altar-cloth, a neat purse to the rector, and a gift to every child in the parish.

Perhaps David Brownson, organist, was chiefly interested in the occasion, for he cherished a mighty secret, not shared even with the rector. He fidgeted about the organ-loft, arranged the music, and imparted to a beetle-browed contralto, a surly basso, and conceited young tenor, such singular commands as these: "Mind that you give her a chance. If she loses confidence, cover her faults. We will have no discords at Easter."

The chimes rang out on the breeze, which was sweet with the promise of early spring. A holy calm rested on earth and sky. The sea rimpled up in blue transparent lines, foam-flecked, and melted away to a tender haze on the horizon, across which the ships passed, like full flower-petals wind-blown. David Brownson, with his sandy hair all awry, and his queer face puckered into a perturbed expression, peered down into the church, and walked to the little door leading to his musical kingdom, consulting his watch as he did so.

He discovered nothing save an indiscretion on the part of Mikey Burke, the organ-blower, in smoking a clay pipe within the sacred precincts, a fault remedied by the simple process of reversing the pipe in Mr. Burke's coat-pocket.

The chimes ceased; a soft rustling of draperies announced the arrival of the Raines ladies. Brownson, with a smothered exclamation of disgust, began his voluntary. In vain the banks of white keys lured his fancy, and the golden pipes waited to swell the grand harmonies which usually came from his inspired fingers. The organist's execution was measured and cold. Truth to tell, he was troubled by the absence of the soprano of the day, and anathematized the unreliability of girls in his thoughts. Very well he realized that the con-

tralto was exchanging significant glances with
the basso, and the young tenor openly smirk-
ing, yet he wove strain within strain of that
deliberate melody, hoping that before he finished she would come. Surely David Brownson had never played in this mood before.

The clergyman, turning the leaves of the
great Bible, glanced up inquiringly. Some of
the congregation craned their necks to obtain a
glimpse of the organist, under the impression,
possibly, that he had changed in appearance
since they last beheld him.

With one final, ill-tempered crash, David
gave the word to the contralto to take the solo
intended for the absent soprano. The contralto rolled forth her deep, powerful notes accordingly.

A quick patter of steps, a rush of garments,
and a girl entered the choir. With flushed
cheeks and sparkling eyes she surveyed the
situation. David Brownson was aware of her
approach, but he did not permit himself to be
moved. It was too late. She advanced quickly to his side.

"Give me the solo."

Still playing, the organist replied,

"You are breathed. Sit down until the
psalm."

"Give me the solo!" repeated the girl, imperiously, at the same time pulling his sleeve.

David smiled grimly; he liked her pluck.
Then she stepped down into her place, waiting
for the contralto to finish, and experiencing
that nervous contraction of the throat peculiar
to young debutantes.

There swelled forth from the St. Chrysostom
choir a voice pure and fresh as a bird's. The
first notes were soft, shy, and exquisitely tremulous, like the fledgling essaying the song that
will later resound through the upper air; then,
gathering volume from the very determination
of the owner, soared and thrilled with piercing
sweetness, until they died away in silvery ca-
dences, guided by delicate chords from the organ, into silence.

A woman's voice, moving the heart to un-
tried depths of delight and pain, fascinating unwilling senses, pleasing even the uncultivated
ear. No wonder Queens of Song have ruled
as Queens of State never have done.

The girl nodded at David Brownson over her
shoulder, and peeped down into the church
through the curtains. A mischievous smile
dimpled her cheek as she spread out her gloved
hands and inspected them.

"If old David only knew! Tidy girls never
lose their gloves, and have to rummage boxes
for them. The tidy girls always have their
worldly possessions so arranged that if they
have a fit of wishing to wear collars and ribbons in the dead of night, they can find those
articles without a candle."

An old woman, wearing an antiquated shawl
and bonnet, had listened to the singing, with
her bony hands clasped tightly together. How
the honest heart throbbed beneath that faded
shawl, which looked as if it came out of Noah's
ark! How another girl's cheek flushed with
ready sympathy down among the congregation!

St. Chrysostom was simply astonished. The
voice had never been heard before. This was
David Brownson's surprise. The battery of
eyes assailed the choir with "Who is it?"
Then the battery of eyes returned to the investigation of the Raines family—a curiosity
shared by the soprano, apparently.

Mrs. Raines, carefully preserved, inclined to
embonpoint—a soft, purring, sleepy woman,
with a guileless manner—of whom her world
remarked that she knew how to use her claws.
The world's verdict was eminently vulgar.
One could not possibly associate the idea of
claws with Mrs. Raines's plump hands.

Miss Raines, stepdaughter, elderly, sharp-
featured, lame.

Mr. Raines, stepson, small, plain, and also
elderly—the gentleman Ethel Hearn had rebelled against in spirit when Peggy pronounced
him her future husband. It was Ethel Hearn
who sat gazing down on the unconscious object
of her sudden aversion now.

"He has a bald spot on the top of his head,
and a mole on his chin. Dear me! how ugly.
Little sister says he has such a good face. I
would rather have more beauty and less good-
ness. The other one is splendid."

The "other one" was a handsome young
man, with fine figure, military carriage, and
drooping flaxen mustache. The head was narrow, complexion pale, blue eyes, keen and scrutinizing, but he was well dressed, wore an eyeglass, and had a languid elegance of manner
very captivating to a girl's fancy. In a word,
Captain Lacer, son of Mrs. Raines by a previous marriage.

The Raines carriage stood before the door,
with prancing steeds in steel trappings, foot-
man and coachman studded with buttons. The
stepchildren always had walked to church.
Mrs. Raines demurred; pedestrianism did not
agree with her. Or was it that one-half of her
life having known no equipage, her declining
days must make the most of one?

Said the lady, arranging her robe, and leaning back among the cushions luxuriously, "You *must* bring me that soprano. Really, she sang like an angel!"

"Best go and see her to-morrow at her home," suggested Miss Raines, who possessed the simplicity of good-breeding.

Perhaps the best trait of this proud family was a lack of ostentation. Mrs. Raines was a fresh tributary, and never wearied of playing the rôle of great lady.

"My dear Hester, why not here?" she inquired, artlessly.

At that moment David Brownson appeared with his protégé, followed by Olive and Peggy. The two gentlemen stood beside the carriage passive spectators.

"Pray bring her here. I am confident that she is the soprano," said Mrs. Raines, beckoning to the organist.

David complied, proud of the praise about to be bestowed on his pupil. Commendation would stimulate her to fresh exertion, he felt assured; and although he despised the flattery of fine ladies, he was willing to hold this cup to Ethel's lips.

What the Raines party beheld was this: The church door was in shadow, the building being of the approved mediæval gloom, and from it the girl came into the broad light of day. She was the type of American beauty; slender and willowy in form, very beautiful in early youth, but suggestive of anxiety for the future. Her features were delicately cut; her skin of that extraordinary fairness which is transparent, and varies with every emotion; mouth small, with sensitive curves, and short, haughty upper lip; hair neither red nor white, but pure rich gold. The chief charm of the face lay in the eyes; for where strict adherence to the caste of blonde beauty would have made the lashes paler, giving that rabbity aspect so often seen, a thick chestnut fringe shaded large, deep-gray orbs, whose only fault was a sparkling unsteadiness of expression. Mrs. Raines sighed involuntarily, and re-arranged the black lace veil over her well-rouged cheeks. Only at one fleeting moment of life can a woman brave unflinchingly the pitiless scrutiny of the midday sun.

"You must permit us to congratulate you on your success to-day. Your voice is lovely. We will see what can be done. You must not stay *here*. When you have leisure, will you come up to the house and sing for us again?"

It occurred to Mrs. Raines that she would vastly enjoy finding a Jenny Lind or Nilsson among the peasant-class, and become patroness of the star.

Ethel Hearn had never been in society in her life, but she understood perfectly well that the rich lady had not proposed calling on her, the choir-singer. She might come up to the house as the trades-people did.

"You are very kind, madam," she contrived to say. Then she turned her lovely eyes to the two men appealingly, as much as to question, "You could not treat me thus."

After that the Raines carriage trundled away, and the Hearn girls took the path homeward. All the pleasure of triumph had vanished from Ethel's face.

"How I hate to be patronized! I will never sing in church again: and when I go to 'the house' we shall know it."

"By Jove! what a beauty!" exclaimed Captain Lacer.

"Very pretty, and so lady-like," assented John Raines, who cared not a straw whether a handsome girl dwelt at the gate or in a larger mansion.

"She did not say she would come," mused Mrs. Raines.

"It would have sounded better to have proposed visiting her," said Miss Raines, who never minced matters.

"My dear Hester, I do not perceive that it was expected."

"Never mind, mamma, I will attend to her." She looked point blank at Captain Lacer as she said this.

"Quite handsome, only so *gauche*," acquiesced Mrs. Raines.

Miss Raines smiled. The *gaucherie* might be applied elsewhere in the brief interview with Ethel Hearn.

"Perhaps she is as good as we are."

"Here? Impossible."

"True. I forgot that we belonged to the blood-royal."

Mrs. Raines winced. Her own father had followed the honest calling of pork contractor. She lapsed into silence. She was never guilty of the rashness of quarreling with her step-children.

"Hester, when you were eighteen you resembled that girl," said the brother.

"I know," replied Miss Raines, quietly.

CHAPTER XVII.

AN UNLUCKY FAMILY.

"GOD gave to Ethel every thing. She has a sweet voice, plenty of wit, and all the beauty the family could muster. It does not seem quite fair—does it, mother?"

The speaker veiled some sadness beneath the merriment with which she thus questioned the decrees of Providence. She was seated on a low stool beside her mother's arm-chair, and they were both gazing out at the sea.

A small, trimly-built girl of one-and-twenty, round-faced, of irregular features, perhaps, and not possessing the dazzling fairness of her sister—a face that interested the most casual observer by the calm reliance of expression, which experience had early imposed on the young life. Olive Hearn, the little sister, as she was familiarly termed, served as balance-wheel to that diminutive establishment beyond the beach, which shared the need of a head with larger mansions. She was the financier, and scrupulously paid every penny due; charmed tidbits away from the young butcher, to tempt her mother's delicate appetite; kept the china closet tidy; and concocted new dishes with the aid of a venerable cook-book, which remained a delightful mystery to Peggy until completion. Moreover, she was chief dress-maker and nurse. There was a beautiful neatness, a dainty precision about her, which was charming. It required a much longer time to arrange her collar and neck-tie than those of hap-hazard Ethel; but, when once adjusted, the result was perfect.

"If ever I saw an old maid!" Ethel would exclaim, giving her ribbon a skillful twist that produced an effect which was all the wearer desired.

I do not use the familiar praise, often bestowed on meek heroines, that Olive Hearn's brown hair was smooth, because it was not. Fashion required a crinkly condition, and Olive knew the fashion as well as any body. Why not? Had she lived in the wilderness she would have found the farmers' daughters worrying their hard-working parents to purchase finery, and she had the superior advantage of dwelling on the outskirts of a summer resort instead.

To search the calendars of crime in these United States would be to find the source of much evil — Dress. Harassed fathers, embarrassed husbands, desperate lovers, each with this goad spurring them to destruction.

A seed of the poison-plant had winged its way into the Hearn home. It took root in different ways. The little sister cut and basted the rich ladies she saw in her mental eye, like the doll's dress-maker, without a thought of envy or resentment. An old alpaca gown might be refurbished and trimmed like the rich lady's silk, by her deft fingers. Ethel, wrathfully rebellious, would toss her worn frock into a corner until her anger against Fate cooled a trifle.

"As for me, I am fit only to be housekeeper, I suppose. A jog-trot!" said the girl, pursuing her train of thought aloud.

"Never underrate yourself, my dear," replied her mother, gently. "God sent you to me when I should have utterly failed without you."

Mrs. Hearn's voice trembled. She was a woman wasted by one of those nervous diseases which have their source in some preying sorrow. Her aspect was melancholy and apprehensive. She always glanced eagerly at an opening door, like a person crushed by a terrible blow, yet anticipating another, without the physical courage to endure it. Pain had blanched her hair, sharpened her features, and hollowed her eyes, was revealed by her weary, listless motions. To such a wrecked nature

Peggy was friend much more than servant, while Olive was the spiritual bulwark.

A great many years before, the sorrow had come which shattered this life. Mr. Albert Hearn discussed his breakfast, kissed the children, lingered a moment to fondle the curls of his daughter Ethel, and took his way down town. Many persons remembered how he looked that morning, good-humored, handsome, the best-dressed man on the street. Jared Hearn especially recollected, for his generous brother had promised to loan him a considerable sum toward purchasing the factory up in the country, which his soul coveted, on that day.

Mr. Albert Hearn entered the spacious building where the Russian Empire Insurance Company transacted business, of which he was president, and opened a letter on his desk. The clerk who brought in the morning mail observed that he was deadly pale, and rested his head on his hand. In those brief moments the wheel had revolved, crushing Albert Hearn. Afterward he was seen writing busily. At noon he passed out, and this side of the grave no one ever expects to see Albert Hearn again. He vanished. In those days such a sensation as his flight occasioned was rare. Now the shock is far more frequently felt. Let those without sin, or who have never known temptation, blame him. Bitten by the mania of speculation, he had staked a little, and lost—appropriated the funds in his charge to cover deficiencies from time to time, hoping to recover the whole amount eventually, and so had stood for a year with the sand crumbling beneath his feet, ever nearer the precipice down which he was destined to slide. The letter had taught him that the position was no longer tenable. In one blinding flash the light had come to him, and it is possible that the weak man did not until then realize his sin. He confessed to his wife, in a hasty note, that he should be a greater disgrace to his family if he remained to be publicly shamed than if he fled. He reminded her that the home in which they lived was her own property. He commended her to the care of his brothers. He promised to exert every energy to repair the havoc done in time, and return to her again.

This was the blow which fell on Albert Hearn's wife at the age of twenty-seven years, and crushed her. She was a light-hearted lady of mercurial temperament, with a strain of Irish wit in her composition, passionately attached to her husband, and always well treated by her world.

Jared and Richard Hearn met in solemn conclave. The plea of helpless affliction in the orphaned family, the consideration of the service the disgraced brother had ever done them, found no place in their thoughts. Indeed, they were disposed to regard the very existence of the Albert Hearn branch as a grievance. They were ambitious men, and they stood on the plane of selfish respectability. Albert had dishonored them. Moreover, the Russian Empire Insurance Company, virtuously indignant that it should have been deceived by so genteel a president, had a clear right to track and arrest Albert Hearn as a common felon, unless something was done. The two brothers reflected, knitted their brows, pursed up their lips, and took their way to the sister-in-law's residence.

It certainly was not so framed in the gentlemen's minds, for they prided themselves on their clemency, but it served as an outlet to their righteous indignation to visit it on the household of the late defaulter.

The house was precisely in the same condition it had been on the morning when the father went away. The blinds were drawn close, to exclude the daylight, and there was an aspect of suspended animation, as if the sources of life were frozen, more sad than confusion would have been. Jared Hearn glanced sourly at the lace curtains, the rich hangings, the graceful ornaments grouped about the handsome parlors. He was a plain man, and had not yet arrived at the grandeur of velvet carpets.

Mrs. Hearn came down stairs, with her little children trooping after. Instinct taught her mother's heart that their presence would soften the resentment of the visitors toward the absent father. She essayed to smile—a pitiful mockery on the pale face—and extended her hand. Neither of her visitors rose from their seats, or noticed her gestures of welcome. They had something more important to consider just then than their manners. Mrs. Hearn would find it useless to propitiate them. It must be inferred that the Hearn politeness was not a gentle courtesy emanating from the heart, but a mask assumed "only when it would pay."

The desolate wife shivered. In her previous experience, it had always been worth while for her brother-in-law to respect her, and she had unconsciously accepted the spurious coin of regard for pure gold. Even now she had faith in them, while they distrusted the motive even of her greeting.

"Send those children away," said Richard Hearn, drawing off one lavender glove and examining his fair, well-kept hand critically, on which sparkled a diamond ring. Richard Hearn hated children.

An angry spot glowed on each of the mother's white cheeks as she bade them run out. Miss Ethel, aged six years, a marvel of prettiness, in white frock and pink boots, made a grimace suggestive of defiance at her respectable uncle.

"You never did know how to manage; they ride rough-shod of every thing here," observed Richard, virtuously restraining himself from any other demonstration of resentment than a frown at the daring child.

Mrs. Hearn regarded him steadily, and compressed her quivering lips. The juvenile element was banished.

"The children are well enough," interposed Jared, stroking his chin, to which was appended a wisp of gray beard, aptly termed goatee, for it imparted to his face a very goat-like aspect. "We've got something more important to talk about, I calculate. Your husband has disgraced us, and we are proud of our good name. I don't reckon that we have had a thief or felon on our list before. There's no good in crying; it won't mend matters. I don't say, though, that you ain't to blame—very much to blame."

Mrs. Hearn raised her face from the handkerchief in which she had hidden it—not her tears, for her grief was as yet tearless—with some faint perception of humor in Jared Hearn's words. Her wretchedness was oppressive enough, but the peculiar susceptibility of her organization to detect the ludicrous cast that glimmer of light over her features. Much was also due to the overstrained tension of her nerves; for three days and nights she had paced the floor of her chamber, refusing all consolation.

Hysteria whispered in her ear, "What possible ingenuity on Richard Hearn's part can twist this matter into your fault? What have you done except to be a loving wife and mother, considering business matters beyond your ken?"

"Any woman is to blame who lets her husband run on so, without saving up and teaching him economy. I always knew that a breakdown would come sooner or later. I've said as much to wife a hundred times. Look at all this trumpery bought with the money of other people!"

"Did you come to tell me what is to be done?" inquired Mrs. Hearn, dreary and rigid again.

Richard Hearn lounged opposite, with one hand thrust deep in his pocket, and the other twirling a tooth-pick. His attitude was far more fitting for a hotel reading-room than a lady's parlor. Mrs. Hearn scarcely recognized him, for he boasted of a reputation as "ladies' man."

"Yes," he chimed in, dropping the tooth-pick on the carpet. "We have got to pay the fifty thousand dollars. A nice business! The alternative, also, is pleasant to contemplate—Albert in prison."

"Where is he?" asked the wife, bowing her head.

"Taken precious good care to get out of the way; and I advise him never to return, even if the Russian Empire Insurance Company does agree to compound the matter," sneered Richard.

"Never to return!" repeated Mrs. Hearn mechanically, almost absently, as if the full meaning of the terrible words had not dawned on her.

"We can ill afford it, but our brother's dishonesty compels us to pay this enormous sum. Of course the house must go for what it will bring." Thus spake Jared Hearn, bringing the palms of his hands together with a preliminary business-like gesture.

Mrs. Hearn started.

"The house is *mine!*"

"And the money is our own," cried the brother, simultaneously. "Is it easier for us to part with it than you?"

There was a profound silence in the room. A fierce conflict raged in this woman's breast. She knew her right to the home, endeared to her by countless ties; her husband bade her retain it. If she relinquished this shelter, her children were cast adrift on the world. Their future was to be decided by the step. On the other hand, to be galled by debt to these men, pitiless to her as long as they retained their own position, was to leave uneffaced a stain on her husband's honor which lay in her power to remove.

"Take the house," she said at length. "And now oblige me, gentlemen, by leaving me alone."

The brothers departed with alacrity; they had gained their point.

"Of course you will go into the country somewhere, and live within your means," was Jared Hearn's parting advice.

She made no response. The iron had entered into her soul. A low, shuddering cry rang through the silent house; later, and Peggy found her.

"We shall do our duty by them," said Jared to his wife.

"Let 'em go to work," she replied.

Mrs. Hearn, in her secret soul, did not object to seeing the rich, extravagant Hearns brought down a peg, but she took refuge in a belief that misfortune would develop to their good somehow, as afflictions are ordered above. The house and furniture were sold for twenty-five thousand dollars, which Mrs. Hearn hurled at her creditors with a feverish eagerness. This sale left her with an income of fifteen hundred dollars, and no home. The matter was hushed up, forgotten in the business community, where fresh waves break ever over sunken rocks.

The Russian Empire Insurance Company announced itself satisfied with the result, and the Hearn brothers gained considerable glory in the transaction. Mrs. Hearn's sacrifice was never known. At that time appeared in the leading journals of England, France, Germany, Italy, and South America, a paragraph warning A. H. of New York never to return.

If the wife had known the place of his exile, she would have taken her pittance to share with him. She did not dare to risk her all in a perilous search which might prove fruitless, and waited for tidings. He was ever the same to her pardoning, pitying love.

"Peggy, you must do better for yourself now," she said, looking around the dismantled house.

"Florence Hearn, you may put me out and shot the door jest because I hain't got a soul to care about besides them children, but I'll come and sit on the door-step, sure as you're alive."

From which easy mode of address it will be seen that Mrs. Hearn was too familiar with her nurse, or that it is impossible to make a servant of a "free-born" American woman, with the power of rising lying ever dormant in her nature.

"There is your brother," objected Mrs. Hearn. "He may leave you his money if you go to take care of him."

"Let him! He hasn't given me a fip, living these ten years," returned Peggy, still unconvinced.

The Albert Hearns hid themselves, much to the satisfaction of their relatives. They changed their abiding-place, always hoping to better their condition, with the restlessness which will cling to us while we are a nomad people. When the parks of Colorado are permanently settled, and the Pacific Railroad is a line of thriving cities, the moss of family tradition and ghostly legends may attach to our names; until then, the generations still living in the home of father and grandfather may easily be counted. We are like the hermit-crabs, always deserting our shells to seek a larger mansion.

For two years the Hearns boarded in the shoe-maker's little red house under the hill, and the children grew to assimilate with the shock-headed urchins of the household. Mrs. Hearn was never the same after the interview with her brothers-in-law. For the first time a cup of humiliation was held to her lips, and imbittered her whole after-life. Gradually the entire charge of the family devolved on Peggy. The nurse had made herself the messenger to the Hearns during the sale of the house, and had given them "a piece of her mind" at parting, rarely spiced with feminine indignation. The spirit of the Old Bay State had been strong within Peggy from the cradle; she was not to be put down by any body.

"Why don't you buy a new gown, Peggy?" asked Miss Ethel. At an early age she was mindful of such matters.

"Because I can't afford it," replied Peggy.

"Why don't you ask your rich brother to give you one?" said the little girl, with the calm persistency children display in pinning older people.

"Law, child, he's dead!"

"Your brother dead, and you have never heard from him!" exclaimed Mrs. Hearn.

"He ain't likely to say nothin' after he's dead, is he? Folks don't, generally."

"Oh, my poor Peggy! I hoped that he would have provided for your old age."

"I guess I can take care of my own old age."

Mrs. Hearn said no more. She inferred that Peggy's pride was more hurt than she was disposed to confess by this slight on the part of her nearest relative.

Peggy, when alone, gave vent to a nervous laugh. "I never told a lie before. I allus hated liars. The Lord forgive me. I reckon He will, this time."

The summer waned, and autumn brought no vivid splendor of changing foliage—only dripping, monotonous rain. Olive Hearn, a serious, thoughtful young girl, stood by the window one day when Peggy went to the post-office. It was always a moment of eager suspense to the mother. O God, if some tidings might come!

A fog hung low over the brown hills, pools of water stood in the road, leaves fluttered from the trees to increase the harvest of sodden, reeking vegetation already under foot. The bell of the little white meeting-house was tolling slowly for a passing soul, and all the village paused to listen.

Peggy walked along the path at a brisk pace. There was a letter for Mrs. Hearn. With whitening lips and trembling hands, she opened it. The missive was in an unknown handwriting, and briefly stated that she could occupy a house for life in the town of Shellport.

"Oh! the sea. To live beside the water," murmured the sick woman.

"Who done it?" inquired Peggy, abruptly.

"One of my husband's family, probably; and I am grateful." She was none the less glad that she need not thank them, the form of the benefit being anonymous.

Then the Hearns went to dwell in the little house beyond the beach. Here the mother discovered her position to be a peculiar one. The dividing-line between classes was more distinctly defined in this town than is usual in America. The native population devoted every energy to making money out of summer visitors. Such an interest develops in a town sordid avarice in undue proportion to other qualities. Not a shop or a house, from the big hotels to the pretty villa, but was a "catchpenny" for the season. The mortal born in Shellport might anywhere be known by the speculative, hungry intelligence of the glance which he bestowed on a stranger. To insnare unwary birds, Shellport plotted in the drowsy, quiet winter, spread tempting nets in the spring-time, and counted its gains, with many chuckles of satisfaction, in the autumn. To such a community the Hearns occupied a false position. They were too poor to hold an equality with the summer visitors, yet above the greedy towns-people.

Jared and Richard Hearn would have sneered at the false pretensions of this feeble mother in dreading to have her children brought in contact with a coarser element of mind than her own. It would have afforded the uncles satisfaction to have Olive and Ethel established in life as the wives of respectable Shellport grocers and bakers, provided their world never knew. And how should their world know? We are too busy climbing upward ourselves to search for the wounded ones who have crept away out of sight to die.

According to Mrs. Jared's theory, people always found their proper level after a while. The lapse of years never softened the sense of injury felt by the brothers that Albert had disgraced them, and forced them to pay the price of disgrace.

The Hearn girls grew up entirely alone. Such an influence does a mother wield, that her choice became their own. If they longed for youthful society, it was not such as they could attain. A part of the false position they occupied was this proud isolation. Not that Shellport cared. The Hearns were evidently poor, did not live in style, or entertain handsomely; and Shellport, measuring people always by the depth of their purse, cared not a straw whether they lived or died. I doubt but such seclusion in a small town is more painful than the prying curiosity of villages.

The element of coquetry in Ethel Hearn was powerful; the incense of admiration from any source gratified her vanity. Herein lay her danger. On the other hand, the Chateaux en Espagne of girlhood—a solitary girlhood—while they were as absurdly ambitious as possible, saved her from stooping to sip at every brackish pool. The like of robes worn by Ethel Hearn were never wrought in earthly loom; before the gems of her *parure* those of royalty might well fade; and Versailles has no more stately salons than those through which she swept, as she sat, with half-closed eyes, on the garret stair, in a patch of warm sunshine, studying her French lesson.

The education of the sisters was curious. The mother shrank from the public school—a small, dilapidated fountain of learning at the best. Peggy upheld her, despite her own strong common sense, and respect for learning.

"They must be taught so that they can shift for themselves, mebbe. They may need to earn their own bread, and never go back on them uncles anyhow," said Peggy.

Then the nurse set herself to accomplishing it. No danger of contaminating her by a journey of discovery through the main street or byways. She found an Italian lady, who, stranded in a foreign land of which she had heard fabulous promises, and was now reaping the sad reality, agreed to instruct the Hearn girls several hours daily for a moderate sum. She educated them after her fashion. Latin became a second mother-tongue. Ethel could glide musically into the liquid verse of Petrarch, when her knowledge of her own national history was far from extensive.

The English branches devolved on the mother; and as attacks of illness were frequent with her, there were sad gaps in the lessons, until Olive undertook to combine student and teacher, by puzzling her steady little head over unfinished tasks at odd moments.

There was a small case of worn, much-used

books in the mother's room, which brought more real pleasure than many a library bound in gold and calf-skin.

"No matter how poor I am, no matter though the prosperous of my own time will not enter my obscure dwelling; if learned men and poets will enter and take up their abode under my roof; if Milton will cross my threshold to sing to me of Paradise, and Shakspeare open to me the worlds of imagination and the workings of the human heart, I shall not pine for want of intellectual companionship, though excluded from what is called the best society in the place where I live."

Shellport boasted a circulating library, kept by a queer old man, where the Hearn girls brought to the light of day many a stray romance, which was read aloud in the mother's presence, and furnished food for endless discussion while in progress of perusal, there being a code of honor that no one should peep ahead in the narrative.

The daughters were thus comparatively well provided with mental culture; but Nicholas Hearn, the male element, was a source of perplexity to the whole household : a red-haired boy, with a droll unconcerned face, and a tendency to frayed elbows. It was impossible to impose responsibility on him, for he shed care from the feathers of his nature as readily as a bird does moisture.

Nicholas Hearn had no pride, no self-respect, as Peggy repeatedly assured him. He consorted with the lowest boys of the town, without feeling himself one whit lowered in the social scale, apparently; he was discovered to be on friendly terms with a pugilist, and he maintained truly amicable relations with a ferocious saloon-keeper. He went to the public school cheerfully, learned what he chose, and no power of persuasion could make him learn that which he did not choose. The future of such a boy presented discouragement even to the mind of Peggy. In the mean while she gave him grumblingly all the stray pennies collected in a tin bank on the kitchen chimney-piece. To his credit be it said, that sorely as he needed pennies at times, Nicholas Hearn never touched the bank without Peggy's permission. He was healthy, noisy, fond of his mother, with a subdued wonder, when he entered her room on tiptoe, that any one could endure such a pent-up life, instead of skurrying across the beach, and climbing about the docks as he did ; boisterously affectionate toward his nurse, and addicted to taunting the girls. The son came like a whirlwind into the quiet house, slamming doors, jarring the china, and upsetting every article which happened to be atilt. There was one redeeming trait that Nicholas developed very early—an electric buoyancy of hope and courage, the gift of perfectly contenting himself with very little. Such trials as came to his boyhood could no more submerge his red head than a cork can be forced to bottom. At the age of fourteen, he was a homely, common youth, without a trace of his father's elegance about him. He formed his own resolution, for he seldom consulted any body. He was going to college. As a preliminary step, he went straight to the clergyman of St. Chrysostom.

The rector was a cold, precise man, of studious habit, who satisfied himself with reaching the heart of his people from the pulpit on Sunday, and then disappeared into his study for the week.

According to his lights, the Reverend Hexham White was strictly conscientious, and he believed he was doing a great duty by the world, in compiling a work on Egyptian relics. Thus, while his eyes were fixed on his manuscript, many shadows flitted across the Shellport sun of which he knew nothing, and the grief of warm human lives was bitter, because the pilot was not at the helm in the hour of need.

"I am going to college," said Nicholas Hearn, entering on the subject of his visit without preamble. "I don't expect that I have learned near enough to pass an examination. You must know lots ; will you teach me? I haven't got any money."

The Reverend Hexham White had never heard the like of such simple audacity in his life. He looked at his pile of writings in a bewildered way, then his glance strayed to an engraving of Christ blessing little children on the opposite wall. The Christian conquered.

"Come here to-morrow morning, and I will find you a place to study."

Nicholas went promptly, and he got on famously with the clergyman afterward. The Reverend Hexham White fitted him thoroughly for college, and he had an apt pupil, for the lad's heart was in the work. Nicholas confessed to Peggy that he was studying with the rector, but prevailed upon her to keep the matter a secret. This step taken, he thanked and left his kind friend. The rector was not made aware that Nicholas Hearn had not the first dollar with which to enter college ; the boy decided not to "bother" his instructor farther.

The latter knew abstractedly that a family of the name of Hearn dwelt in a house beyond the beach, but they might as well have lived in another hemisphere. Every Sabbath he dispensed the weekly ration of spiritual food to serious, devout Olive, in a remote seat of St. Chrysostom's church, but the family did not rent a prominent pew—could not afford to do so, in fact, and they were to him as phantoms. The inference that he recognized only his rich parishioners would be an unjust one; but he walked aloof, and was not likely to see objects not forced upon him. His sympathy was not a divining-rod, pointing the way to the hidden needs of the soul.

Ah! Reverend Hexham White, I behold thee now, sparse, dry, with close-cropped gray hair, holding the golden sands in thy cold hands, and seeing dimly, oh, so dimly, through a narrow casement, the boundless radiance of God's day.

At this time Jared and Richard Hearn received their first direct communication from Albert's family since Mrs. Hearn left her home. It was from their nephew asking them to advance the money requisite to send him to college. Neither of them were college-bred men. Nicholas, entirely ignorant of the wrath his presumption kindled, got letters containing severe advice about learning a trade or going into a store, and some sarcasms as to his lofty aspirations, which failed to singe him in the least. He was not hurt, as his sisters would have been, but a little surprised considering that such rich men might "give a fellow a lift;" then he quietly destroyed the letters, without saying a word to any one. He had a double motive for this secrecy. He would not have the family income pinched, the mother's luxuries curtailed, to give him the money. He kept his own counsel, and awaited his opportunity. Indeed, the opportunity might not have occurred at all to another boy as it did to Nicholas Hearn. At a very early age he believed in the adage that Providence gives us nuts, expecting us to crack them, and he went along his path searching eagerly for the nuts. Wealth did not possess the great value in his eyes which might have been expected, from the beautiful glimpses he obtained. He saw rich boys riding sleek ponies, in natty top-boots and velvet caps, while he trudged through the dust; and it did occur to him that it would be nice to ride, yet the thought had no bitterness of discontent. The rich boys were like the *aristolochia*, growing in a good soil, warmed by the benignant sunlight, and laving delicate stems in the river's flow. Nicholas was the houseleek, flourishing on a particle of sand in a sterile spot.

He scarcely knew what he wanted, except to go to college. Beyond that point his thoughts whirled with dazzling flashes and scintillations. Thus matters stood when Nicholas espied his nut on a high branch, climbed, and grasped it. He went to college.

CHAPTER XVIII.

THE MOTHER'S STORY.

THE day after Ethel Hearn's triumph at St. Chrysostom's Easter celebration was her nineteenth birthday. Mrs. Hearn and Peggy endeavored to keep up the anniversaries of the year to the children all the more tenderly because there was no one else to remember them. The ingenuity of the two women was wonderful. A chain of pleasant associations was made to bind the little household together, the links kept bright by this friction of remembrance.

Ethel's birthday differed from previous ones only in the matter of the mother's gift, which the latter made a mystery.

"Our child has proved herself a distinguished singer, and her present must be musical," she said, smiling. "I shall defer giving it until evening, when I will tell you a story."

The mother's chief talent lay in story-telling. Her descriptions were graphic; she carried the thread of the narration so skillfully that the interest never flagged; and, owing to a latent dramatic power, her look and gesture portrayed the character described. From early infancy the children had clustered about her knee, to catch the words which fell from her lips.

There was a dinner compounded wholly of Ethel's favorite dishes, and Mrs. Hearn was sufficiently well to preside. A green parrot was borne home in triumph by Nicholas from the wharves, supposed to have been obtained in barter with a sailor; a shawl, knitted surreptitiously, was presented by the little sister; and a pair of beautiful kid gloves from Peggy.

Then, when twilight gathered in the mother's room, she produced a small teak-wood box, kept all these years from prying young eyes, as she fondly imagined, and bade Ethel open it. The girl obeyed, and drew forth the gold cord, with the pendant attached, which she had worn on the night of Mr. Raines's arrival. The pendant was a beryl, oblong in shape, framed in dull, yellow gold, which showed the rude work of the Oriental smith's hammer. On the surface of the stone were exquisitely engraved these delicate Persian characters:

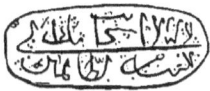

"I have reserved until to-night, children, telling you a story, which seems like a fairy tale, yet is entirely true."

The two girls nestled close to the arm-chair, which was drawn up to the window, from which the faint rose-tints of the dying day could be seen tinging sea and sky. Nicholas held his head between his two hands, as if he feared it would fly off. The son's manners were not less angular after a sojourn at college, and the means which granted him this advantage were permitted to remain a secret to his sisters. Peggy, plying her needles busily, sat just within the door.

"My grandfather was an Englishman. We are all of direct English descent, with the exception of my own father. My grandfather was an honest, brave young man, whose worth was appreciated by his employers. They made him captain of a merchant-vessel."

"What did he look like?" asked Olive.

"My mother had a quaint ivory portrait of him given to her, for the reason that she had never seen him. He was ruddy, fair, and strong; not over two-and-thirty when— But I must not anticipate my story. He married a young girl of his native town on the Devonshire coast, the physician's daughter; and soon

5

after, in all the pride of his new dignity, sailed away to the East, commanding a large ship. Months elapsed; my mother was born; and letters came in which the sailor described the ports he visited. Then tidings reached not only the little sea-port under the hill, but the public, through the newspapers. He had rendered a service to a rajah, one of those cruel despots who wield such tyrannical power over their subjects.

"The rajah, enthroned in his palace, with walls of polished chunam, painted in curious designs of animals and fruits, and carved verandas, was permitted by his British rulers to reap a harvest from poppy, rice, and cotton fields. His city was beautiful to gaze upon at a distance, for the softening atmosphere made the buildings appear like dazzling marble, with slender towers, gilded spires, and cupolas crowning the Moslem mosques. But an entrance speedily dispelled these illusions. The houses were plaster and whitewash; dirt and decay were everywhere visible; groups of ragged soldiery lounged about gate-ways; in the narrow streets mere cells of shops displayed rich wares of gold embroideries, precious stones, and sober elephants wended their way along.

"The rajah's palace was protected by high walls and many courts. There he lived, chewing betel-nut, anointing himself with delicious perfumes, chaining tigers brought from the jungle, and decking them with gold collars, and torturing his subjects. Wherever he went, the people fell prostrate before him, and slaves trembled at his frown, for the prince was a violent man. It happened that an old priest defied him; the Brahman, insolent in the security of spiritual power, protested that the ruler had encroached on the rights of the temple. The position was dangerous. The rajah had never been thwarted, and, moreover, rebellion among the people might be incited by a priest. The holy man disappeared. For a time wonder and fear prevailed in the city, then the excitement subsided. The priesthood maintained quiet. At this juncture my grandfather arrived, and became an interested spectator of a religious festival then transpiring. The rajah was exceedingly devout, and took a prominent part in the services.

"A faquir was brought before him, who promised to counterfeit death for six months in the interest of his religion, provided he could be entombed in the inner court of the palace. The rajah assented. My grandfather watched the proceedings, disbelieving in the fanatic,

and, as an Englishman, was permitted a foremost place' of observation. The faquir passively submitted to being placed in a bag, his ears and nostrils stopped with wax, his tongue thrust back to close the mouth, and buried in the court, with a stone placed above him and sealed. This singular experiment of suspended animation has been frequently tried in the East with success, and the faquir unearthed alive after the lapse of months. My grandfather did not credit it. He had an interview with the rajah, which resulted in his remaining at the palace overnight. This was an unusual concession; but the cause was urgent. The Englishman requested to be allowed to watch the buried faquir, entirely without the cognizance of the household, and also that no guard should be placed about the tomb, as was customary for several nights after the interment of a fanatic.

"My grandfather placed himself in the shadow of the veranda leading from his apartment, which was also in the main building occupied by the prince, and fixed his gaze on the tomb in the centre of the court. At midnight he was rewarded by seeing two figures glide from opposite directions toward the sepulchre. They advanced fearfully, often glancing around, and proceeded to remove the stone slab. My grandfather recognized them as slaves of the palace. The faquir was raised and placed on the ground, where he remained in a sitting posture, motionless. One of the slaves poured water on his head, and soon he entirely revived. The slaves vanished, and my grandfather supposed that the fanatic would make good his escape.

"Imagine his astonishment when the faquir approached, holding some glittering object in his hand. The faquir crawled along, and finally disappeared in the darkness, but not until the Englishman had seen that he grasped a dagger. Thoroughly aroused to danger, my grandfather followed. At first he fancied that he might have personally excited the faquir's anger as an unbeliever, and that he was now seeking revenge. When the Englishman reached the entrance to the rajah's quarters, he was dumb with amazement. The slaves who guarded the place were lying in a heavy stupor on their mats. They had evidently been drugged. No doubt remained of the faquir's motive; he intended to assassinate the prince—a vengeance probably plotted by the priesthood.

"He stepped over the prostrate servants as if he did not fear arousing them, and entered the rajah's inner chamber. The poniard was arrested by a strong hand; the prince opened his eyes to behold the faquir writhing in the grasp of the unbeliever. The holy man broke away and fled. You may be sure that my grandfather did not identify any of the wretched slaves, but the rajah made him a magnificent present. All that a man has will he give for his life; and the rajah was no exception to the rule, although my grandfather would have defended any fellow-creature in distress. Letters were written home descriptive of the gift."

Mrs. Hearn paused, and looked out on the sea, following one of those trains of thought which bring a host of doubts to anxious minds; misgivings as to the wisdom of God in averting to other channels the fulfillment of our right. As if mortals might trace the whole pattern of which they are single threads! She reflected how different the children's lot would be at that moment if the rajah's gift had descended to them, or even a portion of it.

"What was it?" questioned the girls, eagerly.

"A diamond?" hazarded Nicholas.

"A power of money, or an Injy shawl," suggested Peggy, rubbing her nose with a knitting-needle.

"It was a necklace of flexible gold, my grandfather wrote, and one blaze of precious stones. The clasp was composed of large diamonds; on every link glittered incrustations of emeralds, rubies, pearls, amethysts, and sapphires. Three pendants were attached to the clasp, of inferior value, but greatly prized as talismans. Indeed the rajah seemed to consider it the greatest mark of favor to part with the inscribed stones, as superstition ascribed rare virtues to them. My grandfather detached this one, had a scribe translate it, and sent it home: 'O Dieu preservez moi des gens qui ne suivent pas vos chemins droits.'"

Ethel repeated the motto musingly.

"This gift my grandfather felt assured would bring him a fortune. If he could not sell it to some monarch who could afford so costly a toy, the separated gems would be of great value. After that he sailed for home, and the sky clouded just when my grandmother hoped anxiety was past. The *Royal Maid* was missing. She had touched at Cape Town, and sailing away toward St. Helena, vanished forever from mortal eyes. A ship picked up a fragment of wreck known to belong to the *Royal Maid*. Then my grandmother yielded to her grief. 'Perished at sea!' was the knell that rang on many a widowed heart. A year later a letter came from an unexpected quarter — South America. My grandfather had been wrecked

in a typhoon, and had floated for days on a hastily-constructed raft, with a Jew and four seamen."

"They lived on hard-tack and very little water, and after a while began to think of eating each other up," interposed Nicholas, triumphantly.

"Horrible!" shuddered the girls.

"They were sighted by a vessel bound for South America, and were taken to port safely. My grandfather wrote that he had secured the rajah's gift about his body. While waiting for a homeward-bound vessel, a disabled ship arrived, the captain and mate having died of a fever. My grandfather accepted the command. These were his last words. The ship arrived, with scanty crew and no captain. Off the West Indies they were overhauled by a buccaneer, one of the pirates who infested the region then much as the Malays do the Indian Ocean. This robber swept off every coin of gold and silver, and he cruelly shot my grandfather. One of the sailors told my grandmother that the Jew had a surprising quantity of jewels secreted about his person, but the buccaneer stripped him. So, my dears, the brave sailor was killed, and the necklace lost to us forever. I give Ethel the pendant which was sent before, and hope that it may prove indeed a talisman."

Mrs. Hearn had scarcely ceased speaking when the gate swung open to admit a woman, who walked slowly up the little path with the aid of a gold-headed cane. Once she paused and looked back, her sombre form clearly defined against the evening sky, then approached the door.

Perhaps the woman advancing on their path was as unconscious as the Hearns how much she had to do with their future lives.

A visitor was an event. The invalid trembled, and shrank back into her chair. The sisters exchanged a glance of wonder, and gave to their attire a rapid, feminine smooth of the hand. Nicholas alone was entirely unmoved, and sat whistling softly, thinking of the buccaneer. Peggy strode to Mrs. Hearn's side.

"Don't you fret," she said, soothingly; "you sha'n't see any body you ain't a mind to."

"Excuse me as not being well enough to see strangers; say any thing to keep her away," whispered Mrs. Hearn.

The stranger, ignorant of the tumult she had occasioned, rang the sharp, vibrating little bell, and was ushered into the tiny parlor by Peggy. It was Miss Raines. The two girls went in shyly. What could Miss Raines, resident of a great house, wish of them? Miss Raines wished a great deal. She scanned the sisters with the comprehensive glance of a woman of the world, which notes every detail while appearing to see nothing.

Her face was attenuated, not wholly amiable in expression, faded, with cold eyes, and hair like Ethel's rippling above her forehead. It was as if youth rested, lingered, in a golden halo about the head of Hester Raines. She was plainly attired, yet there was an atmosphere of wealth about her—the glimmer of a ring, the whiteness of the wasted, transparent hands. No lady understood better how to behave well than Miss Raines when she was so minded; but she was not always so minded. She liked to thrust little pins of sarcasm into people, then look unconscious. In five minutes she was chatting with the Hearn girls in the most charming, easy vein imaginable.

"Young ladies, I should feel myself slighted that you have not called on me, did I not know you were occupied with an invalid mother. Her right is before all other considerations. I am sure you will forgive me for invading your privacy; I am lonely, and there are so few ladies here."

She addressed Olive chiefly, but her gaze rested on Ethel. What did she want with Ethel? What was the secret of her interest? The little sister asked herself these questions with a thrill of alarm. Ethel Hearn was considered so precious a treasure by her family that it need not have surprised them had she been stolen outright. Olive was flattered by the genuine kindness of Miss Raines, in which she also detected an amend for her stepmother's wounding condescension. After weighing these considerations, the little sister was still dissatisfied. Why did the lady, looking into Ethel's lovely face, almost forget herself, answer at random, as if she saw some fair picture reflected in the soft eyes? Ethel was puzzled, although Miss Raines's curiously expressed admiration brought the dawning of a subtle consciousness. Through every nerve-fibre tingled the first delicate glow of approaching intoxication: she was beautiful, and beauty was power.

The visit was a long one, as if Miss Raines enjoyed a gossip; and when she was gone it was understood that she had invited the Hearn girls to drive with her the next day.

Peggy threw all her ballast of practical sense overboard, and climbed to the clouds of gratified vanity. She would show Shellport what her children were! A real lady had noticed them. Forthwith ensued a brisk discussion as to what should be worn on the momentous occasion. Nicholas, with his hands in his pockets, strolled around his sisters with that increased respect one feels for a relative who has met with some success in life.

The poor mother thought, "Oh, my miserable self! I have lived so long alone that I shrink from a stranger. If she will only do something for my children!"

There is no position more painful for a woman, the mother of a family, than to be swept down from her proper social position by ruin and disgrace, with the years rolling on. Thus ended Ethel's birthday.

CHAPTER XIX.

THE PICTURE.

"WHAT would you like to be?"

"A princess."

"That is sheer nonsense. What do you imagine the lot of a princess to be?"

"It is useless for me to tell you, if it is nonsense. Would it not be grand to have power, to be respected, to be above the vulgar rudeness of the crowd, who jostle you if you are not rich? I hate common people!"

"We all have our dreams, child. Tell me yours."

"I hardly know. Something between a fairy palace and a Fifth Avenue mansion, I fancy."

"Do you mean that you like money?" inquired Miss Raines, with some wonder in her tone.

"Undoubtedly I do." The color dawned brightly in Ethel's cheek. After all her bravado, she was not very successful.

"I never thought of that," said Miss Raines, simply.

"You never needed to, I suppose," responded Ethel, subdued.

"I am not sure that you have correct views of life, but I shall always be interested in you. I never intend to lose you again." She spoke the words with a peculiar, vibrating distinctness which startled her companion.

"You are very good," murmured Ethel, tracing a pattern of the carpet with her foot.

"Bah! I am not good. I am not sweet or amiable—not even a valuable person, that I have ever discovered. I was cut down in my prime by an accident. Well! we will not speak of that. You are very good" (mimicking Ethel's words perfectly). "Where did you learn that conventionality?"

The girl made no reply. She was embarrassed. A degree of intimacy had sprung up between Miss Raines and the Hearn family.

She sent the invalid flowers, she invited the daughters to visit her, but she never presented them to the notice of her stepmother.

Miss Raines's apartments were simple in appointment to the very verge of plainness; there was even a lack of furniture to the eye accustomed to the overcrowding usual in our houses. Mrs. Raines's drawing-room might blossom with the redundant splendor of crimson satin ottomans blockading every step of advance; the boudoir of Miss Raines had only a few slender little chairs, delicate water-color pictures on the tinted walls, rich brown hangings. As with Miss Raines's own person, sharp angularities were concealed by flowing outlines, and thus saved from severity. Her maid alone ever saw the lady's form; there was always some clinging drapery of rich shawl or many-folded lace about her shoulders. The distinct impress of her own individuality was on all her surroundings, which, avoiding stiffness and luxury, mingled the grotesque, odd, and beautiful in abrupt contrast.

"Pray do not attempt to convert me to one style, one reign," she would exclaim. "I should like a suggestion—a mere hint of all ages and lands brought together within my small boundaries." The result was that China and Italy gazed at each other across the room; Louis Quatorze cabinets and the feather-work of the Incas were placed in juxtaposition. She now rose, and placed a hand on each of the girl's shoulders.

"Will you do something to oblige me?" she asked, playfully.

"Any thing," returned Ethel, gratefully.

The result of Miss Raines's whim was that Ethel stood against the dark background of the curtains, wearing a narrow gown of shimmering silk, with fair round arms and shoulders revealed, her hair gathered back, and a rose placed above one ear.

"That will do," said Miss Raines, critically.

The maid, a demure Alsatian, brought a large family portrait, in a massive gilt frame. The mistress knocked the canvas out with her cane, pushed her ancestor unceremoniously into a corner, and held the frame before Ethel.

"I sall be ze support," said the maid, holding the frame Atlas fashion. "Mademoiselle sall be so good as to put shawl over me—so!"

At a short distance the illusion was perfect. The birds chirped and trilled, the world of garden and lawn without was all perfume, motion, glad life. In the room was perfect silence; Ethel in the frame, the maid patiently kneeling, Miss Raines standing, with clasped hands, gazing at her lost youth. The present receded. Time vanished. Even the girl, unconscious of the depths of human grief stirred, felt a faint pulsation of awe steal over her. It seemed as if Miss Raines would never move again—had petrified into an attitude of regret, a sadness which softened her face into tremulous, dreamy rapture, yet held her spell-bound. The maid creaked uneasily; Ethel felt a numb weariness in every limb.

"One moment more, I beg."

Miss Raines went out, and returned with her brother. "Look," she said, pointing to the living portrait.

Mr. Raines did look long and earnestly. Ethel being flesh and blood instead of canvas, flushed; then amusement afforded by the maid's attitude overcame her gravity, and she laughed irrepressibly. The light on her face was like a rift in the clouds of memory to the brother and sister.

"My dear Hester, is this best?" he inquired.

Miss Raines elevated her eyebrows comically. "Why not? Only I have tired the poor child."

Ethel, in her quaint dress, slid down on the stool of the cabinet piano, and glided into a low, sweet cadence, possibly with a view to exorcise evil spirits. Her fingers wandered over the white keys; she breathed forth, not a trivial song, worn by a thousand repetitions, but the wooing, soft utterance of her own soul, filling the room with tender hope. The harmony fell like balm on the wounded soul of Hester Raines.

"Child, you may understand my liking for you by-and-by. I don't expect it now. I do not even ask you to like me; only be patient."

Surely the world is full of marvels! Miss Raines had asked Ethel Hearn to be patient, and try to like her.

CHAPTER XX.

CAPTAIN LACER.

"I THINK we shall obtain a better view from the far rock. Please come. Grant me that much, my time is so short."

Thus spoke Captain Lacer, in the tender June twilight. He had met Ethel quite accidentally, on the way from Miss Raines, and joined her. Nor was it the first time. Indeed the young lady had learned to expect an escort down the sheltered avenue, and found it altogether pleasant.

"I will go half-way," she laughed, not insensible to the flattery of the invitation.

Ethel Hearn was just at that perilous crisis in her youth when she was ready to fall in love with any person in the garb of gentleman, since vanity and the entire novelty of the situation would temporarily blind her to the true instincts of the heart. Had fate given her the opportunity, she would have been a coquette. Was she not to enjoy her chance now? The captain was handsome, gentle in manner, and respectfully admired her. So the two young people strolled along the sands, the soft obscurity folding the water-line in front, and closing noiselessly behind. The evening seemed like life, the past a dream, the future a wish.

"Strange how we are brought together. Is it destiny?" asked the young man, with tender attuning of mood and voice to the hour. He drew nearer to his companion as he spoke; they were the only moving objects in sight.

"I suppose it must be the destiny of good or evil. Oh, look at the gull catching his supper." Ethel edged away from him almost imperceptibly. She was ignorant, but she had nice instincts. The allusion to the gull was inopportune; her cheeks burned at the thought of her awkwardness, but sentiment made her uncomfortable. It was a weapon she dared not handle, yet dreaded to be considered uneducated in its use.

The captain was aware of the repulse, without appearing to perceive it; but he was too wary a tactician to press an advantage yet. He turned the current of talk cleverly on to sea-birds, of all things in the world, and even skipped a stone at the diver in a boyish fashion, which wholly diverted Ethel. Then he returned swiftly with,

"I have found your favorite violets, after searching the garden over. May I put them in your hair—just once? No? Well, I must carry them instead. Are you cold? Such a flimsy covering."

He drew the fleecy shawl closer about her, with a lingering touch. The girl was very fair, and tempted caresses. She smiled brightly, and glanced up into his face. It was nice to be taken care of in that fashion, and quite different from Peggy's prosaic chidings concerning night air.

"Will you answer a question frankly?"

"Yes."

"Two months ago we were ignorant of each other's natures—"

"And now?" interposed Ethel.

"I never intend to lose sight of you again," said Captain Lacer, firmly.

"Indeed! What if we had remained ignorant to the end? The world would have still moved, I suppose."

"Ridicule me as much as you choose, Miss Ethel," he returned, seriously. "No doubt I am very absurd. I am not such an idiot as to fancy that you cared—I mean that it makes any difference to you having ever met me. I was alluding to my own good-for-tune."

They took ten steps in silence; then Ethel stole a glance at him through her lashes. Was he angry? How proud and handsome he looked! What a noble carriage, with the head erect! She repented having vexed him. What would he think of her?

"I am glad, too," softly, and a little shyly.

"Are you, really, Ethel? Tell me—"

But Ethel would tell nothing. She sprang up the rock, and stood on a jutting edge lightly. The evening breeze fanning the sea seemed to sway her slender form, and she trilled a weird little siren strain. Captain Lacer was watching her curiously; but for the first time that night she reached beyond her companion. She sang to the ocean that touched the brink of far-distant lands; to the mysterious depths where forests grow, branches of purple fuci, blue and green algæ, above a carpet woven of silky mosses, and where phosphorescence illuminates the dim halls with stars and quivering bands of flame from moving creatures. Who has not spent a season in an undulating range of country, fresh and pleasant to the eye, yet where a weariness, a longing, comes after a time—an aridity of all the senses? So a mill-pond, wind-ruffled, produces sudden ecstasy, and explains the want. The desire is for water; the senses are athirst for a wide, changeful sweep of river or lake. Is it not Ruskin who affirms that a picture without water produces a sense of suffocation? As the mountains stir the souls of the highland people, so the ocean had educated the Hearn girls. They never wearied of it. In this theatre tragedies of passion were enacted, with crushing billows and spray clouds, while comedy smiled in dancing wavelets, bearing toy-ships of the children.

The sisters liked to linger on the edge of the storm, as it were, to feel themselves the whirling plaything of the advancing tempest of scudding clouds. When the blue dome of sky was reflected in sapphire depths below, and the air seemed liquid sunshine, they danced along, instinct with the pleasure of the day.

"Oh, how nice it is to live in such weather," Ethel would exclaim, the enjoyment active, buoyant, stimulating.

"Miss Ethel, it is growing late—and pardon me for the suggestion—but should we not return?"

Here was a check to the wayward song indeed! To be lured on to the distant rock, and then reminded by the gentleman of the lateness of the hour! Captain Lacer was not as desirous of recalling Ethel to a consideration of proprieties as to himself. She stepped down from her height without a word. Then came a revelation. The captain was a selfish man, of warm passions. She was beautiful, and her voice kindled fire in his veins. Propinquity brought inevitable fascination.

"Would you grant me a favor if I asked it?" searching the gray eyes for his answer.

"Perhaps."

"What a guarded assent. You are so cold to me! My request is that you keep these violets, and a year from to-day look at them, thinking of me. Will you?"

It was the paltry detail of a flirtation, perhaps, or it might have some deeper, sweeter significance.

"Where will you be?" the young face growing pensive.

He had imprisoned her two hands before she knew it, and was wooing her impetuously. "I shall be where you place me."

Every moment of happiness may inflict some corresponding period of pain elsewhere. At home the mother was saying, with a flush on her cheek,

"Your uncle wishes Ethel to visit him, and improve her voice." She did not add that she had petitioned Richard Hearn to do this thing for her child. He responded graciously that Ethel might come for three months. Since she had sung at St. Chrysostom's, Mrs. Hearn had determined to do something for her advancement. The mother had a double anxiety for getting her youngest daughter away now. The whole household had merged from pleasure to dread concerning Miss Raines's whimsical fancy for Ethel. She was a rich, elderly lady, to whom the girl possessed the novelty of a fresh toy; but while she found amusement in petting Ethel, might not the latter become imbued with false ideas regarding her own home? The question was asked in the darkened sick-chamber, by the mother; in the china closet by the little sister, sorting dishes; and in the kitchen by Peggy, as she brought her flat-iron to bear with unusual energy. Another reason was still more urgent. The captain was always strolling about the place, haunting Ethel's path, where Miss Raines's sharp glance could not detect him.

"I can't see any thing uncommon in that ere capting," blurted Peggy. "Why does he come snoupin' around at dark?" Takes mighty good care that nobody sees him. S'pose he'd feel ashamed, likely, to have his folks know!"

Ethel would smile in a superior way. Young or old, it is hard to make a woman believe that she is not an exception to all known rules.

"Lord, child, he'd no sooner marry you than me. I've seen that sort afore in my time; wants a gal with lots of money to buy 'em.

No! They don't marry poor gals such as you be, but they stand in the way of honest men marrying 'em, if they can."

How Ethel's eyes flashed. The captain should see if she was good enough to marry him or not. Of course, she had thought of it. Few girls ever see an eligible man without a rapid inventory of his qualifications, wondering dreamily what *may be*.

"Peggy, you are a fool," cried Ethel, thus hard pressed.

"Mebbe. I've got plenty of company if I am," returned the old woman, sententiously.

But Peggy's arrow rankled. Ethel was haughty and indifferent for a while, and the change only piqued the captain.

Olive and Peggy received the tidings of Richard Hearn's offer with positive relief. The sisters had never been separated, and Ethel's departure would be like depriving her of a limb, Olive felt, yet she rejoiced. She had early learned to set aside herself wholly for others. In an unobtrusive way Olive Hearn gave the best portion of every thing to her mother, sister, even to Nicholas, and accepted the crumbs so quietly that it required more than a glance to discover that she was not equally well supplied.

"Where is Ethel?" inquired the mother, with the shade of reproach in her voice which invalids acquire when they feel themselves neglected.

"She has not returned yet."

Peggy stole out, with her apron over her head, and peered keenly in all directions. Olive followed. Two figures were on the beach, moving slowly in the opposite direction. Peggy gazed after them, with the helpless anger of the sheep-dog at beholding one of the lambkins strolling in a friendly manner with the wolf.

"I'll go and fetch her. What business has she stragglin' round this time o' night when her mother wants her?"

"Do not go, Peggy," urged the little sister, earnestly. "She might be vexed if she thought we were watching her, and did not trust her. She is so young and pretty, and she has had very little fun in her life."

Then Olive laid her head down on Peggy's arm, and began to cry softly. It was all so strange. Ethel has stepped out into a world, whither she might not follow. Oh, patient little sister, were you thinking of a night in "the season" of whose gay existence you knew nothing, when the music came from a neighboring ball-room to the silent chamber where you listened? Thrust outside the gate of unknown pleasure, how the music pulsed and throbbed through young frames, with the irresistible impulse to fly and circle over the polished floor among the gay multitude, bringing to your heart a certain wistfulness while Ethel burst into passionate tears! "Why are we not like other girls, with fathers and friends?"

Peggy gathered up the little form, and carried her into the house, bidding her keep the mother from worrying. For another hour Peggy stood, a grim sentinel, behind the syringa-bush, sweeping the beach with her glance. She longed to run after the fugitive, but Olive's warning restrained her. She magnified the artful wiles of the adversary; she underrated the sagacity of her dove. At last her weary eyes discerned two specks, which grew into the familiar shapes of Ethel and Captain Lacer. The old nurse was further made aware of the pleasing fact that the gallant officer had offered his arm to the lady, and she had accepted it. Peggy involuntarily stooped, and a wrinkle deepened in her forehead. Ignorant of the stern face behind the syringa-bush, there was a lingering leave-taking at the gate.

"Good-night. You will meet me there to-morrow," said the captain, softly, and departed.

Peggy made the guilty one aware of her proximity.

"You there?" inquired Ethel, with a nervous laugh. Her cheeks glowed like damask roses, and her eyes sparkled like twin stars. The stimulus of excitement is the very wine of life to American women.

"I'm ashamed of ye, Ethel Hearn."

Now Ethel was a trifle ashamed of herself, but she resented reproach. She could never endure fault-finding. Smooth her silken plumage, and she was winning, lovable; ruffle it by disapproval, and she grew angry.

"Indeed! I hope you may never be more seriously disgraced. Had I known that I gave you the trouble of playing *spy*, I would certainly have come before." She swept to the door with lofty dignity, only to encounter the little sister's troubled face.

"You will be sorry for speaking like that. Ask pardon."

But Ethel twisted away her shoulder from the warning touch, and remained obstinately silent. Peggy strode into the kitchen, took a pinch of snuff, and shuffled her cards reflectively. The mother was in a state of feverish anxiety to get Ethel away at once.

"I can go to-morrow. I have only to bid Miss Raines good-bye," said the girl, airily, already pleased with a prospect of change.

"We can do that for you."

"What!" exclaimed Ethel, amazed.

She has been very kind to you, yet there can be no friendship where people are not of equal social position. She will have ample opportunity of being kind again if she chooses. Leave the matter to us."

Ethel Hearn went away. Miss Raines was offended. She had plans of her own for the girl. She made no inquiry; as she readily divined, she was not to know. The captain smoked, strolled, and waited in vain. His mother gave him much good advice about settling in life. Peggy could not resist saying to Miss Raines,

"Would you kindly tell that capting, ma'am, that Miss Ethel's gone away for good?" Which caused the lady to open her eyes precisely as Peggy intended.

"Perhaps I am indebted to you for the flight of my protegée," she said at dinner.

Captain Lacer laughed consciously, and pulled his mustache. Mr. Raines looked at them in silence.

CHAPTER XXI.

A STRANGER WITHIN THY GATES.

NICHOLAS HEARN returned from college one dark night unexpectedly. When the little sister ran out to greet him, she discovered a second taller figure in the background.

"My friend, Nelson Thorne, has come to make us a visit, and try my new steam-power," said Nicholas, with charming hospitality.

This announcement threw the small household literally on its beam-ends. A guest was an obstacle before which even Olive's clear sagacity wavered. While she was being introduced, and welcoming her brother's friend, she was rapidly asking herself such mental questions as these: Where was she to put him? What would the larder furnish for the supper of two hungry men? The little sister groaned in spirit as she led the way into the house with some cheerful inquiry concerning their journey. How could Nicholas be so careless! When Nelson Thorne beheld the tiny proportions of the establishment, he realized that he had made a mistake. He had no more idea of the circumstances of his college-mate than the man in the moon. Nicholas had importuned him to come, and, with his customary good-nature, he had yielded.

The young hostess rapidly whisked all traces of feminine presence from her own chamber, flashed in to tell the mother of this unexpected calamity, and informed the gentlemen that their meal was served in a surprisingly short space of time.

You can not summon a banquet fit for the gods with one wave of a wand, in an American country town. The butcher and baker are locked up, probably; the kitchen-fire is low. If you give the guest that portion which was to have served for breakfast, wherewithal shall that meal be furnished? Olive and Peggy, caught on the horns of this dilemma, gazed at each other in silence, until a happy inspiration came to the latter in the one word "Chickens." The little sister brightened, then gloomed.

"I hate to kill my pets. Pray spare the top-knot."

How those collegians ate! Famished wolves are no comparison. Peggy hovered over the ruins of the feast in dismay.

Said Miss Hearn to Mr. Hearn, with pardonable acerbity, behind a closet door at a safe distance from the visitor's ear,

"May I ask where he is to sleep?"

"Oh, we can give him a shakedown somewhere."

"He is not a horse, but I hope we know how to treat him."

The three young things passed a merry evening after all. The little sister seldom harbored malice long. She enjoyed the exciting descriptions of college life, the matched games of ball, the battles and controversies, the injustice of certain professors, and the meanness of certain tutors; the clever tricks; the details of how the president was "done." Olive forgot the cares of breakfast, the possible sacrifice of the top-knot, in this stir of healthy animation which had come to her sober life.

Peggy in the kitchen, rendered gloomy by the discovery that not a crumb of bread remained to the whole loaf, sat, finger on lip, studying the cards.

"He's the knave of hearts, and he brings trouble."

"A very nice girl. A fellow might fall in love with her if he had time," reflected Nelson Thorne, betaking himself to Olive's clean little chamber, unconscious that the young lady in question was sleeping on an improvised couch on the parlor floor, with her head under the table. He had seen enough to resolve on leaving next day after the experiment. At noon of the next day Nelson Thorne lay senseless in a turnip-field, having been hurled to a distance by a force of nature which Nicholas Hearn had not learned to manage.

CHAPTER XXII.

LOVERS.

NICHOLAS HEARN, in his college progress, was diffusive. He either lacked concentration of purpose, or attempted to grasp too much at one time. His future life alone could determine by development whether his industry equaled his enthusiasm. He was not as brilliant as original in the researches of study; he was always unearthing questions of which his mates seldom thought, and his instructors delighted in him. If in geology he was hammer and anvil, in the laboratory he was a fire-brand. Daring were the intimacies induced between inflammable gases at the hands of Nicholas Hearn. The forces of galvanism and magnetism fascinated him; chemical affinity and mechanical motion filled all his waking thoughts. Platinum and steel, iodine and naphthaline, yielded their secrets to young Nicholas, as they had done to greater men; sand whirled and danced on plates of glass; even gold was refined to a purple residuum.

The professor said that he would be a famous student if— The "if" was Nelson Thorne knocked senseless in a turnip-field. Nicholas desired to become an inventive force, and tried his little golden key in all the ponderous locks of nature, hoping to throw wide the portals to some fresh realm of wonder. Might he not discover, at least, some lost art of the ancients, and restore it to his century? Life was too serious for Nicholas Hearn to rest content with the fame acquired by coining a word, like the witty Frenchman, Victor Roqueplan's invention of "chic."

A continent to cultivate meant more to him than a bonmot, although the polish of civilization and the bonmot would come well afterward. The bent of his nature was to do battle, not idly dreaming, somewhere where there was a work imperatively set him to do.

At the time Nelson Thorne came home with Nicholas, steam had acquired to the latter the attraction of a mighty monster, to be approached gingerly, but, if once tamed, converted into an obedient slave. He proposed to saddle and bridle this steed, as it had never been curbed before. A miniature engine was constructed in leisure moments, to demonstrate the theory that greater pressure could be used than had ever been considered practicable, by the employment of proper valves. Nicholas infused all the ardor of his heart into the valve. He built a cloud-castle occupied by the mother, where he should dwell, with the debt of his education paid, and have a laboratory of fabulous resources, while working over scraps of iron and tin.

At last he rushed out, glowing with excitement, and encountered Nelson Thorne. One young man, without thought of the clear purity of the day, had bent to the task he was for the time absorbed in; the other came swinging along from the river, with a grand play of lung and muscle, his whole frame expanded by healthy exercise.

"I've got it at last!" cried Nicholas.

"Hurra! old fellow," responded Nelson, heartily.

He believed in Nicholas, although he preferred out-of-door sports to the other's chosen studies; while Nicholas, in return, gloried in Nelson's strength and beauty. Then they came to Shellport. The engine was set up a short distance from the house, and looked so very insignificant that Nelson was careless of his proximity.

"Perhaps you had better stand back," suggested the inventor, on his knees over the fire.

Nelson had no time to respond. Lo! The steam monster rose in wrath, wrenched off the valve, which struck Nelson violently on the head, and spurned the shackles of the puny engine with a resounding explosion. The receptacle was small, but the power within was mighty.

Olive and Peggy rushed out of the house in alarm. There sat Nicholas on the ground, gazing around at the ruins in bewilderment. Nelson lay very still. Peggy gave her boy a little shake.

"Are ye hurt? Bedlam's let loose, I believe."

"I think wrought steel might stand the pressure," quoth Nicholas.

Olive raised Nelson's head on her lap, in sickening fear. Blood trickled down his forehead, and he had fallen heavily in a rough place among stones. The nurse came out in full force in Olive. She was tender, but calm, although she could have cried with pity over the manly strength laid low. Perhaps his brain was injured! Perhaps he was hopelessly crippled!

"Shall we keep him here until a doctor comes? or shall we move him to the house?" she questioned, looking up at Peggy and Nicholas.

"I can lift him a'most," said Peggy.

"Oh, Nicholas!" cried the little sister, in one uncontrollable outburst of regret. "Why can't you rest contented to be like other people, instead of doing these dreadful things? You may have killed him!"

"I?" said Nicholas, aghast.

"Just keep quiet, child. Talking don't mend matters," interposed Peggy, who always espoused the cause of the oppressed one in her little flock. So, with the aid of a passing laborer, Nelson was borne back to the house, and, when the physician came, his injuries were found to consist of a broken limb and a wounded head. Events followed in quick succession. The little house beyond the beach missed Ethel; but Nelson Thorne had almost taken her place, and was rapidly becoming one of them.

Peggy, stalking solemnly about her own duties, was more of a tactician than the household dreamed of. She assumed chief charge of Mrs. Hearn; she directed Nicholas into the groove of caring for his mother; yet if a wise measure occurred to her respecting the comfort of their guest, she made Olive her deputy, as if the idea originated with the girl. Ah, wise old Peggy! Were the subtle agencies at work in two young hearts thus brought into close contact, the one helper, and the other helpless, known to you? Cool hands smoothed the pillow beneath Nelson's restless head; a sweet voice soothed him to sleep; in his pain and weakness, he found an unfailing sympathy, although he was ignorant at the moment of its source. To the little sister, used as she was to illness, his dependence on herself was touching. Often she reflected with satisfaction that he needed her, would suffer by her neglect or absence, as she looked at the handsome face no longer blooming with health. This superabundant life, that would never otherwise have known her influence, hung on her vigilant care through all the stages of dangerous fever delirium. Thus to the Hearn home, small and humble as it was, came the dawn of a joy such as the Raines mansion had not known for many years, finding root, as it did, in the noblest sources of the heart.

Nelson Thorne returned to life, and found the little sister ministering to him. The strangeness of his surroundings; the unaccountable languor of illness; above all, the delicious novelty of a feminine influence such as he had never known, seemed only a dream. As his strength came back, the natural tone of health gradually re-asserted sway, and the dull oppression was lifted from his injured head; yet this new element in his existence did not fade away, but became a steadfast fact, over which he pondered with closed eyes. Then dawned a day when he stretched out his hand to Olive, an unwonted glow on his pallid cheek, a soft, beseeching entreaty in his beautiful eyes, and he said, quite simply,

"How much you have done for me! I suppose I should be dead but for your kindness. Kiss me, dear."

And Olive, bending low, kissed him as she never would kiss but one man in her life.

"Thou, and no other,"

was her creed.

CHAPTER XXIII.

AN INTERRUPTION.

THE treasures of a lifetime may be found in one golden grain of the life-sands. The monotony of months and seasons, following in smooth routine, may be broken by a marvelous change which will ever after prevent the years from settling back again to the old groove. Olive Hearn was transfigured, and on Nelson Thorne fell the reflection of her radiance. It was all so wonderful! The circumstances of their meeting and loving were so extraordinary and unprecedented that they were never weary of dwelling on the theme.

Down through the starry silence of night had slanted a falling light, vivid as the fire of comet or meteor, assuming, as it approached, the pure lineaments of an angel form. It was not Iris crossing the rainbow-bridge, Venus undulating through space in her chariot, buoyant as the sea-foam from which she sprang, nor stately Juno, with her jeweled train, but a little child-soul, ignorant of sorrow, fed on no earthly perfumes, and reared on the celestial heights of paradise. In obedience to an impulse, mysterious and inscrutable, which yet thrilled the universe, the child-soul came to forge two destinies into one. On the threshold the presence paused; snowy pinions fanned the slumberers; two hearts were poised in the balance—one pure gold without alloy, the other, alas, only veined. Then the rapid quiver of wings clave the air, and earth was left to its clay again.

Time, as counted by Peggy's kitchen clock, no longer had any control over the small household. There was a perpetual confusion and upsetting of all routine, which the little sister strove, shame-facedly, to remedy entirely without success. She was the cause. When the young housekeeper put coffee into the tea-caddy, and absently administered Nelson's hourly medicine to her brother while she conversed with the real invalid, Peggy gave it up and retreated to her own dominion. Yes, it had all happened; yet repeated assurances of the fact would not render it one whit more tangibly real. A ring sparkled on Olive's finger, pledging her to Nelson, sent by Experience Thorne. Mrs. Hearn strove to enter into the happiness of her child, and stifle all appearance of regret at losing her. Peggy was satisfied, for the handsome lover had a rare gift of winning good opinions.

Nicholas was unfeignedly amazed, but dropped the matter as beyond his ken after several days of fixed staring at the young couple, devoted his thoughts to adding an iron cap to the valve, and procuring a patent. In his mother's sick-room he unfolded his plans to an unwearied listener. Never, by word or thought, did she discourage him, and the son came away from her presence strengthened and refreshed. Blessed maternal faith and patience! Thus, when sentiment in the parlor became oppressive to Nicholas, he ascended to the mother's chamber to discuss mechanics.

Experience Thorne made several visits to Shellport; first when he was summoned to his son after the accident, and during several stages of convalescence. He scanned the family carefully, but his gaze rested longest on Olive. The son, from long habit of boyhood, rather dreaded the severity of his criticisms on the kind friends he had found.

The little sister had a skirmish with him at the outset, and came off victorious, to Nelson's secret amusement. She found Experience Thorne pouring some favorite medicine into a glass of water preparatory to administering it to his son.

"You must not give him that," said Olive,

arresting his hand, and looking unflinchingly into the stern face.

"May I ask your reason?" he found words to inquire when he had sufficiently recovered from his first surprise.

"I have the doctor's orders to obey. It is not honest to him, you know, unless he is to give up the case altogether; and I am sure," with a glance at Nelson, "you will not insist on that at such a crisis."

Experience Thorne corked his bottle, and put it in his pocket, without further opposition. Some murmured remark he did make about the wisdom of the present generation, which was only to be expected. A faint smile flitted over Nelson's face, and his respect for the little sister increased from that hour.

"I like that girl," was the father's comment, made quite abruptly.

This commendation made the task of filial reverence easier when the son was able to write a few straggling lines announcing his engagement. Perhaps Nelson Thorne was never more surprised in the course of his life than when his father responded in person to this letter. It had never seemed as if an extraordinary interest in the marriage of his son would move him, yet here he was discussing affairs eagerly with Mrs. Hearn, sounding Olive on her preferences, and urging all speed in the wedding. The young people should live with him if they could content themselves, and when he died all his possessions should be left to them. In the mean while Nelson must bestir himself; he had idled long enough.

"I look to you to make a man of him. A woman's influence is so great," he said to Olive.

Nelson made a lordly sort of lover. He grew hourly more fond of his little Olive, but he received worship rather than gave it. No wonder she was fascinated. Beauty of the manly type, the bloom of glorious, robust youth, and, most captivating consideration of all, he preferred her to all the world.

Happiness of this kind comes usually once, at least, to every woman's lot, but it rarely has the ingredients the cup possessed for Olive Hearn. She would have been grateful for the proffered love of any good man, even if she could not have accepted it, but the offering dazzled her when it came from this young god, with a wide field of choice open to him. In the stories told by the mother, Ethel was always the fairy princess, and Olive the hearth-flower. These roots struck deeper into the little sister's natural humility than the story-teller realized.

"I do not know how you can prefer me to other girls. If you had only seen Ethel first!" she would say to this hero, with the light of perfect trust in her clear, serene eye.

The response was some re-assuring caress. At times this modesty annoyed him; at others, afforded gratification. What right had the best girl in Christendom to lay herself at his feet, as it were? Pleasant the task of raising her, however. As for this Ethel he heard, so much about, she must be pretty, certainly, and all that, but he would willingly balance his choice against any power of attraction she might possess. Soon must come a change from the pleasant, idle life of convalescence and delightful petting, to which the soul of man is not insensible. Especially grateful to Nelson was the delicate, womanly influence, reared as he had been in that dark city home. Change was coming, although they rested on the very brink in calm content.

They were seated by the parlor window one sultry morning, Nelson in the large arm-chair, the little sister reading "Lucille" aloud. The young man's gaze rested placidly on the dainty figure beside him, and he imprisoned her disengaged hand in his broad palm. There had been active discussions as to whether Nelson resembled Alfred Fargrave or Luvois. Olive insisted playfully that he was like the former. Her voice trembled as she read,

"I follow the way
Heaven leads me; I can not foresee to what end.
I know only that far, far away, it must tend
From all places in which we have met,
Far away!—onward—upward!"

"Ah, how common and mean we seem after that!"

"Nonsense," returned Nelson. "Lucille is an ideal woman."

"I know," assented Olive. "All the greater pity."

"The reality is so much better, my dear little girl." A warmth of affection underlying the insignificant words brought a becoming blush to Olive's cheek.

"How is mamma, children?" inquired a sweet, demure voice.

There stood a girl in the door-way, smiles of saucy amusement dimpling her face, a presence of exuberant life and loveliness. Nelson sprang to his feet. Surely he had seen her before. Where? In church, when he was a lad. But she was young.

"Do not rise, I beg. I know all about it," pursued the stranger, with that indefinable mockery in her tone, while her glance broke in a thousand sparkles over the young man. He reddened uncomfortably; evidently she was making fun of him.

"Oh, Ethel dear, we did not expect you so soon," said Olive, embracing her joyfully.

"Very likely," replied Ethel, making a little moue, which a handsome girl can only do successfully. "Well, brother-in-law, do you think you would recognize me again if we happened to meet?"

"I beg your pardon," began Nelson, confusedly.

"Granted," said Ethel, with airy impertinence. "Where is that explosive brother of mine? Cupid loaded the boiler, I suppose. Such a fortunate accident! Why am I home so soon? You wish to know, little sister. Well, as a poor relation I was not a success, my love."

Ethel was gone, and appeared no more that day. She must stay with her mother, she said. Nor was she more companionable the next day. After breakfast she appeared, equipped for a walk.

"You do not know Nelson a bit," demurred Olive.

"I shall have plenty of time for that agreeable employment. When you are married, I will spend half of my time at your house," said Ethel, drawing on her gloves. "After brother-in-law recovers the use of his limb, he may escort me out," she added, inclining her head gracefully, and glancing roguishly at him from beneath her silky lashes.

Every thing was just the same as before, Nelson kept assuring himself. Olive read, Nicholas came and went; yet he vaguely regretted the absence of this girl, who was so "awfully pretty," and "set a fellow down confoundedly."

CHAPTER XXIV.

A POOR RELATION.

IT was impossible to conceal the reason for Ethel's return from her mother. Up stairs the whole history was revealed, which the girl's pride forced her to conceal beneath light words in the presence of Nelson Thorne. Ethel had received her first sharp lesson, and was still wounded.

Richard Hearn had invited her to his city home in the summer season, when his world was out of town; not with premeditation, but because his wife advised it. Ethel found the family to consist of her uncle, tolerant of her presence, surprised by her beauty, and disposed to patronize her; for it delighted the heart of Richard Hearn to consider himself rather an easily-imposed-upon, generous man; her aunt, handsome and cold, apt to mourn over the follies of society, and the price of her rich toilets as diverted from missionary channels, yet wearing them all the same; and the daughter, Clara Hearn, a high-shouldered, plain girl, fond of horses and talking English slang. No amount of costly apparel could ever make Clara Hearn elegant; she was one of those daughters who suffer from comparison with their own mothers. Behind her back Mrs. Hearn's dearest friends remarked, "What a pity it is that poor, dear Clara is so shockingly plain. Her mother was quite a beauty once."

Ethel, sensitive and proud, was received amiably by her uncle, with scrutinizing disfavor by her aunt, and pleasantly by Clara, as a companion of her own age. The first walk taken by the cousins was marked by an event to both. Captain Lacer, in search of fugitive Ethel, and surmising that she was in the city, met them. What more natural than that he should join the young ladies? What more natural than that he should be impressed with the stately exterior of Richard Hearn's residence, and proceed forthwith to inquire what that gentleman's standing actually was. The girls went home brimful of the adventure. Mrs. Hearn, in India muslin and mauve silk, stood at the window using her eyeglass.

"Who was that gentleman?"

"A friend of Ethel's. No end of a swell, mamma."

"My dear child, is this best? You came here to study."

"Best," echoed Ethel, coloring brilliantly.

"One does not have the latitude of the country allowed in town, you know. Are you engaged?"

"Oh no," asserted Ethel, hastily, yet with a little complacency. She could marry Captain Lacer; even her aunt perceived that already.

Mrs. Hearn tapped on the glass softly, and made no further comment.

The captain called, sanctioned by an introduction to Richard Hearn at the club. He greeted Ethel with a tender familiarity when they were alone, but he rode out with Clara Hearn, because Ethel had neither horse nor riding-habit. Ethel attributed the captain's search for her to his acknowledged devotion, and accepted the triumph. She believed that she liked him very much. She was prepared to consider herself absolutely happy in marrying him. Fancy had less to do with this resolution than circumstances, but she was not aware of it. The captain had sought her; longed to see her; determined to win her at all costs before leaving Shellport; afterward he had wavered in his resolution. He was madly in love with Ethel when he came, he assured himself; but beyond was Clara Hearn, flattered by his attentions, an only daughter, and the inheritor of Richard Hearn's wealth. It is not an elevated type of humanity to contemplate, but one found every day. He preferred Ethel—she was his fancy, his day-dream; but his mother's lesson was bearing fruit, while the pressure of debt warned him to stifle sentiment. The settlements of Mrs. Raines's fortune rested on the tenure of her life; all other property belonged to John Raines. With Clara Hearn as his wife, Captain Lacer could lead the life of his choice; without, her he must be banished to some remote fort or station, and an existence of moping poverty. The young man felt himself aggrieved, miserable, ill-used; but there seemed to be no help for it, he must give up Ethel, and take her cousin.

"Where did you meet Captain Lacer?" inquired Mrs. Hearn.

Ethel stood at the window watching the departure of Clara, with the gentleman in question in attendance, with a wistful longing to be one of the party. Ethel was not as patient as the little sister; there were envy and jealousy in her heart. She would look better in the saddle than Clara, and the captain's defection stung her keenly, although she did not fully understand it as yet.

"At Shellport."

"Do you visit the Raines family?" Mrs. Hearn was smiling, and smoothing her laces with a caressing touch.

"Yes," said Ethel, flushing uncomfortably.

"I was not aware of it." Volumes can be condensed into a sentence.

Mrs. Hearn had no desire to make Ethel's stay an agreeable one. Ethel was a dangerous guest, and the lady understood to perfection the art of making an unwelcome visitor uncomfortable, without any act of overt rudeness. Moreover, she was getting the best of this affair, so plainly was it to be seen that Captain Lacer's interest had been wholly transferred to her own daughter, much to the mother's satisfaction. Clara would have money—Captain Lacer, family; the alliance was in every particular desirable. Ethel was walking through a path of thorns. She missed the sympathy of her own family, she longed for Miss Raines's kind indulgence. Her musical studies led her through a vale of discouragement. The Herr Professor was saturnine in disposition; he raved over false notes in a terrifying outburst of mingled English and German; he rapped his pupil's knuckles smartly at the repetition of a mistake; he was chary of praise. How gladly would the girl have returned to good David Brownson, less learned, perhaps, yet far more gentle.

It was already late in the summer, and the Hearns were making preparations for a speedy departure to a fashionable watering-place, when Captain Lacer requested to see Ethel one day. It is needless to add that the relative from Shellport had no place in these plans. If she continued her lessons she was to remain in the deserted city house, where Richard Hearn would be detained much of the time by business. The aunt had no intention of taking Ethel where she would cast her own daughter in the shade. Who can tell what difference it might have made in Ethel's whole life, had her aunt set aside self, and given her this one sip of innocent pleasure? Certainly it would have softened much of the angry bitterness with which she was disposed to regard life—not life really, but her experience of it. Ethel entered the parlor, haughty and indifferent. Time was when such a summons would have made her nerves quiver with pleasurable anticipations; now she knew that she had nothing agreeable to expect. She hated Captain Lacer very cordially. The emotion he had aroused in her heart was not sufficiently powerful to stand the test of needless humiliation. His value was not enhanced by loss half as much as her own pride was wounded.

"Do you want me?" she inquired, elevating her eyebrows. Her first salutation had been a trifle sullen. He looked at her regretfully a moment before replying. She might have been his own; he knew that she loved him, and he must give up all. Men like Captain Lacer are turned aside by straws; it does not require mountains to check their progress.

"I am all attention, only permit me to remind you that I go to my professor in ten minutes."

"You are cruel. I always bored you, though."

Ethel remained obstinately silent, looking at the carpet. Could she ever forgive this man for the position he had placed her in? Among strangers, only too ready to find fault, he had heaped additional mortification on her, when there was much to bear besides. The silence was growing awkward, the captain felt ill at ease, and Ethel would not help him. He had come dreading a scene, and how was he getting through with it?

"I want your assistance—ah! that is, will you say a good word for me? You knew me before, and we have been such excellent friends, Ethel," he said, imploringly, taking her hand.

She knew what was coming, but must needs affect ignorance. She withdrew her hand.

"Say a good word?" she repeated. Was he afraid she would tell of him?

"I am going to propose to your cousin; in

fact, we understand each other," said the captain, in desperation, flicking his boot with his cane. "I thought I would tell you first."

A mist swam before Ethel's eyes, her hands grew icy cold, yet she steadied her voice to reply. "You wished to prepare me for the shock, Captain Lacer? That was very kind. What is it to me?" She tried to look at him steadily, but the rebellious tears would come. She could have struck herself as she felt them coursing down her cheeks.

"At least, we part friends," he said, again extending his hand. The scene was coming; he anticipated it with nervous trepidation, and he was by no means sure of the result. He would have liked to venture on a warmer salutation, only something in her face withheld him. Indeed, he was loath to give her up.

"Friends, if you choose. Now I may go to my lesson."

She got away after that. The face she turned back toward the parlor door on the stairs was actually ugly with vindictive wrath. Ethel's anger could have moved mountains at that moment of intense resentment. "Oh, I am poor now, but I may be even with you yet," she said, with a quick sob.

"Poor little girl. How hard to have to give her up. She stood it like a brick, too, by Jove!" soliloquized Captain Lacer, surveying himself discontentedly in the pier-glass. He went to his club, and drank brandy-and-soda, yet he was dissatisfied for the day, and many days after.

The Hearns went away, with Captain Lacer in attendance. Mrs. Hearn, always wearing that meaning smile as of amusement at somebody's expense, gave Ethel a cool peck of a kiss, and hoped she would practice faithfully. Clara was really affectionate, bestowed on her cousin a lovely pearl fan of no earthly utility, and promised to write faithfully. After that, Ethel, with a certain stubbornness of pride, held to her music, and wandered about the silent house, until her uncle came home at night. The two were amicable. Neither were demonstrative—one from a feeling of superiority, the other from restraint.

Richard Hearn knew nothing of the little tragedy of Captain Lacer. Clara's success elated him; for the paternal eye had never been blinded to her defects, and he was willing to support so noble a son-in-law for the connection. It never occurred to him to rank Ethel as a rival to his own daughter, while his wife kept her own counsel about many things. When tidings were received that the ladies would return for a week, en route to the mountains, Ethel's resolution failed.

"I can not bear it," cried the girl, with an impatient stamp of the foot.

She told her uncle that she was going home, and she went.

CHAPTER XXV.

THISTLES.

"YOU will hurt yourself."

"I expect to prick my fingers many times before I learn wisdom. There! I *will* have it."

A bright September day, with the atmosphere sparkling and pure, and a breath of the night's frost lingering. Here and there in the hedges a scarlet vine gleamed among the green foliage, and the maples showed a few leaves of pale gold, but for the rest summer reigned.

Two girls were on the bank, the warm shadings of their shawls and hat-feathers giving color and life to the spot. A young man accompanied them, previously listless, now roused to animation by the saucy-defiance of his companion, who persisted in gathering her own thistles.

"Ethel will never allow me to help her," he said, reproachfully.

"I do not need you," replied Ethel, blushing deeply, and with an expression of annoyance.

"Wait until an emergency comes," laughed Olive.

Then they seated themselves on the slope to patiently convert the thistles into balls of snowy down—Ethel, more perverse than usual, at a short distance from the others. A chord was out of tune; there was the jarring strain of discontent in Ethel that morning. Nelson's frequent languor, in which he took refuge occasionally, after his illness, assumed also the moodiness of abstraction. The little sister was cheerful, and gently rallied her companions on their evident depression. Whereupon Ethel roused herself to a tone of badinage.

"We shall see whose pon-pon is the prettiest," she said, gayly, brushing the purple flower-tip against her face, and inhaling the faint sweetness.

"What if mine turns out best?" retorted Olive; and indeed soon held up, gleefully, a compact little globe of the finest spun silk that glistened in the sun.

"Sing to us, dear. Nelson would like the serenade on—"

"A serenade by daylight? No, I thank you." Ethel would never sing to her sister's lover; every entreaty had failed to make her. The temptation was great now, too great to be resisted. The clear voice breathed out the simple pathetic song of the Douglass, "tender and true," ending in a passionate appeal:

"Do you know the truth up in heaven, Douglas?"

Nelson Thorne flushed and paled as he listened; his was a nature luxuriant and impressionable to such influences as Ethel's smooth voice produced. His heart beat in his throat, and suffocated him, but he made no comment on the song. Olive rather wondered at his silence. Ethel was intent on her work again. The thistle burst its bonds of tough scales; already its promise was fair, when—an ugly worm crept out of the core. She flung it away with an exclamation of disgust.

"Try another, or take mine," suggested Olive.

"No; no."

The girl bent low over a bush, that they might not see her gathering tears. A fig for the thistle! Ethel was miserable, and resented intrusion. Every thing for Olive, even sound flowers; nothing for her but worm-eaten buds. The sufferings of youth, so keen, so insurmountable, in the estimation of the sufferer, were usually counteracted by Ethel's buoyant health and consciousness of beauty. But to-day she could only think of the stings, the regret of passing youth, the wound of the captain's marriage.

"What good is it to be handsome, if I never see any body in my prime," she was thinking, as she stared into the bush, where a delicate forest of leaves and twigs rose above her head.

Olive slipped her arm around her neck.

"Is any thing the matter?"

"Nothing. I am watching a spider crocheting with its legs for a needle, and running from loop to loop. I wonder if this example of industry furnished the model for the modern mat, wrought in baser cotton," said Ethel, calmly, and successfully diverted attention to the busy insect.

Nelson, watching them, noticed the gold cord which slipped from beneath Ethel's dress as she stooped.

"Please allow me to look at it," he said, with sudden animation. But when he drew from his pocket a second pendant of dull gold, framing a beryl identical with the first, it was the girl's turn to be astonished.

"Oh, where did you obtain it?" they exclaimed.

"I found this three years ago on the floor beneath my father's desk, where it had fallen without his knowledge. He allowed me to keep it. I carry it for luck, I fancy, and as a curiosity, besides."

"What did he tell you about it? Where did he get it?"

"He told me nothing."

Then Olive repeated briefly the mother's story, and Nelson listened with interest; yet when she had finished, he said,

"I dare say they make these things by the bushel in the East, to sell to travelers as antique relics."

This was so tame and practical a view, that the little sister could not help bestowing a glance of some contempt on Nelson.

"Yours may be," she said. "You shall have another thistle, Ethel, as good as mine.

Nelson, give me the knife. No, I am going myself."

"I shall not make another," called Ethel, hastily.

Nelson took a few steps after duty, paused irresolutely, and came back to inclination. Neither spoke, but it was a troubled, eloquent silence. Ethel sat gazing straight before her to the horizon limit, as if unaware that his gaze was riveted on her.

"I was wondering what we all shall be by the time we reach over yonder," she finally said, in a low tone, pointing to the clouds.

"Never mind. Oh, you have hurt your hand."

She trembled at his tone, but she passively allowed him to brush the blood-stains from her finger with his handkerchief. Ethel never flirted with Nelson.

"How have I vexed you? Look at me once. You never look at me now."

Ethel's mouth framed the words that never came; he drew nearer to catch them, and the two beautiful faces just touched. The next moment Nelson, with pallid lips, as of one in deadly pain, was kissing the stained handkerchief passionately, murmuring hoarsely,

"I will keep this until I die!"

And then the fire leaped from Ethel's veiled eyes; she swept away the stained cambric, ran swiftly down to the brink of the little pond below, wrapped a stone in it, and tossed it far out from the shore.

"Never do that," she said, with a tremulous attempt at firmness.

Olive was approaching over the brow of the hill with her harvest of thistles; Ethel paused by the pond-brink, in advance of the others, looking back with regret, almost despair, and between was the young man. Above all brooded God's clear sky, where one day we shall see as we are seen.

CHAPTER XXVI.

PERIL.

A DREARY day in May. St. Chrysostom had chimed in the Easter season without the voice of Ethel Hearn. The Raines family were in town, with the exception of the stepmother, who had gone to Europe with Captain and Mrs. Lacer.

The routine of life was unchanged in the small house. Nicholas and Nelson Thorne would graduate soon, when the latter would take unto himself a wife. This same bride in prospective went cheerfully about her home, where the most trifling details assumed a deeper, holier significance. Ethel had no part in this joy beyond transient satisfaction in her sister's happiness, and she evaded the proffered kindness of Miss Raines, from her very connection with Captain Lacer. She detested to think of him, and all associations belonging to him. Thus the elder lady made but trifling progress in any of her schemes for the girl's advancement, from a willful misunderstanding on the girl's own part. Perhaps these very obstacles enhanced Ethel's value in Miss Raines's estimation. Did wounded pride occasion sudden blushes and tremors, when a well-known step was heard on the walk, the impulse to hide for hours unnecessary stiffness and haughtiness of manner in welcoming the visitor afterward?

Was Captain Lacer responsible for the varying moods, the undertone of unhappiness, the lack of interest in any stated employment? She always felt bound to make herself disagreeable to Nelson Thorne, and the effort cost her some secret tears; for, in so doing, her love of approbation must needs be set aside. The young man, on the contrary, was always striving to please her, to win some kind word of acknowledgment from her, and patiently endured her most extravagant whim without reproach. This contrast was always rising up before Ethel, and added to her discomfiture. Here was a cause of no small trial; Ethel wishing to be gentle, winning, good, and appear at her best, yet not daring to obey the dictate of her own heart.

"She's moping over that 'ere capting," reflected Peggy. "Might have known how he'd turn out; but she'll get over it. Ethel's not of the pining sort."

Yet Ethel nursed her wrath; found consolation in having a grievance the like of which was never imposed on a girl before.

The fog came creeping in over the sea, swathing the promontory in soft folds of vapor, and gathering in drops on trees and roofs, like gems on the margin of a veil.

Ethel Hearn, in a reckless mood, was defying the fog, and walking steadily onward. Her cloak was wet, her slender feet made tracks in the damp sands, but she did not heed it—rather enjoyed getting thoroughly drenched and wretched. She watched the break of the waves, glimmering weirdly through the mist, and glanced from side to side in supreme satisfaction at her own loneliness. She liked to get away by herself now—she scarcely knew why; her thoughts were not active, and she seldom used to enjoy solitude.

"I suppose this is something like our lives," she soliloquized, sweeping the dim obscurity with her hand. "We never see one inch ahead."

Then some element of the day entered into Ethel's soul. She was treading the shifting clouds instead of firm earth, with the monotone of the sea rising about her. She was the centre of a white sphere, with walls of opaque crystal—moving whither? What more natural than that out of such unreality should grow

Nelson Thorne, eager, radiant, breathless? She might have stood dumbly gazing at him—a spectre—for whole minutes before she turned and ran over the sands, obeying blind panic, as swiftly as ever Atalanta sped before her male competitors. Long striding steps followed, and Nelson held her close—a captive.

"Always luring me on, and flying before me. It drives me mad! I have got you fast, and I will keep you," he said, a passionate exultation glowing in his face entirely foreign to its usual expression.

Ethel braced herself against the arm that held her. "Of course, mere brute force can always triumph, yet gentlemen seldom use it."

Nelson's arm sank, and Ethel's heart smote her. Poor fellow, he was never brutal in his life, she knew. He took the margin of her cloak between finger and thumb to prevent further flight.

"Does that offend your ladyship?"

In spite of herself, she dimpled into a smile. Instantly the savage look flashed back into his face; he wheeled around to prevent her further progress.

"You were not angry after all. You like to torment me. Good fun for you, no doubt!"

"Please let me pass, Nelson. I did not mean to tease you. Surely I need not quarrel with my second brother." The words told; his lips quivered with pain. As for Ethel, if she had strength to reach home she would never risk another interview of this nature. She was striving to be loyal to Olive.

"Do not go on. Stay here," urged Nelson, in troubled tones.

"Are you expected?" she asked, quickly.

"No; I came to see you. I could stay away no longer."

"Hush," entreated Ethel, in a shocked whisper, growing white, and forcing back her tears.

The moment had arrived toward which every ripple of laughter, every glance had converged, since the day Ethel returned. The flame leaped its chill barriers, all the more intense for long repression.

"You love me," cried Nelson. "I know that you do. Oh, my darling, she would forgive us. How can we help being more to each other than all the world besides?"

Ethel essayed sarcasm, and smiled weakly. If help did not come soon, all would be lost; and the woman saw further than the man; beyond this bridge of transient pleasure was a realm of endless pain. On the contrary, Nelson, grown reckless and audacious in his unhappiness, closed eyes and ears to every thing but the fact that they were alone together, reading each other's souls. He had gained possession of both hands, and was raining passionate kisses on them. Gradually a wild, sweet triumph dawned over Ethel. She was loved despite all obstacles, and when she had been purposely ill-natured, dreading the new influence in the household. Why not enjoy the moment?

"You might help me," she whispered.

"We will help each other," he murmured, re-assuringly.

Fulfillment of delirious dreams! The fair face was nestling against his breast; his arms held the treasure; their lips met. At last! at last! The fog changed from ghostly white to tawny orange, a light breeze stirred along the sands, and parted the fleecy mantle in rifts of gold. Olive, secure and trustful in her happiness, judging the stainless honor of others by her own, saw it all. One low groan of mortal anguish was wrung from her heart, then came blessed, merciful darkness.

Mr. John Raines, bent on his own affairs, yet destined to play a part in this domestic drama, discovered her all alone.

"What can have happened to the poor child?" thought the gentleman. "Dear me! This seems to be a most unfortunate family."

With that he raised her, and Olive's first impulse was to efface any suspicion of the truth from Mr. Raines's mind.

"I can not imagine how it happened," she said.

"You slipped, and turned your ankle, perhaps," he suggested, offering his arm.

"Possibly," assented the little sister, steadily; but she accepted the arm, for she was giddy and stunned. What had happened? Was she still in the body or out? Ethel stood at the door, anxiously watching her approach. Again the great pain quivered through Olive's frame at sight of her sister. The younger girl was not one whit behind her in self-command; she ran down the path with eager inquiries; she supported Olive, and thanked Mr. Raines for his assistance. She even managed to inquire about Miss Raines. They entered the house, closed the door, looked at each other earnestly, and Ethel cowered down at Olive's feet.

CHAPTER XXVII.

AFTERWARD.

WHEN the little sister opened her eyes, misery awaited her waking moments to fasten on her for another day. She felt a sickening dread of the burden, a longing to creep away somewhere and be at rest. Where were all her bright dreams of a home of her own now? Of what use was all the pretty finery prepared by her industrious fingers, when her thoughts flew faster than her needle? She put away the linen and embroidery drearily, and turned the key on them, with the heart-ache one feels in laying aside relics of the dead.

There had been tears and lamentations, reproach for Ethel, but never from the lips of her sister. Olive could not bear to look at Ethel, to feel her near approach, yet she was able to restrain her own speech by a resolute silence.

Nelson, torn by conflicting desires and a sense of duty, had begged to see Olive once more, when she sent him down the ring selected by Experience Thorne for her to wear, and she had refused.

"He says that he will never trouble you again," said Peggy, very grim in appearance at this crisis.

"I can not see him," asserted Olive, lying on her bed in the darkened chamber, with a handkerchief over her eyes. When Peggy reached the door she bethought her of an expedient.

"Tell him that I will see him later; in a month, perhaps."

After all, how natural it was he should prefer Ethel. By-and-by, when he had forgotten her, she might be the means of bringing them together. The woman's soul cried out against being forgotten. She did not wish to live to see them married. And so the days went by, with Olive Hearn fighting a desperate battle in the little chamber before she conquered. In the mean while, Nelson was on the rack. He had a long interview with Mrs. Hearn, from which he emerged pale and grave. Then followed a stormy one with Ethel. The elder sister would have made him a loving, faithful wife; the younger one captivated his fancy by the charm of lovely features, waving hair, grace of motion. Olive would have made sacrifices for him, which he might have accepted unconsciously; for Ethel he would have sacrificed all.

The latter sat by the window of the parlor, pale, distressed, sullen. Nelson stood gazing out at the spot where Nicholas had placed the engine, wondering moodily if it would have been better had he never come. Then his glance fell on the golden head beside him, and the harsh thought melted to one of tenderness.

"I know that I must appear a scoundrel to her, but in time—" he began drumming on the pane.

"Time can make no difference, so far as I am concerned. How is it treating my only sister, who has been so good to me? Do you suppose I don't know, just because I am heedless and careless? How could I look any of them in the face again?"

"Then I have lost all," responded the young man, slowly.

Ethel's sole reply was a low sob. Nelson turned to soothe and comfort her directly. He knelt down beside her, and put one arm around her slender waist. The color dawned again in his face as he whispered, eagerly,

"Come with me now. Matters could not be worse. We can get married, and then return to be forgiven. I will take all the blame. They shall not scold you, love. Say yes! Come."

He turned the pale face gently until it rested against his cheek, and renewed his petitions in her ear. Then Ethel drew a long, shuddering breath, and considered. She longed to throw herself on his broad breast, and allow him to take the responsibility. How sad and miserable they would be when he was gone! But then the little sister, robbed and wounded, left desolate! Ethel drew back.

"If we have patience, I am sure it will come right eventually. Will you wait for me, dear?" he pursued, hopefully, and still fighting for the ascendency.

"Good heavens! Have you no conscience, no remorse for what you have done? Is it a trifle in your eyes to ruin a life? Nelson, you will be sorry for all this some time. Try to be brave and good now. You must go away. Do not tempt me."

"If Olive forgives me, will you marry me?" Nelson had risen to his feet.

"No."

"Will you marry another man?" he asked, desperately.

"Yes, I shall accept my first offer," said Ethel, with whitening lips.

"Can I do any thing for you? I am going."

"The greatest kindness you can do me is never to see me again." It was impossible not to feel a yearning toward him. Ethel never moved from her seat, but Nelson did not forget for many a year the look she turned on him at the door, as of one receding mute, helpless, and without personal volition. And Nelson went away without consolation or hope. The young man's lines were no longer cast in pleasant places. Experience Thorne was horrified at the denoucment. He visited wrath and invective on his son for the insane course he had pursued.

"What! Was it not sufficient for you to gain the love of the good one?"

"Ethel is equally good," retorted Nelson, hotly.

"Pooh! A jade. A meddlesome jade!"

After a pause, the father inquired, with cutting irony,

"May I ask what your future intentions are?"

"I am going away. I have always been a source of contempt to you since early boyhood. I have tried to be respectful, and as there seems to be nothing remaining to be said, I will leave. I am now old enough to exercise discretion about my own affairs."

Nelson had never thus defied his parents before.

"I might have known it would end so," said Experience Thorne, bitterly.

Nelson took this reproach wholly to himself, as a more tender-hearted father might have foreseen; but Experience Thorne's words had a deeper meaning. "And now she will marry somebody else," the elder man pursued, slowly rubbing his hands over his knees. "A good man, capable of being respected, I hope."

Nelson started: he had not thought of Olive in the way of marrying. He went to his room, rich with the mementos of his boyhood, and buried his head in his arms on the table. On the wall gleamed the letters, placed there so long ago by his father:

"Unstable as water, thou shalt not excel."

He felt like a criminal banished from his own kind. He was an exile thrust forth from the paradise he had so lately occupied, shamed, remorseful, and with wounded self-love. While he rested there in silence, Ethel Hearn, the other culprit, was approaching timidly her mother's door in much the same mood, her only refuge to throw herself down beside that mother, sobbing piteously,

"I don't know what to do. I am in the way. Oh! mother, I cared for him too."

The little sister, standing by her window in the darkness, saw God's glory as on a curtain, with the pale, aurora fires scintillating over it. The curtain stirred and throbbed with undulatory ripples from horizon to zenith, the effulgence of an unseen splendor, as if moved by the current of a divine will. If the cloud drapery were furled, what wonders might be revealed! The sorrow of Olive Hearn faded, was swept away in the contemplation. How insignificant she seemed compared with the kindling of the heavens by the torch of nature. Then, just as she seemed about to be crushed by a conviction of her own insignificance, she remembered a tiny insect traversing the garden fence, clad in armor of frosted pearl, with jeweled wings, and eyes like ruby points. Surely she was not smaller in the great Master's estimation than the minutely perfect insect.

"There remaineth a rest for the people of God," said Mrs. Hearn, solemnly and wearily. She had come to Olive in her need, and the girl's heart went out to her. She could utter no words of commonplace condolence. Life had been to her so grievous an ordeal that she could only point to the hereafter of peace, gazing also at the cloud-curtain.

"How I have neglected you!" exclaimed Olive; and the reminder was salutary.

The little house pursued its usual routine.

When Nelson Thorne raised his head in his silent chamber, he had formed his resolution. Having learned to despise himself, he determined to make the world respect him. The war-note thrilled through the land, and Nelson became a soldier.

CHAPTER XXVIII.

THE MEMBER FOR MILLVILLE.

THE residence of Jared Hearn was a marvel in its way. There were wooden towers and gables, projecting windows and balconies. It had the appearance of crowding its neighbors on the village street, and a small fountain, crowned by a flesh-colored cupid, ornamented the patch of greensward between the entrance door and the highly-painted fence.

Over the way Mr. Pettigrew acknowledged no such supremacy as the meek little houses around accorded. Mr. Pettigrew boasted also a gabled mansion; and not only a fountain in the front yard, but statuary, and a conservatory. In a word, Jared Hearn and Eliphalet Pettigrew were rival manufacturers. If the Miss Hearns were given a horse by their fond parents, the Miss Pettigrews at once "set up" a pony carriage. If Mrs. Pettigrew appeared in church draped in a new lace shawl, Mrs. Hearn might be relied upon to sail up the aisle the very next Sabbath in one of richer quality. Nor was the competition confined to the feminine portion of the families alone. The *Millville Free Lance* was known to be the organ of Jared Hearn, while the *Advocate* was as loyally enlisted in the cause of Eliphalet Pettigrew and his calicoes.

Millville thrived apace under the stimulus of this zeal, having already sprung from village infancy to the middle growth of a town, and aspired, at no distant day, to becoming a city. If Mr. Pettigrew paved a street, Mr. Hearn was spurred on to pave two thoroughfares. Millville also projected gas-works and a branch railroad, but here matters became involved hopelessly. The two proprietors could never be expected to unite in pushing the same railroad or the identical gas-works contemplated, so, for the nonce, Millville was left in darkness, and to follow the old track. For the rest, they were the best neighbors possible; both deacons of the Millville church, and vied with each other in decorating the sanctuary. Both were shrewd business men, and fully intended to extract the money's worth out of "the hands." In appearance they differed; Mr. Pettigrew being short, stout and pussy, with an altogether jolly aspect, as of a man who thought much of his dinner; and Jared Hearn tall, thin, hard-favored, with the soured aspect of one whose digestion is a burden.

Mrs. Hearn was in her medicine-closet, surveying the shelves with a reflective eye, while a poor woman waited at the door.

"I am not sure that some 'oh be joyful' would not help your cramp more than the elixir, Betty."

"I think it would, ma'am," responded Betty, with the slightest possible twinkle in her small eyes.

Mrs. Hearn, without further comment, poured some Holland gin into a small glass—the liquor which she had designated by the above enlivening name. The manufacturer's lady was an excellent housekeeper and manager, but she appeared to the greatest advantage in the medicine-closet. How comprehensively her glance swept the rows of patent remedies for every known ill flesh is heir to! How vigilantly she watched for symptoms in her family, so accurately described on labels! Although not an educated woman, she was, in one sense of the word, scientific; she personally tested every fresh discovery emanating from the apothecary's shop. Her children grew up pale and sickly. Whether there would have been less nervous headache, fewer fainting-fits, with plenty of fresh air and exercise, is a question which never disturbed the mother. The Miss Hearns, with education completed, and nothing whatever to do, languished in the sitting-room over worsted-work, music, and French, finding excitement only in watching the advent of a stranger at the Pettigrew's opposite. Lina, in the kitchen, bared plump arms to wield the scrubbing-brush, and wore roses of health in her cheeks, such as never bloomed in the parlor. As utterly useless girls are reared in country as city, and they are the children of industrious parents. Jared Hearn toiled early and late, with furrowed lines growing ever deeper in his care-worn face, and Mrs. Hearn was far more frequently to be found in the kitchen than any other portion of the house; yet their daughters, one step removed from necessity, rather prided themselves on their entire ignorance of work.

"I'm afraid your father will get one of his attacks after this excitement. He's run down with business considerably already." Thus spake the mother, entering the room where her daughters sat, wiping her hands on her apron from force of habit rather than necessity for the operation. "Dear me! It puts me all in a flurry to think of it. Father's heart is set on beating, and if he does we shall have to live in Washington. Seems as if I should sink right through the floor when I think of facing the nation like that."

"It will be splendid," commented Susie, drawing her worsted through the canvas, with a yawn.

"For mercy's sake, ma, don't have it traveling through the town that you are afraid," said Sophia.

"I don't intend to," replied Mrs. Hearn, in rather an aggrieved tone. "Look, girls! Quick! Isn't that Judge Blank and Bell going into the Pettigrews? I declare! S'pose they'll talk him over in no time. Bell's setting her cap for Silas Pettigrew. *They* say it would be a good thing. Well, father can do without him, I guess. That girl is coming to-day."

"That girl" was Olive Hearn, descending from the train at the very moment, and welcomed impetuously by a red-haired youth.

Nicholas Hearn had lost no time after he graduated in seeking employment. He had the debt of his college term to pay to the benefactor he had found, and he was firm in the faith that he should be able to accomplish it. As a first step, he asked to be taken into the service of Jared Hearn, for the reason that in a manufacturing town he would have opportunity for study.

"Perhaps I may be his chemist yet," said Nicholas the sanguine, and went with his mother's blessing. Two weeks later, Jared Hearn invited Olive to visit his family—an offer eagerly accepted by the mother, as giving the little sister a change at the time when the daily round of her life was irksome. Whether the uncle, thus reminded of their existence, really felt a desire to see his brother's children, or the mother obtained the invitation, Olive never knew. The first greetings over—and Nicholas did not before appreciate how fond he was of the little sister—she asked,

"And how do you like it?"

"So so," replied Nicholas, swinging her bag as they walked along. "Family well enough; work hard; pay scrimpy. I say, Olive, Uncle Jared is a screw. I'd be ashamed to do things he does if I was a rich man."

"We must not judge him, dear."

"Of course not, Mrs. Goody. There's a great row going on here. A week will decide whether you have an uncle who is an M. C. or not. It is Pettigrew *versus* Hearn; and don't they go it! Even the factory hands meet at night, and pound each other black and blue. Here we are."

Having fortified his sister with this amount of information, Nicholas deposited her in the large mansion, and sped swiftly back to duty on a high stool in the factory office. Olive was received politely by her uncle and aunt, with visible curiosity by her cousins. She was not ushered into the state guest-chamber furnished with blue and gilt, yet in the smaller one accorded her sleep was equally sweet. The little sister, observant of trifles, compressed her lips, and wrote home the most flowery epistles, for which she may surely be forgiven.

The waves of strife ran mountains high in Millville. The whole town was agog with excitement, and the good minister could not, for the life of him, help giving his sermon a political tinge. In the stores old and young politicians uttered their opinions freely, while seated on barrels chewing tobacco. In the dramshops fusil oil heated the angry debates among the hands. The rival editors were perpetually hovering about the telegraph-office, and staring haughtily at each other. But when Mr. Pettigrew encountered Mr. Hearn, the two gentlemen shook hands with great cordiality, and inquired very particularly after the health of the respective families.

As the important election-day approached, Mrs. Hearn had recourse to the medicine-closet, anticipating collapse. Behold the morning ushered in, fraught with brilliant victory or defeat. The gabled houses, standing face to face, represented the extremes of a seesaw, and Millville stood on tiptoe to watch the result.

Nicholas, at his desk, was undisturbed by the general excitement, for his mind was straying on other things. Leaning his head on his hand, he traced a plan on the paper before him. He was disturbed by the hasty entrance of his uncle. The face of Jared Hearn was pale with anger.

"How do you dare to come here and disgrace me! I took you out of charity, too."

This was not strictly true. The uncle had taken a new clerk in the person of his nephew, because he thought the nephew might be useful. What if Nicholas proved an inventor, might not the benefit accrue to himself? Mrs. Hearn, in recommending her son, had not failed to set forth his talents, and the description had made a certain impression. It happened that Millville, almost hysterical from the sensation, was laughing at Mr. Hearn, and he could by no means endure the ridicule of his fellow-townsmen. We Americans are remarkably sensitive to ridicule at all times, but Jared Hearn was additionally so, from the weekly flaying of the *Advocate* since his nomination.

Nicholas dropped his pen, and looked at him.

"Hold me up to be the laughing-stock of the whole place, will ye? Like your impudence! I dare say your mother is at the bottom of it all," fumed Jared.

"What have I done?" cried Nicholas.

"I am to stand any thing for the sake of your valuable services. As if there were not forty lads in this very village who would do better than you, and for less money."

"Suppose you explain."

"You have chosen to associate with George Whitby because he is the worst enemy I have. He gathers every knave he can find at his place, to plot mischief and defeat my election."

"George, the blacksmith? Ha, ha!"

Jared Hearn looked at his audacious young kinsman with lowering brows, and Nicholas knew that all was over. Now George, the blacksmith, a burly giant, whose stentorian voice rang out above the blows of the hammer, was a good fellow in his way. A natural power of attraction brought Nicholas to his forge, the attraction of a furnace, glowing with a tempting invitation to fuse metal, and much practical sense in his own walk of life, on the blacksmith's part. Concerning the political prejudices of George, Nicholas had no thought. His stay in Millville had been brief; but during that time he loved to loiter in the forge when his day's work was done, and the shadows played odd tricks with the giant's form, as he came and went through the ruddy fire-glow. Dear to the heart of a college graduate is it to impart knowledge, and Nicholas found an interesting listener in the blacksmith. The grain of a man's coat never had much weight with Nicholas Hearn.

Lo! Millville observed the intimacy; the *Advocate* smacked its lips, and inserted a malicious little sting to the effect that, if our fellow-citizen could not control the vote of his own household, he need not expect to rule Millville. A very near relation was understood to be ringleader at George Whitby's shop. To Nicholas the accusation seemed ridiculous.

"You are mistaken. George is a good man, and—"

"You teach me! I am rightly served for having any thing to do with you after your father—"

"Stop! Not a word about my father." Nicholas was angry at last.

"Hoity-toity! Pay me the twenty-five thousand dollars he cost me, and I will gladly be silent."

"I will pay you some time," taking his hat from the peg, and preparing to depart. Then Nicholas went out without another word. Jared Hearn knew that he had gone too far, had said more than he intended, but he would not retract a word. Anger is a terribly expensive luxury; still, the candidate for Congress had a nervous headache that morning, after a sleepless night.

Verily one does not know what a day will bring forth. Olive sat by the window, watching the little fountain in the yard, always aspiring in a slender spray, always sinking back. The Miss Hearns were acting as a reserve corps behind the closed blind to report the condition of the popular mind, as evinced by the appearance of the village street. A letter was given to Olive, directed in Peggy's queer, cramped handwriting.

"DEAR GIRL,—You must come right home. I can't find Ethel. Your mother don't know.
"PEGGY."

Olive sprang up wildly.

"I must go," she said.

At the door she encountered Nicholas, not less agitated, although from a different cause.

"We can take the four o'clock train," he said, hurriedly.

"Yes. Do you know already?"

"Do *you* know?"

Rapid explanations followed, and Olive's visit was thus brought to an unexpected close. Her departure had the advantage of saving her from the indignation of her aunt, who had not yet learned of the enormity of Nicholas Hearn's offense. The young man did not see his uncle again, nor did he demand any salary.

"I should like to see him offer to pay me, after telling me that my father was a thief," blazed hot-headed youth. But to the credit of Jared Hearn be it said, that he did not offend youth's susceptibility in any such way.

When the brother and sister were seated in the cars, a large man pushed his way through the crowd on the platform and accosted Nicholas. It was Giant George, expressing his good-will in this conspicuous way in the eyes of all Millville.

"I am sorry to lose ye," he said, heartily, and touched his hat to Olive with the dignity of one of nature's noblemen. "When you are a great man, don't forget me. If ye ever want a hint that I've hammered out, drop me a line and welcome. I hope you've got our wheel all right."

"No; I left it on the desk."

"May I get it?" asked George, quietly.

"If you choose. Good-bye."

Giant George stood on the platform, hands in his pockets, a cigar in his mouth, as the train glided away, and a cheer floated to the car from the town. It was the decisive hour. Millville was shouting itself hoarse with enthusiasm; the *Advocate* unfurled the stars and stripes to the breeze at this auspicious moment; the blinds of the Pettigrew mansion flew up, revealing the Miss Pettigrews with pink bows in their hair; the blinds of the Hearn house remained down, and behind them sat Mrs. Hearn, dissolved in tears, a camphor-bottle in her hand. Eliphalet Pettigrew was the member of Congress by two hundred majority.

The blacksmith made his way to the office door of the Hearn factory. Perhaps he was thinking of a time when the proprietor had refused to loan him a sum sufficient to start in life, and had demanded even the payment of rent in advance. Result: George had appealed to Mr. Pettigrew, who had built him the forge on easy terms. Jared Hearn was not so much an unjust as a cautious man; he liked to see his equivalent before taking a risk. The world repays us in our own coin. Mr. Pettigrew made a warm partisan by a really generous action, and Giant George was worthy of confidence, while Jared Hearn made an enemy. The blacksmith pushed boldly into the office. "Mr. Hearn, I'll trouble ye for a paper left here by your nephew," he said.

Mr. Hearn held the paper in his hand at the moment. His reply was to place it in the desk and turn the key.

"It is useless, as far as I can see. I will communicate with him about it," he replied, coldly.

CHAPTER XXIX.

ETHEL.

THE summer evening was closing in, and the Hearn house at Shellport looked deserted, save for a star of light in the mother's room.

A slight form, veiled, and carrying a small traveling-bag, emerged from the door. It was Ethel. She glanced back wistfully at the little house, and a great sob shook her like a reed. If she might only turn now, and throw herself on her mother's breast, telling her all! But that she could not do. Even heedless Ethel had learned not to worry the mother by useless complaints. The star of light glimmered in the window; even then her courage wavered, when Peggy's ungainly shadow was thrown on the curtain. That turned the balance. She fled from her home as Joseph Rost had done. These two young creatures of different races, destined never to meet, yet bound by a common interest, pursued the same course.

Ethel believed she was going for the good of her family, and she also intended to punish Peggy in her flight. Peggy would be sorry that she had talked to her with such severity. She had told Ethel that the little sister's misery was entirely her fault; that every act of Olive's life had been a voluntary sacrifice for her; and when this prize—a good husband—had come, she must grasp at it too. Every word uttered by Peggy stabbed the listener's heart with fresh pain. How could she help Nelson's falling in love with her? How could she help loving him in return?

"If I was only dead and buried, I should be out of people's way," said the girl bitterly, with tearless eyes.

"That's no way to take things," said Peggy, softened.

"What am I to do?" in a dull, constrained tone

"Try to mend it somehow."

All day Ethel went about declaring mentally that she would mend it ; at evening she disappeared. Ethel Hearn knew no more of the evil of this earth than a baby. Her experience had taught her that there were ill-natured people, hard in their dealings ; but of lower depths of sin she was ignorant. She lacked even the education gained at school among school-girls. The mother held a theory that a young girl's mind should be kept like snow.

Ethel stood on the pier, with ten dollars in her purse, going forth to make her fortune. Her castle of independence was altogether a superb structure. She was very much in earnest. She was not the fairy princess awaiting the prince ; marriage had no longer any place in her thoughts. She would rise by means of her own exertions, work ever so hard to attain perfection, and become a great singer. She did not intend to see Miss Raines, or tax her uncle's bounty; she would keep entirely to herself until she learned something. Perhaps Olive and Nelson would be wedded by that time. A second sob welled up from her heart. It was so terrible to be thrust forth from home in this way; and even if she had no exact perception of her audacious recklessness in taking this step, she shivered with dread at the uncertainty of her future—through such deadly perils do young girls pass in our midst. Better the Old World chaperonage. Better convent rule, if we neither shield them, nor train them to a true knowledge of evil. Too often the wild boar tramples our vineyards, dims the purity of "the polished corners of the temple," while we comfortably reflect : Our American girls are to be trusted. Why not, mesdames and messieurs, adopt foreign espionage and careful selection of associates, when we are so fond of imitating Europe in dress, manner, and language?

The steamer swept up to the dock, gemmed with light from bow to stern, and Ethel flitted on board with the rest of the passengers. At another time she would have been amused watching the variety of faces; now she nervously shunned observation, kept her veil down, and followed a family, with a timid desire to appear to be one of them. Ethel took a stool behind them on deck with an envy bred of her own loneliness. The lady was a mere bundle of rich wrappings, sallow, peevish, and dictatorial. The husband was fat, smooth, urbane; and it seemed to afford the wife pleasure to find fault with him when not snifling disdainfully at a gold vinaigrette, or giving directions to a French *bonne* concerning the sharp-featured little children. There was a perpetual stir about them, a truly aristocratic current.

"How people gape on steamboats! Really, we must charter a boat for our set next summer," said the lady. A sudden gust of wind swept aside Ethel's veil. The small, beady eyes of the fat gentleman fastened on the face beyond his wife's bonnet in surprise and bold admiration. Another passenger also saw Ethel; a large, handsome woman, attired in black, with a profusion of jet and lace, and hard, cruel eyes. The woman quickly concealed her interest in the solitary young girl; so did the fat gentleman. The supper-gong sounded, one by one people dropped away, leaving Ethel almost alone. The woman in black rose and paced the deck with the noiseless, agile step of a cat.

"Are you alone, my dear?" a soft voice inquired.

Ethel started, and looked into the hard eyes, which resembled the jet ornaments in surface glitter, without depth.

"Will you go to supper with me?"

"No, I thank you," rather coldly. Ethel was on her guard; the stranger evidently was a lady, perhaps some friend of Miss Raines, and would tell her all about it. The woman still smiled.

"If you wish any thing, I shall be glad to help you. My room is No. 95. Accidents occur in the night at times, you know."

Ethel shuddered; then, fearing she had been ungracious,

"I am very much obliged to you."

The woman went to supper with that feline step.

This episode cheered Ethel. How easy it was to make friends away from hateful Shell-

port. She might confide her plans to the stranger, and ask her where to go. O God, was this to be the end?

"Thou child of many prayers,
　Life hath quicksands, life hath snares."

Ethel sat gazing at the sea, reflecting that every surge of the steamer carried her farther away from home, and wondering when she should return to it. The fat gentleman approached the unconscious fugitive eagerly, after a cautious glance around.

"Pardon me, but you are alone, I perceive. Allow me to do something for you. There is less wind over here."

Ethel was puzzled and embarrassed. He was the father of the little children, a married man, and therefore one in whom to have confidence; yet there was a look in his face before which her soul shrank. The instinct dormant in every woman's nature caused her to recognize in him an enemy.

"Let me see your eyes once more! You are so beautiful."

"Sir!" said Ethel Hearn, springing to her feet.

He grasped her arm, dared her to make an outcry, as that would bring public notice of a damaging nature to herself, and poured rapturous flattery into her ear which she only half understood. Then he deliberately pressed his full, red lips to her delicate, quivering mouth. Now the fat gentleman, in his right mind, would have gone to no such extreme. He had dined before he came on board, and was in that condition of wine-drinking which made it problematical whether he would fall asleep, or be guilty of some excess. Do not misjudge him, kind reader; he would never have addressed one of his own social position as he saw fit to accost a girl traveling alone, who had doubtless run away from somewhere. If the woman in black had been there, Ethel would have rushed to her for protection; instead, she was seated just within the door watching.

How the girl loathed and abhorred the coarse face barring her flight! Thoroughly aroused to danger, angry and terrified, she eluded him, and flew around the corner of the cabin. Three yards more would have brought her to the woman in black, seated on the velvet sofa, but between stood a man—John Raines. The power of speech had frozen on Ethel's lips by the time she reached him; only two desperate little hands clung to his arm as if they would never again become disengaged, and she simply looked at him. There are fleeting expressions on faces which we never forget. John Raines never quite lost interest in searching Ethel's eyes for the look he found in them that night on the boat. A wild animal, brought suddenly to bay on the precipice brink, startled with a dawning perception of evil, yet sinless, may have the same trembling expectancy. Two wells of pure light, dilated by this terror, with an underlying delight, incredulity, and gratitude for his presence there, Mr. Raines read, "Take me to Miss Raines!" That was the true chord to strike with this brother, unerring tact might have taught her, yet she was ignorant of it. Fear had quenched her heroism. Miss Raines was always good to her.

"You are frightened," he said, re-assuringly.

"That man," gasped the girl.

At this moment the fat gentleman, feeling himself to be in no very graceful or dignified position, passed, with a hasty bow to Mr. Raines, and vanished.

"He frightened me," whispered Ethel, pressing closer to her preserver's side.

"The low hound!" muttered Mr. Raines. He did not consider it necessary to inform her that the fat gentleman was a member of his club.

"I am so glad! Pray don't leave me. I was going to the lady, who spoke to me, but I had so much rather find you. Oh, there she is."

Mr. Raines glanced at the woman in black within the door, and the gravity deepened in his face. He drew Ethel's hand within his arm with a tenderness she could not understand.

"Do you believe the lady knows Miss Raines?"

"No, my dear," he replied, quietly.

It became distinctly understood, by two persons at least, that the young girl had found a protector. The full significance of the fact was felt by Ethel alone. She forgot that she knew Mr. Raines slightly—he might have been her champion for a hundred years, to warrant the confidence reposed in him. And in his heart he was touched by this trust. Ethel recoiled from telling him what the advances of the fat gentleman actually had been—she felt too deeply humiliated, with his kisses still burning on her lips, and he asked no questions.

To the girl's mercurial spirit the terrible journey, fraught with perils, became, if not actually pleasant, curiously novel and comfortable. Mr. Raines was taking care of her. Of course it was not like having Nelson, or even the captain, yet it was very nice.

"You are chilled and tired. You must have supper, and go to bed," proposed middle age, sedately.

"And lose all the beautiful evening?" queried youth, with a pout of dismay. "I thought you were to talk."

"Supper first, and the talk afterward," he said.

An hour later these two, brought together unexpectedly, were seated in a sheltered nook; Ethel well wrapped up in the gentleman's shawls, gazing dreamily at the water, and her companion studying her downcast face. Mr. Raines regarded her first with the forbearance any person would receive from him as his sister's favorite; again, with the pleasure a very plain man feels in dwelling on female beauty; and again, with profound thankfulness that he had found her. Then came a natural doubt as to what reason could have induced Ethel to leave home. What had she done to necessitate flight? Without instruction in the art of pleasing by some subtle influence on an impressionable temperament, Ethel had grown quiet, watching the waves, while these reflections troubled Mr. Raines. At last she raised her eyes to his.

"I will tell you why I am here, if you will please listen."

"Certainly."

"You are very good. I do not know how you could be so good to me if you were not Miss Raines's brother;" and moved by a sudden impulse of gratitude, Ethel touched one of his small hands with her lips. Mr. Raines made the most comical grimace of amusement and disapproval.

"Mademoiselle, if you do that again I shall punish you."

Ethel feared she had made a mistake. She was a country girl, and did not know how to behave with a gentleman like Mr. Raines. With glowing cheeks and drooping lashes she drew back.

"What is the matter now, petite?" he inquired, still amused, and with a caressing intonation very winning to the ear. Ethel struggled with her tears—tears of mortification and sudden homesickness. Oh, how she wished she was back in the little sister's arms, in that safe haven, the mother's chamber, even under unjust Peggy's wing. Her reply was a mute, beseeching glance of the tender eyes, which Mr. Raines probed, lingered, and finally lost himself in. Ah, daughter of Eve — country bred, indeed!

"Now for the story."

"Not much of a romance. Peggy scolded

me about my sister, and I thought the best thing I could do was to leave home. I wish I was back again!"

"School-girl tragics," mentally observed Mr. Raines. "Nurse gave my doll to sister, and I will hide to frighten her. My dear little girl, don't cry. Allow me to suggest that these boats return to-morrow. It is not as if you had crossed the Rocky Mountains."

"Mr. Raines, I was not going to your sister, but I will now."

"Ah?"

"I intended to learn to be a singer."

"Yes. Where?" The first plump question.

"I hardly know. In some school, perhaps."

He made no comment. Hester should talk to this fledgeling. In his very fear for her his manner became more cordially kind. After that Ethel's spirits rallied by one of those marvelous transitions so incomprehensible to the masculine mind, while Mr. Raines was charmingly entertaining. It is not your very young man who is a good conversationalist; his talk may be original, his ideas fresh, but both lack the riper reflective power of the educated, traveled, mature man. Ethel found herself comparing Mr. Raines's easy flow of words on any topic with Nelson's monosyllables. A girl, brimming over with life and interest, ready to be amused, is a stimulus to exertion which few men can resist. Certainly the hours were passing much more swiftly to Mr. Raines than he had anticipated. He no longer insisted on youth's retiring. Indeed, it was his own proposition that they should go into the cabin, where the great chandelier globes glittered on Ethel's

crown of yellow hair. The procession of restless men, perpetually pacing through the saloon, turned for a glimpse of her face, until Mr. Raines frowned and looked at his watch.

"Am I to go to bed?"

It then became apparent that Mr. Raines no longer considered it desirable for Miss Hearn to be subjected to the scrutiny of the staring crowd. Accordingly she went, with a parting smile full of sweetness for her protector. Ethel's smile was gentle and winning; no spasmodic expansion of the features, revealing the teeth, but a gradual curve of the lips, spreading onward into lovely dimples of the cheek. Mr. Raines departed for his book. Returning half an hour later, he found the woman in black tapping on Ethel's door. He strode to her side.

"What are you doing here?" he demanded, sternly.

She quailed; but covert insolence shot an arrow: "I did not know she belonged to you."

When Ethel opened the door Mr. Raines stood alone.

"Are you sure that you are comfortable, my child? Do not unbolt your door again unless I request it. There are thieves on board; a lady can not be too careful."

Ethel promised, and laughed to herself afterward. "I suppose middle-aged men get like that—fussy."

Mr. Raines folded his cloak about him, and took possession of a sofa opposite Ethel's door.

"A true knight of forty-five guarding his mistress's bower. A new rôle for you, John Raines," he reflected, grimly.

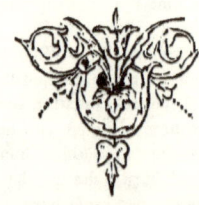

CHAPTER XXX.

UNDER MOB RULE.

WHEN Mr. Raines opened his eyes a girl, fresh and pure as the dawn, sat patiently watching him.

He had slept late, overcome by his vigil. Many of the passengers had departed, yet the girl did not arouse him. Her rest had been sound, and her heart was overflowing with gratitude to Mr. Raines for this instance of watchful care. Asleep outside her door! Had it been Nelson, she would have been amused, a trifle condescending. But Mr. Raines!

"Oh, how kind of you! What a miserable night you must have had, and all for my sake."

"Pooh! it is nothing. I would have done the same for any one," he said, crossly.

Mr. Raines's waking sensation was irritable. The pleasant sentiment, the merry jests of evening vanished in the clear, practical morning. With a nervous horror of making himself ridiculous, he felt convinced that he was playing the fool. He had not intended to be discovered in the rôle of guardian, only the stupor of sleep had overcome him. How was the girl to understand his anxiety? Good heavens! He could not have acted with greater gallantry had he been in love with Ethel Hearn, while in reality nothing could be more absurd than such a supposition. A reserve and constrained silence ensued. Ethel's warm thankfulness flowed back into her own heart, and chilled it. She would call on Miss Raines, and return home by the afternoon boat. After all, her own people were much kinder, even when they scolded, than strangers.

Mr. Raines busied himself with preparations to land. Ethel silently assented to all plans; there was no conversation between them. A carriage, with negro coachman in livery, awaited Mr. Raines's arrival. The latter placed Ethel in the carriage, and the girl, whose tastes were luxurious, became too much absorbed in admiring the satin hangings to observe that the master stood conversing earnestly with the servant. Sambo's ebony face had the peculiar gray tinge which fear lends to the African physiognomy. At length Mr. Raines sprang into the carriage. Ethel immediately resumed an indifferent expression, as if she had not the previous moment been patting the crimson cushion with an appreciative touch.

"Friends?" he inquired, amiably, extending his hand.

Ethel willfully ignored the outstretched palm, and sat with haughtily drooping eyelids. The next moment she repented of her petulance. Mr. Raines unclasped his portmanteau, and took from it a silver inlaid box. Ethel watched him askance.

"Do you know how to shoot?"

Offended dignity was lost in amazement. He displayed two silver-mounted pistols, small and elegant in shape.

"One for you, and one for me," he pursued, with assumed playfulness. "You pull the trigger—so. The next time a fat gentleman insists on talking to you, for example, you can use it. There, put it in your pocket."

Ethel looked at him with dilating eyes.

"What is it?" she asked, breathlessly.

They were on a broad thoroughfare, which presented the unusual aspect of entire desertion. Far ahead a red glow was discernible in the sky from burning buildings. Out of the strange silence grew a low, sullen murmur, the most fearful sound which ever smote on a city's listening ear—the voice of a mob. The coachman checked his horses, gazing wildly from side to side in search of escape. The murmur increased, advanced, broke into a shout. Then the carriage swerved to the right, the negro lashing his steeds to mad speed. Flight was the one instinct left to him, flight from a brutal multitude thirsting for his blood. Ethel was answered. She understood the gift of the pistol now.

"Oh, I am sorry that I refused to shake hands. Pray forgive me."

"Child, there is nothing to forgive," replied Mr. Raines, drawing her close to him. "Listen to me. We are in danger. Much depends on your courage. The city is delivered up to rioters. One can never judge what insanity will do. Can I trust you to use the pistol, if necessary?"

Ethel blanched with horror at the suggestion. How unreal it all was! For a moment she quailed and trembled.

"Yes," she finally said, lifting her eyes to his to gain courage.

Then Mr. Raines touched her cheek with his lips, prompted by her helpless dependence on him, her beauty and docility; and if Ethel was conscious of the caress, she was grateful for it, as effacing the stain of the fat gentleman's bold salute.

The bewildered coachman had made a fatal mistake. In avoiding Scylla the carriage plunged into a Charybdis of seething humanity. The mob, in its apparently aimless course, had stretched vast arms across the town, and that portion which the coachman had mistaken for the main body proved to be only a branch. The wide-spreading limbs of this monstrous growth of evil passion carried poison; but, ah! the cruel venom of the central body, the blind, insensate fury of revenge! A gentleman's carriage, driven by a negro, was greeted with yells and execrations. Greedy eyes peered into the windows at Ethel sitting rigid and silent, rude hands plucked at the fastenings of the doors.

"To resist would be to have the whole pack of wolves on us. Wait!" muttered Mr. Raines, scornfully calm. The fury of the onset was directed against the harmless servant. The mob was ripe for plunder and destruction wherever impulse might lead, but its watchword was, "Down with the negro!" The slave was being freed in the South to rob the mob of lawful work in the North. Away with law, order, and government! Rule by violence and bloodshed! Thus clamored the Old World importation of rioters. Sambo stood on the box, praying piteously to be saved.

"He has done you no injury. I will give you any thing to spare my servant," cried Mr. Raines.

"We may take what you've got without, guv'nor," said a wag in the crowd. This witticism was greeted with an appreciative shout.

Mr. Raines groaned aloud at his own helplessness. Ethel hid her face in her hands. When she looked up again the negro had disappeared into that angry sea, surging and flooding the street. Their turn next. A burly form was thrust into the carriage close to Ethel's shrinking form.

"Out wid yer watches and money!" commanded a rough voice. The girl turned wildly to Mr. Raines for protection. A gun in the hands of a reckless boy sent a bullet whistling through the window. The sudden report thoroughly aroused the trembling horses; they bounded forward, breaking loose from the men who held them, and cleared a way through the crowd. The carriage jolted over some obstacle; Ethel's nerves told her that the soft, yielding thing was a human body. They seemed to be impelled from one peril to another. They were the shuttlecocks tossed from one form of death to the next on that awful day.

Away flew the frantic horses along the street, faster and faster, as no restraint curbed their progress. Ethel neither wept nor spoke. She was frozen in that phase of mortal terror which mechanically awaits the end. Only once did she arouse herself. Mr. Raines forbade her to jump from the carriage, and endeavored to climb to the box by breaking the glass sashes. The aperture was too small; he drew back with bleeding hands.

"Will no one help us?" he exclaimed. "Has the whole town gone mad?"

"I don't think any one can help us but God," said the girl, in a strange, far-away voice. She tore her handkerchief into strips, and bound up his wounded hands. Then a great terror swept over her.

"Are we going to die?" she inquired, incredulously.

"Heaven forbid!"

Then there was a lurch, a grinding crash from the overturned vehicle, a final, desperate struggle of flashing hoofs and delicate limbs, and the horses sped away free of shackles. Mr. Raines extricated Ethel from the ruins. What next? The accident had carried them three miles from Mr. Raines's residence. Where was safety? Without his companion Mr. Raines could have run many risks, and he did not dare to leave her sufficiently long to procure assistance. They were in that portion of the city which borders on the water, a sort of rough upheaval of lumber, coal heaps, and quarried stone, with an occasional factory (silent and deserted that day) rising above the surrounding disorder.

Mr. Raines went to the corner of the street to reconoitre. He had no sooner left her than Ethel discovered a party of workmen approaching from the opposite direction. She ran after Mr. Raines, who without more ado led her into the adjacent lumber-yard, and behind the shelter of a pile of boards. The laborers, disintegrated atoms of the mob, paused to examine the wrecked carriage. Their words were distinctly audible to the hidden listeners. Mr. Raines pressed Ethel's hand re-assuringly.

"Hiding at noonday from desperadoes! Fate is playing odd pranks with us," he breathed in her ear.

"Don't pity me! I shall break down if you do."

"It was not that, you good, brave child. I was thinking how it would seem when we get through it all safely."

There was comfort in this reflection. Safe at last! Just as if Mr. Raines did not know what to say at the right time. One of Ethel's dimples was coaxed into sight in a faint smile. The workmen tramped on. They might emerge from the board castle, but Mr. Raines lingered. Perhaps he dreaded the next step and its unknown perils.

"We must agree on a course of action—and —allow me to be your hair-dresser, for indeed I fear to venture into the presence of King Mob with so much living gold visible."

Then Ethel discovered that the upsetting of the carriage had disturbed her coiffure. Imagine the self-forgetfulness induced by terror that she did not perceive it before. Extremes meet. The deepest tragedy may have its farcical side. John Raines found himself gazing delightedly on the silky masses that Ethel's fingers wove into smooth braids, and once he patted her head softly with such approval as ten years of age might receive.

"I could have seen you for years in my sister's rooms without knowing you, petite," he said, half absently.

"Certainly without noticing me," added Ethel, winding the last band around her head, and putting on her hat.

He actually laughed, displaying dazzling white teeth. "As to that, what need have you of the attention of an old fellow?"

Ethel's eyes clouded. "Great need of your care," she said, soberly, and, remembering her mistake of last night, colored beautifully.

The streets still presented that strange desertion, in which there was also a fear. The two pedestrians made as rapid progress as could be expected, when it is considered that

Mr. Raines always guarded a retreat in event of coming unexpectedly on the foe. Occasionally they met frightened citizens, each intent on his own danger, or flying to the rescue of his family. The soldiers had not yet appeared on the scene, although rumor stated that a gun-boat lay ready to sweep the vicinity of banks should rioters attempt to despoil them.

"We are near my uncle's house, I think," said Ethel, wearily, after an unusually tedious detour to avoid a fired building. "Shelter is every thing."

The mob, slaking its thirst at every pool of revenge, discovered that it owed Mr. Richard Hearn a grudge. He was the rich man, the oppressor of the poor—at least one discontented artisan was of that opinion, and the mob was remarkably unanimous in sentiment. Just as our wanderers reached the edge of a park, the human storm burst opposite in full fury, and the point of attack was undoubtedly Mr. Hearn's elegant residence. The crowd streamed in from every by-way—ragged boys, armed with sharp-pointed staves, excited, brazen women, swarmed, as if summoned by the tap of an evil genius's wand.

Hasten within the sanctuary of the church, standing solemn and pure amidst the turmoil, before some wandering glance falls on Ethel, and the tidings run from lip to lip that she is a lady!

Mr. Raines could not pause to reflect on what might ensue if the church door was locked. No, it yielded to his appeal; they entered the vestibule, and he turned the ponderous key behind them, with a sigh of relief.

"If the fools hold any thing sacred, we are safe here."

"But my uncle," suggested Ethel.

"They are not likely to commit murder."

The interior of the church was lofty and dark; the transition to quiet calm marvelous. They threaded the aisles, followed by hoarse shouts of the crowd, horrible even at that distance. If any thing could have surprised on that day, so replete with strange incidents, it must have been to find before the altar a child's coffin, the tiny inmate, white and still, decked with flowers that breathed a mild fragrance around, as if the child-life yielded a faint sweetness insufficient to permeate a great world.

"Come away," said Mr. Raines, hastily, without looking at the altar, when he divined what was there. But Ethel paused. The little coffin touched her strangely.

"Perhaps we were sent to guard it. Every

one has fled. The poor baby left alone, just as I should have been without you."

Mr. Raines hesitated, then returned to her side, and looked at the child without repugnance.

The property of Mr. Richard Hearn was being roughly handled by his enemies; the family were forced to escape through the stable to a place of safety.

We did not realize it at the time; we can not appreciate it, now that it is past. The mob held sway, like a drunken despot, for three days.

With regard to Richard Hearn, one spark of angry vengeance in the discontented artisan kindled many sparks of wanton mischief, until the mass was ignited into a full blaze. It battered his foundation, forced an entrance; there was an ominous shivering of mirrors, a crash of falling pictures and furniture. Delicate articles of *bijouterie* in Mrs. Hearn's boudoir were tossed out at window to friends in the crowd, and gilt-bound books rained down on the curbstone. Then the brazen women reappeared, each carrying an apron-ful of booty, the glittering spoils of a lady's wardrobe.

In the church the two living human beings were scarcely less silent than the dead child. Ethel leaned her head against a stone pillow, while Mr. Raines, in sheer weariness, lounged among the cushions of an adjoining pew. He closed his eyes; he must have slept; and when he looked at his companion again she was marble pale, with tears slowly coursing down her cheeks.

"Are you ill, or hurt, Ethel?" he inquired.

"No; I am very hungry."

They had been all day without food, in the midst of plenty. He rose quietly.

"I can get you bread, at least."

"No, no! Don't leave me alone! Indeed I do not mind." John Raines had never had a woman wholly dependent on him; the sensation was novel, but it brought no exhilaration.

Suddenly the girl became transfigured before him; a red glow crept up her gown to her face and hair, changing the latter to molten gold, thence bathing the stone pillar in rosy flames. She might have been one of the early martyrs, bound to this stake, consumed by this fiery splendor, gleaming like a star out of a darkened world. In reality, Ethel Hearn was vividly illuminated by the light of her uncle's burning home. No one knew how it happened, unless it was the urchin with matches who could trace the tiny blue flash which ran and hid cunningly, then leaped into free life above of devouring flame. Miss Raines opened her own door that evening to admit her brother and Ethel Hearn. The servants had run away.

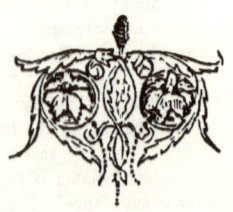

CHAPTER XXXI.

JOHN RAINES.

"WHY not marry her yourself?"

"Eh? What put such a thought in your head?"

Miss Raines sat bolt upright, with her hands crossed on her knee, as she asked this abrupt question. She had come to her brother's library after Ethel Hearn was asleep. The room was wholly in shadow, with a gleam of polished mirror, the cases of books dimly revealed by the radiance of the shaded lamp on the table. John Raines had his fancies. One was for rare, faded old volumes, vellum-bound; another for the Apollo who stood disclosed in graceful outline of marble on an ebony standard; and yet another whim was a clock like that of Linnæus, in the window, divided by lace curtains from the room. He could only imitate others, he would affirm, and persisted, so far as it was practicable, in counting the passing hours by means of the floral group ranged in a circle. The lotus spread pure, snowy leaves to the early sunbeams, and the daisy opened a crimson star to greet the day; but John Raines liked best to watch the tender primrose unfurl velvet petals in the effulgence of sunset, and the cactus bloom with starry splendor at midnight.

This brother and sister were understood to be very dear to each other. One cloud had rested on their attachment, and over that she still brooded at times.

Mr. Raines flushed an uncomfortable red, and looked inexpressibly horrified at Miss Raines's proposition. He glanced around involuntarily, as if about to escape from the very idea. Good gracious! Had the girl actually mistaken his pleasantries and formed an attachment for him? Here the good sense of John Raines re-asserted itself, a glance at the mirror over the chimney-piece rendered such a construction improbable. Miss Raines did not, apparently, observe his discomfiture. "He receives it precisely as I expected. There is no great harm done yet," reflected this wise lady.

"The idea!" he repeated, with increased vehemence. "I shall never marry, of course."

"Why?" inquired Miss Raines, turning her quiet glance full on him.

This question was unpleasant; he had a reason, yet it was altogether unnecessary to explain.

"How can you be so disagreeable, Hester?"

The corners of Miss Raines's mouth showed suppressed amusement.

"Does the girl know? Has she—"

"Has she fallen in love?" The sentence sounded so absurd as she deliberately finished it. "Not that I am aware of. She has never confided any such precious secret to me."

"Of course not," said Mr. Raines, conclusively, relieved, and a trifle piqued.

"Dog in the manger," thought the sister again. "I am interested in this girl," she continued, aloud. "I intend to do something for her. She is what I should have been if the accident had not befallen me. I recognize the same traits daily of my younger self, and to watch their development is a perpetual source of wonder. So like! Ah, me! only without the arrogance my birth and wealth gave me, therefore much better. I should like to see you married. What a different home this would be with a beautiful wife and children, instead of presided over by me, a stiff old maid. Do not interrupt me; I know. Perhaps I am selfish; but my other self, sans crippled limbs and soured temper, must marry well; and I should choose you out of all the world."

Miss Raines's clear voice trembled with unwonted emotion. She was honest in what she said, yet there was a reservation which was not honest.

"My dear Hester, I like the girl for your sake. We will see what can be done for her. I can not marry her to oblige you, can I?"

He patted her shoulder re-assuringly. Miss Raines's features contracted a moment; then she said, lightly, "I suppose every thing is changing. Beauty like that to go begging! Men must be made of ice instead of the old fire and passion. Ah, my little Ethel, could you be established as the fashion, how quickly would one sheep follow another in pursuit of you! Well, my lord, I have given you the first bid for my fair slave, now I will summon others."

"What do you mean by that threat?" He was still smiling.

"I intend to introduce the most eligible men of my acquaintance to my pet forthwith. Good-night!"

Pretty Ethel asleep up stairs knew nothing of these plottings concerning her welfare. Miss Raines stood beside the bed looking earnestly at the girl.

"There may be time yet before Hortense comes."

Mr. Raines, left alone, wandered restlessly about the library. Of all Hester's absurd whims, this was the most ridiculous. She *was* whimsical. All women were. He was to marry this protégée to accommodate his sister. Surely that would be a *mariage de convenance* of a unique sort. He would do any thing else for Ethel. She was a dear little girl. So pretty and piquant, altogether a bright element in the household. If Hester wished to turn the establishment inside out for company, to amuse Ethel, she must have her own way. Yet the suggestion annoyed her unaccountably. They were living very quietly and comfortably as matters stood, with Ethel to sing in the twilight, and Ethel— There! best not to make any change until the autumn. He would advise Hester. Of course the latter thought of his happiness; he firmly believed that.

Then out of the very quiet of night was born the shadow of a desire which stole over him in soft reverie. The smoke of his cigar wreathed in fantastic shapes before his half-closed eyes, and assumed the fleeting form of filmy draperies, even of a well-known face, for imagination was busy within him. While the flower clock grew in the window, a soul flower expanded an alabaster chalice to catch the dew of life, with which to enrich and beautify a sterile nature. The dawn found him still in the chair where his sister left him. Certainly this was a very extraordinary predicament for a sedate, middle-aged gentleman, even if habitually late in retiring.

At the breakfast-table his manner was cold and slightly embarrassed. Miss Raines watched him with covert amusement behind the coffee-urn. Ethel was frank, and oblivious of change. She claimed his attention with playful exactions, unmindful of stiff rejoinders, for Ethel was sure of indulgence from her haughty, sarcastic hostess.

Occasionally he stole glances of critical disapproval at the girl, seeing her in a new light, which melted as they rested on her fair, happy face. Ethel was very happy indeed.

"I must go away," he announced, after breakfast, pausing by the window, irresolutely.

"Oh, must you?" inquired Ethel, with a shade of disappointment in her tone. The soft flattery of the regret expressed was very winning, but it only served to increase Mr. Raines's alarm.

Ethel came in from the conservatory as she spoke, her hands full of rosy blossoms. She had a rare appreciation of flowers, not your humble, out-of-door wild growth, but gorgeous exotics, and she was in league with the gardener. She was really attached to the master of the house: she recognized in him a gentleman, contrasted with the Shellport trades-people, contrasted with Richard Hearn's surface polish of manner.

"I am sorry. See! If you will stay, I may give my loveliest flowers," she said, wafting a delicate spray toward him. Ethel knew that her pose was graceful, felt the exultant thrill of her own beauty and health, quite as much as she thought of Mr. Raines at that moment.

Sunshine, warmth, perfume, and youth! He looked at her with suddenly dazzled eyes, as he had done on the steamboat, then turned away hastily.

"I *must* go away!"

Miss Raines had watched them from her arm-chair. Had she feared the result, rest assured that Ethel Hearn would never have come about her brother in that fashion.

"Then we must be twice as agreeable," said Ethel, going over to her friend.

Mr. Raines glanced back at the door. Ethel was adorning Miss Raines's hair with her blossoms, drooping slender tendrils each side of the pale face. The brother departed. The sister made no comment. Two days later, Ethel looked up from the book she was reading aloud, at the sound of carriage-wheels.

Mr. Raines had returned. His sister suddenly snatched her companion to her breast and kissed her, then said, "Will you go down and welcome him in my place?"

Ethel flitted down the stairway, pausing on the lower step to exclaim, "We are so glad to have you back again!"

Mr. Raines stood at the door without replying. The hall was shaded and cool, after the sultry street; while the light from a window above streamed down on the girl as she hovered there, just above him, in delicate summer raiment. Was she sent down in that ray of brightness to his sober life?

CHAPTER XXXII.

GREAT NEWS.

ETHEL was gone. The blinds of the sick-chamber were always closed now, excluding the sweet summer days. The little sister, forgetful of her own sorrow, was a cheerful presence again. She was finding peace in these days. In her own humility she did not blame Nelson, was even learning to hope that all might yet be well between him and Ethel. They were so well suited, and would make a noble pair. She had heard from Nelson before he went to the war, and often her thoughts, her prayers, followed him to the battle-field.

Nicholas, on his return from serving Jared Hearn, had met with a disappointment so unexpected and severe, that even his sanguine disposition yielded to utter despondency. Awaiting him was an ominous missive, stating that his safety-valve was already anticipated. Poor Nicholas! He fancied that his one little idea was owned by himself alone, out of the whole universe, instead of realizing that many minds ponder on the needs of the age. The plans that hinged on the valve! The mother was to travel in the warm countries, Olive own a piano, Ethel have unlimited gowns, and Peggy her heart's desire, whatever that might be. Now, instead, Nicholas might bury the tiny hope in the grave of silence. The mother comforted him, and watched for the reaction. It came in a glow of youthful patriotism. Soldiers were needed, and Nicholas, pushing his papers into a corner, hastened to the front.

Peggy was morose. The Raines family were not at their place this year. Ethel had not returned. Her flight had been explained in a charming note from Miss Raines, written with all possible dispatch after Ethel's arrival at her door. Without positive prevarication, she shielded the girl from blame. She begged Olive to forgive her for keeping her sister, while assuring her that Ethel should be her first care.

"Had you not better add a few lines?" Miss Raines suggested, as she folded the note.

"Oh, I can not!" exclaimed Ethel, in agony.

She had confessed much to her friend. The elder lady believed that she read the other's soul like an open page; yet there were folded leaves, as there are in all natures. Ethel had been the cause of a difference between her sister and lover. Absence might heal the breach. That Ethel herself loved this hero, Miss Raines did not divine.

The little sister's reply was dignified and simple. She thanked Miss Raines for her kindness, and did not reproach her sister. Inclosed was a smaller letter to Ethel, full of affectionate solicitude, begging her to write to the mother, who missed her sadly, and speaking hopefully of a speedy return. And Ethel wept bitterly as she thought of the lonely little home, wrestling with her own heart. "I must not return until I have accomplished something," she sobbed, and allowed the opportunity to pass.

One of the Raines's servants brought a letter to Olive. She turned faint and giddy as her trembling fingers closed over it.

"Has any thing happened?" she faltered.

"Nothing bad, miss," said the groom, touching his hat with greater respect than ever before.

Olive sank into the first seat, and opened the envelope.

"Peggy! Peggy! Come here."

The old woman obeyed, and at the same moment a light, unsteady footstep, crossing the floor above, descended the stairs. Mrs. Hearn stood on the threshold, a very wraith of a woman in flowing garments.

"What has happened? Is it about your father, at last."

"Oh, mother dear, how stupid I am to frighten you," said Olive, with a tremulous smile, winding her arms about the tottering form. "We have good news. Can you bear to hear? Ethel is married."

Mrs. Hearn's lips quivered without sound, she looked at Olive once—such a look!

"We could not keep it from you," said Olive, tearfully.

Peggy led her mistress back to her room, passive. There was a gray shade on the nurse's face also.

"It's to him, I 'spose," she whispered, later.

"Yes. Mr. Raines."

"I told ye so, long ago. It was all in the cards."

Night settled down on the household, each striving to understand the new state of affairs. How wonderful to think of Ethel married. Of course they had always looked forward to such an event, yet the fulfillment was unexpected. It was not at all remarkable that Mr. Raines should have fallen in love with Ethel, but the marriage was painful to contemplate, as transpiring entirely without their cognizance. Was it an elopement? Did Mr. Raines wish to wean Ethel entirely from them? Oh, why had she thrust them out of her confidence at such a crisis? Such were the little sister's first reflections. As for Mrs. Hearn, she lay on her bed in silence, with her hands clasped over her eyes.

"Go to your supper, my dear," she said, pushing Olive gently away, as she hovered anxiously near.

"What will you have?"

"Nothing."

"You must. A drop of chicken broth. A cup of tea?"

"Tea, if you choose."

Left alone, Mrs. Hearn murmured,

"Married, without me — her own mother. Ah, I hope the child may never need me again. I have done the best I could for her."

The little sister went down with an aching heart to the lonely supper-room. She spread the letter open, instead of eating. "Read it again," said Peggy, coming in with the tea-pot, and preparing to listen, with folded arms.

"MY DEAR, DEAR MOTHER AND SISTER,—When this letter reaches you I shall be married to a good, kind gentleman, who will devote his life to me. We never thought that there would be a rich Mrs. Raines in our poor little family, did we? Miss Raines is satisfied, and likes me for a sister. I hope you will be pleased, too, for indeed I could not have made a better match. I am very fortunate for a girl in my position. Uncle Hearn may know me now, as I shall rank above him in society. Oh, how splendid it will be, my darlings, to be a lady. I am coming to you to-morrow. Do not allow dear Peggy to fret about preparations; we stay at the house.

"Ever your affectionate   ETHEL."

"She is better off," said Peggy, with an involuntary sigh.

"I never could understand her leaving us," said Olive.

"P'raps I know. I scolded her, and she deserved it. She took the life out o' your heart, child, and I told her so."

"You did?" said Olive, regretfully. "Then you were very unjust. Just as if she could help it—or—"

Here the brave little sister laid her head down on the table and began to cry. "You sent her out into the world, poor child! She might not have found friends; we read of such things."

Peggy was dumb. Remorse for her own harsh words had weighed on her ever since Ethel's flight. The old woman went away in silence; it was not best to condole with Olive, who would be ashamed of her tears presently. Peggy had not dwelt with the little sister these one-and-twenty years without understanding her peculiarities. In the kitchen Peggy glanced around for help. The clouds were very dark. "Shouldn't wonder if it killed her mother," she said, from a habit of speaking her thoughts aloud.

First she refreshed herself with a pinch of snuff, then, slighting the clairvoyance gift as a broken reed, she lifted from a shelf a large Bible, with worn cover. Peggy's selection, after adjusting the silver-bowed spectacles, was the Lamentations of Jeremiah. Her theological views were peculiar. In fact, no one exactly knew what she believed, as she maintained unusual reserve on the subject. With her, reading the Scriptures was not so much a habit as a resort in emergencies, when her courage was spent, and then she invariably turned to the grand, stern prophets of the Old Testament.

In this way was the news of Ethel Hearn's marriage received by her own family.

Olive speedily dried her tears, recovered her composure, and went into the kitchen to make overtures of peace with Peggy—poor old Peggy, who always did her best for them. This accomplished, she returned to the mother's room, reproaching herself for having given way instead of making the others happier. Mrs. Hearn lay in precisely the same attitude, with her hands over her face, the cup of tea untouched beside her. Her daughter, so young, and patient, and hopeful, stood regarding her with unutterable tenderness; then the grief of her heart found utterance against her will.

"Oh, mother, you have me left."

Mrs. Hearn was not insensible to this appeal; she quickly withdrew her hands, and looked into the clear eyes of her child.

"I am selfish. But you do not know how hard it is to bear all alone—all alone! If your father were only here to share it. My own daughter to go away and marry a man I never saw!"

Then she burst into nervous, feeble weeping, which somewhat relieved her. Olive soothed her, suggested hope in every form which her office of consoler could discover, and thought of Ethel with sudden bitterness, for thus wounding her mother. The little sister's efforts were so far successful that when she cracked a poor little joke about one old maid being left in the family, by a wise dispensation of Providence, the mother smiled faintly.

In the mean while Peggy, seated before the open Bible, was arguing with Deity, entirely without intentional irreverence.

"It ain't right for one young thing to hev' all the trouble. Any one can see that. It don't matter for an old body like me to live shet up so. One place is as good as another when you get to be sixty odd. Then, as if it wasn't enough to be always planning and fussing for her mother—bless her!—that beau had to come and make her happy for a spell, only to shoot off agin. It's enough to break any camel's back, the way she's had to excuse Ethel to her mother, I declare."

Oh, Peggy, would you disarrange the pattern, weaving through all the ages, with dark and bright threads, under the All-seeing eye? What if the noblest natures are purified in the chasuble of affliction? And what if reparation to Albert Hearn's wife should be the loving fidelity of one of Albert Hearn's children through all these weary years?

The clock struck twelve. The strokes rang on Mrs. Hearn's brain with painful distinctness. She raised herself and listened. A dim light burned in the hall; Olive was sleeping the dreamless sleep of youth in an adjoining room; even Peggy had succumbed to bodily weariness,

closed her Bible, and gone to bed. For the mother there was no rest. The shock of excitement had brought the enemy of her life trooping back with all his legions. She had been aroused from a doze by a thrill of agony darting through cheek and temple. The veins of her temple projected like knotted cords, a chill perspiration rained down her face. "Let the child sleep while she can," she thought, fearful of arousing Olive. "To-morrow will be another day, alterday, as good King Taldemar said." Then, with her brain on fire, she rocked herself, repeating: "Alterday, Alterday," unconsciously. The pain fiend put her to inconceivable torture in the application of his Inquisition, as if to wring a groan from her lips, which would bring a small, white-robed figure to her side. Darts of flame flashed before her closed eyes. She buried her head in the pillow, clenching her teeth on it.

"I wonder who bought my daughter's wedding clothes. Oh, Albert, we are brought very low when strangers pay for her trousseau!" Wounded sensitive-plants do not close in sleep. She rose and paced the room with her light step. The poor woman was beside herself in the terrible anguish of suffering, yet she must think—think with an acute perception of evil, and no power to see good. At one moment she leaned far out the window, inhaling the grateful dampness of night, the next she immersed her face in ice-cold water, then she recklessly beat her head to deaden sensation. Suddenly the fiend whispered, "Morphine." Mrs. Hearn shivered, and glanced toward a closet. In the closet was oblivion. She returned to her bed resolutely. Some slight noise just then aroused the little sister, who crept in as she was in the habit of doing several times in the night. She thought that her mother looked haggard and white, but the invalid feigned sleep. A fierce contest raged within the latter's breast. At length she went to the closet; she would merely look at the remedy. There it stood, a small phial, filled with a colorless liquid. Insignificant in appearance, but gazed at by the yearning eyes of misery so often, and bringing a fatal death in life to its votaries. This bottle had a history in the Hearn family. Mrs. Hearn had used it, until Olive had observed, with inexpressible horror, that she was drifting into a habit of requiring the narcotic at stated hours. There had been a struggle—drunkards, whether of liquors or drugs, being self-deceptive—and the daughter's firmness won. Mrs. Hearn promised never to touch the medicine without Olive's entire consent. Again she resisted temptation, and returned to bed. Her best resolutions faltered. The fiend—surely never her own better nature—waxed defiant. What was honor to torture? What right had Olive to exact such a promise from her poor mother, for a principle? Principle! Her trembling hands clutched the bottle.

Olive knew what had happened when her mother opened her eyes at a late hour next day. Abashed and humiliated, Mrs. Hearn avoided her daughter's gaze. "I have broken my promise. I could not endure more," she whispered, hoarsely. "Oh that death might render me no longer contemptible!"

Olive refrained from mentioning the medicine again, only, with ever-increasing pain, kept the phial replenished. Later, Mr. and Mrs. Raines came. Ethel was all smiles and pretty triumph. She put her arms around Peggy's neck at the door, and the old nurse thawed into a proud smile.

"I am so glad to be home once more!" said the bride, embracing Olive. Then she added to her husband, "This is your new sister," and Mr. Raines obediently kissed Olive, although the little sister did not care much about being thus saluted.

Ethel left them in the tiny parlor to make the best of each other's society, while she ran up stairs to the mother's room. Olive dreaded this *tête-à-tête* with her brother-in-law, and sat casting about in her mind for some topic of conversation which should be conventional. Mr. Raines, also, conscious of some awkwardness, stood before a choice engraving, a relic of Albert Hearn's better days, which gave Olive the opportunity to study the back of his head, and speculate on how soon he would be bald. Fortunately, he found something to say about the famous original of the picture, which he had seen, before they congealed into statues. Olive was interested, against her will, in Tintoretto, although she still regarded Mr. Raines with asperity. What business had a plain, small gentleman to marry handsome Ethel? Suppose he *was* rich. He had need to be, one would think, to balance things.

Observe, the little sister was not at all worldly-wise, nor did she judge mankind by a fair standard in comparing them with Nelson's extraordinary beauty. Mr. Raines read this hostility at a glance. He was a trifle offended, and a good deal amused. Perhaps Mr. Raines was more in the habit of playing the great gentleman than was good for him. He certainly had not expected to sue for pardon when he entered this humble domicile, and elevated a

daughter by marriage, yet Olive lost nothing of his respect by her entire unwillingness to receive him. He frowned once at the picture, then turned to his companion. There sat the little sister, on the extreme edge of her chair, in a stiff, old-maidish attitude, intending to be elaborately civil, and not in the least aware of her failure.

"You do not forgive me yet, I perceive, but you will in time, I hope. I shall try to make the child happy; and," freezing a little, "she was not forced to marry me against her will."

"Oh, I am sure not," stammered Olive, blushing violently.

"You must not consider her lost, although it is natural for families to feel such partings keenly, especially women. You will judge me more leniently when your own turn comes."

"I shall never marry," said Olive, promptly, glancing at him with a quick suspicion. Could it be possible that Ethel had told him about Nelson?

Mr. Raines made no immediate reply; his smile said more plainly than words: "Young ladies more frequently form such resolutions than keep them." Ethel returned radiant with satisfaction. She had resolved to make all amends to her mother, and had succeeded. She glanced with some curiosity at Olive, then approached her husband.

"Mother wishes to see you."

"Is it not too much for her strength?"

Ethel looked at him beseechingly, and Mr. Raines, being on his good behavior with his wife's relations in this first interview, obediently went.

Mrs. Hearn's chamber was very simple in appointment, but exquisitely clean. The robe she wore had been bleached to snowy whiteness by Peggy's hands; her hair was becomingly arranged, and a knot of lavender ribbons at the throat gave a tinge of color to the faded face. A cool, green, twilight chamber, with a pervading atmosphere of fragrance from the lilies in the vases. It was none of Mr. Raines's affair that the little sister had toiled in the hot sun after the lilies; had paused on the threshold to note the artistic effect of light or shade on her invalid; had even consulted Peggy as to the advisability of allowing him to sit in a cane chair, or the arm-chair, with a cashmere shawl draped cleverly over the back to conceal its shabbiness. When he entered this hushed room, and encountered Mrs. Hearn's earnest gaze, he realized the wrong Ethel had done. The mother desired to see her daughter's husband alone. The interview was long and quiet.

Ethel held court below stairs, with Olive and Peggy for subjects. How pretty she was! And with what pride did she sketch the future of Mrs. Raines!

"Do not forget the mother," Olive warned.

Then the bride flitted into the dining-room, reached to a shelf for a little volume of Tennyson, and overturned a port-folio of sketches. How came a sheet of paper in her hand, a mere suggestion of the low, curving shore, with the fog rolling in from the sea? Instantly the scene flashed back to her, this fickle Ethel, assisted by circumstances to forget, rushed over her with an overwhelming mastery and intensity of vain longing, which blinded her eyes with sudden tears. Oh, the beautiful young face bending over her that night! Oh, life, full, perfect, self-sacrificing, if shared with him! Gone, gone, never to return in time or eternity. "I am glad I closed the gate!" she said, passionately.

The little sister's arms encircled her.

"My dear, the step you have taken was terribly rash. God help you!"

Ethel proudly dashed away her tears.

"God helps those who help themselves"—the soft lips uttered Miss Raines's hard philosophy already.

"God has helped you all your life, Ethel Hearn. The time will surely come when you will need him."

How meek and tame the little sister was! Fate brings to each of us our allowance soon enough; Ethel had gone forth to meet it with eager, outstretched hand, while Olive had patiently awaited it.

Up stairs Mrs. Hearn was saying:

"Had I been consulted about your marriage you should have learned this before."

"It could have made no difference, I assure you."

Then Mr. Raines came down stairs, knowing more of Ethel's father than she did, and the visitors departed.

"You may hold my parasol."

"With pleasure. I believe that I will send out to Europe for a coral handle and point-lace cover. Would you like it?"

"Of all things," assented Ethel, with sparkling eyes. After all, it was nice to be Mrs. Raines, and have a husband devoted to her. Ethel looked at him complacently. What could she not make him do? Alas! that woman should believe her power to be unbounded. As it happened, Ethel Hearn was not the romance of John Raines's life.

CHAPTER XXXIII.

THE HERMIT.

DOWN by the river the old house stood, holding its secret close. Joseph Rost had nearly wrested it away, but death had checked the progress of Joseph Rost, and saved the house. Saved? Daylight disclosed fresh lines and crevices in its aged front, like the wrinkles of laughter in an old man's face. Above the decayed walls rose the marble Virgin in stainless purity. The flowers and weeds grew rank in the garden, the humid steps were again untrodden; the very layers of dust, gathering in impalpable folds, had settled on every projection as before the coming of the Jew.

The sole occupant of the place was the Indian woman, who glided swiftly among the trees, collecting the simple necessities of her life, bright-eyed, alert, and ever watchful for the return of Bernardo.

On the morning of which we write, she was melting the berries that furnished the candles of her altar, in an iron pot, over some crackling branches, when she felt her skirt pulled. Turning, she saw a large, rough dog of sagacious aspect. The Indian passively watched his movements. The dog whined, fawned on her, licked her hands, ran a short distance, paused to see if she followed, then returned to repeat his entreaties. The woman went to her room, returning armed with a Mexican dagger, bow and arrows slung over her shoulder, and a rifle in her hands. Apparently satisfied with this curious mixture of barbarous and civilized weapons, the dog bounded through the thicket. The Indian followed. A man hung limp in the lower branches of a small tree. He was evidently injured, and had made great exertions to climb the tree out of reach of some enemy. "Alligator," muttered the Indian, and began to search the underbrush carefully, aided by the dog. A hidden object presently stirred the leaves cautiously. Beware of the cruel jaws, the slimy length of hidden reptile! The dog shrank back, trembling. The Indian surveyed her antagonist contemptuously, from intimate association with the monster since childhood. Her keen glance told her that the alligator was already wounded in the head. Measuring her aim critically, she fitted an arrow into the bow, and sent the barbed agony home through the eye to the sluggish brain. The creature moaned like a human being. Then the savage burst forth, coursing like a lava torrent of fierce delight through her veins. Generations of warrior ancestors impelled her to crush and trample a fallen foe. The war between reptile and man dilated her nostril, and flashed in her eye, as she plunged her dagger into the helpless carcass. She despised the alligator, she wreaked vengeance on it, she wrought herself into a frenzy over the work.

But when the wounded man opened his eyes he was lying on a soft blanket in the Indian's room, and she was skillfully binding up his wounds with bruised leaves and aromatic-scented herbs. The faithful dog lay stretched across the threshold, afraid to approach his master without the Indian's sanction. The man smiled faintly, and nodded a friendly greeting. She replied gravely. These two knew each other; they were neighbors, after a fashion. He had appeared five years before, built a cabin in the fir plantation half a mile up the river, and sat watching the rippling water all day. He lived as a hermit withdrawn from the world. Often he met the Indian, in lonely rambles; once, indeed, she had brought him a gift of yams, and asked his opinion about Bernardo's long absence.

"The alligator tracked me unexpectedly, and snapped at my leg before I could get away. I shot it once."

She mixed a bitter draught, while he spoke,

in an earthen vase, bade him drink, and soon sleep settled gently on his eyelids. They formed a singular contrast of races: the Indian's bronzed face, thin, eager, self-contained; the sleeping old man, with beard and hair like the silk of milkweed, or cotton in the pod, regular features, and a transparent fairness of complexion.

The dog suddenly pricked up his ears, but his sense of hearing was scarcely more acute than that of the woman. She passed rapidly around the house and confronted strangers coming up the path from the beach, as she had faced Joseph Rost before—two young men in blue uniform, one tall and handsome, the other small, red-haired, and ugly. The latter accosted her with easy familiarity.

"We are glad to find you well, aunty. We are going to make you a visit."

"Did Bernardo send you?" she inquired, slowly.

"I am sorry to say that I do not know Bernardo."

"This is no place for strangers, then. Why do you come?"

"Do not chaff her, Nicholas. You little know the breed," urged his companion, in an under-tone.

"We will not trouble you," said Nicholas, good-humoredly. "We want to see the house, and a queer old place it is. We must behold it, by fair means, if possible, by foul, if not. Does she understand that, think you? Come, let us ransack before night, and then camp somewhere near. Mind you, I believe that old fellow was cracked who left you the pocket-book. Men have dreamed of treasures before. Still, the description tallies, and it serves as a lark." So saying, Nicholas Hearn gave a resounding blow to the door, which fell open, and they entered the hall—desolate, chill, silent, and void, with the ashes of the Jew's fire still on the hearth.

The Indian hesitated, watching their movements with glittering eyes; then she went away.

"Let them touch one of his things!" she muttered.

The two young men explored to their hearts' content. To be sure, the doors were fastened leading from the hall, but they were off on furlough, and there was ample time to dig for Captain Kidd's treasure, as Nicholas called it. Nelson was becoming more impatient; some portion of Joseph's eagerness seemed to have been his inheritance with the pocket-book. The wounded man's slumbers were broken by a cheery voice.

"Hulloa, aunty! Have you got any thing to eat? We are starving."

The hermit opened his eyes, with a great start, and looked at Nicholas Hearn standing at the door.

"Dear me! a sick man. I am sorry to disturb you!" exclaimed Nicholas, in dismay. "Are you the master of the house? I wish you would make the old woman feed us; she's uncommonly rusty, you know."

A strange dread and awe rested on the hermit; he made no reply, but continued to gaze at the intruder gravely. A voice was speaking to him out of the remote past like an echo of his own life.

"He's cracked, too," thought Nicholas, and bore the investigation patiently until he should speak.

"Where did you come from?"

"Down the river. We are off on leave, and wish to explore this old house. There is no harm in that, is there?"

"Certainly not. I will speak to the woman, and you will find food at my cabin in the fir plantation above. Will you come again?"

"To be sure I will—as often as you like; and we must nurse you well. Is it fever?"

"No, no, an alligator attacked me. Your accent is different—did you—live—north?"

"Yes. My home is Shellport. Do you know that place?"

Nicholas was fondling the dog.

"No. And your name?"

"Nicholas Hearn. Why, what is the matter?"

The hermit had quietly fainted.

CHAPTER XXXIV.

FOUND.

AN hour later the two young men were contemplating with the satisfaction of weary travelers a fire blazing on the broad hearth of the old hall. At first they had discussed sleeping on the ground, as in camp; but had finally decided to allow themselves the unusual luxury of a shelter of any sort. Not having old Jake in the capacity of steward, they had been obliged to act as their own purveyors, even going as far as the hermit's cabin to borrow from his stock of provisions. Nicholas had not yet given a full description of his interview with the stranger.

"You saw him well out of it, of course," Nelson, who was on his knees sorting hard bread out of their knapsack, observed.

"I should think so," replied Nicholas, with his gaze fixed on the coffee-pot. "You should have seen the old woman pounce on me! She ordered me off, with such a look. But I was not to be disposed of in that fashion. I know something about doctoring; I studied medicine once for a while."

"Oh, Nicholas! what have you not studied?" exclaimed Nelson.

"Knowledge is power," said Nicholas, gravely, raising the lid, and squinting into the coffee-pot. "I felt his pulse, and all that, and when I found he was coming around I walked off. Catch me worrying the poor man again; his nerves are too shaky. Indians are capital nurses. What did make him faint, I wonder."

"The poor soul has been so long out of creation that he is like the wild animals. Fled from some real or imaginary evil, and is half insane, probably. In Europe he would have become a Trappist, and his name have perished with him."

"Strange! when there is so much to be done in the world," said Nicholas; and losing himself in this thought, staring at the fire, permitted the coffee to boil over.

Nelson and Nicholas were the best possible friends, from the very contrast of their natures. Nelson was the practical financier, Nicholas the nerve force. Their interests did not clash, thus creating envy, but followed widely different channels. As soldiers they worked shoulder to shoulder. With regard to the disagreement with the girls, Nicholas saw no occasion to take up cudgels against his college mate, and believed it would "all come right" some time.

How it was to come right, Nicholas did not trouble himself to decide; he was sorry for any unhappiness, but rather thought that, if the girls had something to do, were deeply versed in science, for instance, they would find no time for moping. As for Nelson, he was a man, with a man's work before him. Nicholas did not see any necessity for pitying him.

The supper was dispatched with relish, albeit frugal, and then they filled their pipes.

"Oh! did I tell you I got a letter from home just before we started?" said Nicholas.

It was a full minute before Nelson trusted his voice to inquire:

"All well?"

"All well, and Ethel married."

"Married!"

How the fire leaped and dazzled! How unnaturally loud sounded the tones of his own voice! Did he actually shout the word, or had Nicholas repeated it? Or were his senses stunned with that singing in his brain? Ethel married! Gone, lost to him forever. In the selfishness of his pain, he never once thought of the little sister. To be sure, he had not hoped for any thing but wide separation, yet— Olive might have forgiven him in time. It was torture to consider this girl of his brighter fancy as belonging to another man. What did the old clock know about it? He found himself asking this childish question, because he fancied there was intelligence in its ghostly silence. When had the pendulum swung the sad refrain "Never—forever," and whose life had been ticked away?

Nicholas Hearn, who was entirely devoid of imagination except in the speculations of his own future success, did not particularly notice his friend's abstraction.

"By Jove! I am glad Ethel *has* caught such a fish," he continued, warmly. "It is not only that he is rich, although that is a comfortable thing too, but he is as good as gold. I shall never forget him! I declare, if he wanted my head to-morrow, I would give it to him in a minute."

If Mr. Raines accepted the gift of Nicholas Hearn's head so generously proffered by the owner, it would never be as an ornament, but rather from some internal quality of usefulness. Nelson would scarcely have been human had he not sneered a trifle when his heart-strings were thus trampled upon.

"He seems to be a favorite. May I ask his name?"

"Mr. Raines."

"What! that old fellow? I forgot; of course, money is the first consideration. A good match to wed a grandfather! How girls *do* sell themselves!"

"I should say he was worth every inch as much as Ethel," replied Nicholas, quietly.

Then it did occur to him that the subject must be a painful one.

Nelson said very little more that night. He replied in monosyllables when Nicholas rambled off in ghostly dissertations suggested by their surroundings, and the fun it would be to search the old place. With a feeling of positive relief, Nelson bade him good-night, after each had placed his heavy boots for a pillow beneath the blanket, soldier fashion, and lay down beside the replenished fire. Nicholas fell asleep. Nelson lay looking at the glow on the ceiling from the coals, as Joseph Rost had done, with throbbing, aching brain. Joseph had thought of Rachel as Samuel's bride, with much the same bitterness that Nelson now thought of Ethel as the wife of John Raines. The solemnity of the night, the lonely desertion of the place, weighed on his spirits, because a part of his misery. If he had only known before! He would have rescued Ethel at all hazards. People might have thought their worst. His father could have still further de-

nounced him. Olive—here came a sharp twinge of pain—well, Olive would have considered him the mean hound he was. He writhed at the idea. How dreary and long life would be; how blank and devoid of interest! Again he felt the golden hair drift across his cheek. Again the gray eyes, deep and dreamy, were raised to his, while the ghostly clock above his head surely ticked "Never—forever."

It was not the clock, it was the stroke of conscience vibrating through his being. This was his punishment. The measure he had meted out to Olive, his chosen wife, was now his portion. He had been unfaithful to her, and Ethel unfaithful to him, in turn. If he could only act, it would be savagely, but he was restrained by wide distance. The powers of good and evil were testing the manhood of Nelson Thorne that night. Had his father known it, what passionate prayers for his deliverance would have come from the strong man's soul!

Thus the darkness gathered around them; the hermit, intensely wakeful, in the out-building, and the young soldiers following the clue of a letter which might prove as delusive as a vision.

It may have been hours later that Nicholas Hearn was aroused to a condition of rigid wakefulness. He did not fear any thing mortal, tangible, but on the barrier of the unseen world he had never stepped. A cold current of air awakened him, without a transition state of drowsiness, every faculty unnaturally alert and keen. On the other side of the hearth Nelson was sitting erect, and between stood an old man in a green coat, holding a glittering chain of jewels in his hands.

"Father, how came you here?" asked Nelson.

The old man did not heed the question. He stood there with an expression of musing admiration on his face, turning the necklace through his fingers, or laying it against the relief of his coat sleeve, to bring out the lights. Nicholas observed, with horror, that a long silk scarf of curious netted work was tied around the stranger's neck, and the ends trailed behind on the floor.

"Father, father, speak to me!" entreated Nelson, almost wildly, rising to his feet.

Nicholas mechanically did the same.

The old man glanced quickly over his shoulder, not at Nelson, but beyond, and concealed the chain in his breast. Simultaneously the two young men extended their arms to grasp him ; the fire leaped up, distinctly revealing his figure, then went out. Nicholas clasped Nelson's hands across a vacant space.

"The fellow told the truth in that letter," said Nicholas, when a torch was kindled, shedding a pale gleam on the two startled faces. "We have seen the ghost."

"Ghost!" interrupted Nelson. "That was my father."

Nicholas regarded him in astonishment.

"We must not let these things turn our brains. They are queer. Perhaps science may find a solution for them some time."

"Science!" repeated Nelson, impatiently ; "I tell you it was my own father. Don't you suppose that I know him by this time ?"

"Look here, Nelson, your father does not wear his hair in that way, or clothes of that cut. I never saw the like out of a picture."

"True, but the resemblance is remarkable," replied Nelson, with a sigh of relief, wiping his damp brow.

They made a tour of the premises, and discovered nothing. The next morning the young men started in search of game and fish to replenish their larder.

"We must lay in some provisions, and perhaps to-night the goblin will be so obliging as to show us where the jewels are hidden," said Nicholas, lightly.

Nelson was gloomy and silent ; he could not so easily shake off the influences of the previous night.

All day the hermit watched, with feverish eagerness, for a glimpse of Nicholas Hearn, but the latter never came. He had, however, inquired of the Indian about the sick man's condition. At last the hermit could endure suspense and disappointment no longer ; he begged the woman to fetch the young man, but the Indian came, and went sullenly, neither promising nor refusing. In her heart she was jealous that he was not satisfied with her care. Then he coaxed his dog to go, and the animal, already on excellent terms with the intruders, went. Toward evening the sick man heard approaching footsteps, and the color deepened in his cheek.

Nelson brought him some birds, fruit of the day's shooting. The color faded in the hermit's face.

"Can I see—the other one ?" he asked, hesitatingly.

"He believes he had best not come until to-morrow."

"Why ?" suspiciously.

"Because you are not strong yet."

"Is your name Hearn also ? Are you brothers ?"

"No ; friends."

"I should like to see him."

"The hermit evidently likes you best," said Nelson, afterward.

Nicholas went, to humor the sick man's whim, and Nelson suddenly decided to explore the room described by Joseph Rost. The interview with the hermit was unimportant. When Nicholas returned, his comrade was rolling a canvas which he put in his knapsack. They agreed to take turns in watching that night, and draw lots for the first choice.

"Don't you see how much easier it is ?" argued Nicholas. "Ghosts always point the way to secret treasures in stories—get out of their graves on purpose. If the old chap—I beg his pardon, the apparition—don't enlighten us to-night, we will tear the house down piecemeal."

They spun a coin, and the lot fell to Nicholas. His companion rolled himself in his blanket, and fell asleep ; Nicholas sat bolt-upright, his funny little eyes roving around the place. He smoked a pipe, yawned, looked at the clock, then took a wooden model of a lock from a convenient pocket, and studied it attentively. Nicholas was a good soldier, wiry, active, courageous, but all the military drilling in the world could not have banished the lock from his mind. It was to be burglar-proof, easily adjustable, small, yet strong. In the insignificant invention Nicholas again saw a cloud castle rising which should own in him a master. Suddenly he looked up ; the clock case had a curious brass lock.

"I might get an idea from the old thing," he soliloquized, placing the torch on the mantel-piece, and cutting around the lock with his penknife.

Angry eyes were watching, stealthy steps were drawing near. The wood was old, the lock, with one wrench, lay in his hand, but the rude shock had wrought more than Nicholas in his wildest dreams anticipated. The clock rested in a niche, but the jar slipped the door off the hinges.

"I did not mean to do that," thought the young man, peering into the case.

In the back was a panel which had once been concealed, but was now revealed by the warping of cracks. Nicholas's heart began to beat with excitement. A touch of his penknife opened the second door, and in a space of the wall behind was a small wooden box.

A quick hand swept down the torch, a fierce

throb of pain darted through Nicholas's shoulder. He sank to the ground with a groan.

"What is the matter?" cried Nelson, aroused as if from a nightmare.

"A light—quick!" panted Nicholas.

When the torch was relighted, they were alone. Nicholas Hearn had been stabbed in the back, and the niche behind the clock was vacant, except of a log-book.

Outside a man climbed the vine ladder leading up to the statue of the Virgin quickly. He was small, and bent in figure, with greenish eyes and a crafty face. Then all was still. In the mean while the hermit had passed an eventful night. Toward evening he dozed. He was aroused by the dog. The animal was behind his master's couch on the floor, as if to get beyond the Indian's reach, and gave vent to a dismal howl. The sick man opened his eyes, and beheld the Indian woman scowling at the dog, while she prepared a fluid in the vase.

"Too tired, make you sleep," she said, placing the vase within reach of his hand.

"You are a good doctor; what should I do without you?" he returned, gratefully.

She looked pleased. One of those sudden impulses or convictions which flash through the mind at times seized the hermit. He raised the vase to his lips, then quickly poured it on the ground when her back was turned. Why did she wish him to sleep? She had given him no drink the previous night. Why was the dog uneasy? Was her anger kindled against the young men? He must watch. For a long time the woman appeared to mean nothing unusual; she moved about quietly, the hermit pretending to sleep, while the dog kept between his master and the wall. Nothing sinister, only she looked at the sleeper occasionally, and once stole up to examine the empty cup. Heavens! she could not intend to murder him. He must not die now. The sick man's heart gave such a bound of alarm that he feared she would see the blanket heave. Like a shadow she moved to the door, and melted into the darkness of night. He raised himself, and listened intently. The dog growled; his master's hand gripped his collar to command silence.

If he could only have followed, instead of lying bound to the floor by weakness! Perhaps the young men should have been warned of danger. She might surprise them in sleep. Why should she? Surely his brain was sick with morbid fancies, as well as his body. He tried to compose himself in vain. His thoughts must follow the stealthy figure in the darkness.

There sat the man with one hand on the dog's throat, straining his senses to catch an unusual sound. What if he shouted? That would bring the Indian back sooner than help, and when she recognized in him a foe, a spy, what dreadful form would her anger take in his helpless state?

Suddenly she sprang into the room, and threw herself on her couch. The hermit had barely time to drop back into his former position and keep the dog quiet. The woman held a small box, which she thrust beneath her body for concealment. Not a sound broke the stillness. She lay perfectly motionless. At last, when her fears of being followed seemed to be allayed, she rose, and went out. The hermit, wrought to the highest pitch of anxiety, crawled on his hands and knees to the door. Peering into the night, he at last discerned her by the ruined part of the wall, where a wild fig-tree grew. She lifted a heavy stone, put something—probably the box—among the rubbish, and replaced the stone.

She had returned to her bed, the hermit having crept back with infinite pain and difficulty, when steps were heard approaching, and a torch flared. The light fell on the Indian's impassive face awhile before she appeared to awaken.

"I want your help," said Nelson Thorne.

"Help?" she repeated, stupidly, rubbing her eyes.

"Yes; my friend has hurt himself a little."

"Me come. Hush! he sleep."

The hermit clenched his hands beneath the blanket; the dog wagged his tail, but never moved. The woman calmly gathered up her herbs and accompanied the young man. Nicholas Hearn had received a wound in the shoulder, which was not deep enough to be dangerous. The inscrutable bronze face stooped to examine it. For a time she busied herself in preparation, then, as she spread a green leaf over the injured part, a grim smile just curved her lips. Nelson mistrusted her, and he was ordinarily the most unsuspicious of mortals. This duty performed, she stalked away.

The door leading to the back of the house was slowly opened, and the hermit crawled in with his dog. He checked Nelson's exclamation of surprise by an imperative gesture. He was deadly pale, trembled excessively, and drops of blood trickled from his wounded foot. Nelson held his flask to the old man's lips.

"We have not a moment to spare. The woman did it. Oh! is he much hurt? You must take me. If I am left, she will hunt me down, and I wish to live now. I have deceived her; she believes that I am still asleep in the dark yonder. I have the box here."

"We need not run away from a woman," said Nelson, contemptuously.

"True, but from an Indian? I think she considers you thieves of some sort, and will have vengeance, for I have robbed her. Quick! the boat before dawn."

They made their preparations silently and rapidly. At the door Nicholas paused, bade his companions wait, and went back for the lock of the clock case and the log-book. Assuredly, Nicholas Hearn could not be said to neglect his opportunities.

Down to the river and the boat. Out on the rippling tide, the hermit steering, with his faithful dog between his knees, Nicholas crouched on the next seat, and Nelson pulling sturdily.

Push off from the dark bank, with the old house shrouded in its tangled thicket, and the savage, in her lair, guarding the treasure of a dead owner. The loud report of a rifle broke the stillness; Nelson rested on his oars and listened intently. What was it? Only this:

Reuben Wentzel had tracked the two soldiers when he found that he could not obtain possession of Joseph's pocket-book, and had hovered near the old house for two days, sleeping in the hermit's deserted cabin. He had taken care not to be seen by a soul, and he had discovered that the vine ladder was an excellent perch at night, commanding as it did the ingress or egress of the young men. As regarded the Indian woman, Reuben knew absolutely nothing. This night he had climbed until he reached the niche of the Virgin, and found a resting-place on the ledge beside the white figure. He may have dozed in the weary vigil, when a noise startled him—the shipping of an oar. What! had they accomplished their purpose, whatever it was, and gone? He pushed the statue with his elbow, perhaps in his haste to get down, and the marble form, glimmering weirdly in the night, toppled forward, and disappeared with a crash. Ah! Reuben Wentzel, better to have been aware of the foe crouching panther-like among the shrubbery. Then the shot rang out, and Reuben Wentzel fell.

After that Nicholas was very ill. They made a camp for him, and removed the Indian's bandage. Whether the application was poisonous, or the fatigue of the journey injurious, was questionable. The hermit inclined to the former belief. The old man watched unweariedly, forgetting his own sufferings in anxiety for the

other's recovery. Gradually it dawned on Nelson that this interest was remarkable.

But there came a day when Nicholas was so much better that they could discuss matters and examine the box. The hermit had insisted on keeping it closed until they could all investigate its contents. There the necklace lay, destined never to gladden the eyes of the diamond brokers; concealed by the old master from Bernardo, who must have been ignorant of its existence. Had not the old house held its secret well? The sunlight smote sparks of flame from the jewels, and a clear lustre, like drops of water strung together, delighted the eye. A chain of translucent emeralds was held by a rim of diamonds, pearls, rubies, and sapphires.

The three men were silent, dazzled, stupefied. Nicholas first recovered himself.

"Well done, old fellow! I congratulate you. Only think of that letter being true after all! I never believed a word of it."

The hermit glanced up inquiringly.

"We will share it. Our friend here has earned a portion," said Nelson.

A light broke from the old man's eyes; he clutched the chain eagerly, then he grew ashy white, as he groaned:

"How much is it worth? Not fifty thousand dollars, surely."

"Perhaps. Why, Nicholas—I never thought of that!" With eager fingers Nelson drew out the pendant which he always wore.

He blushed even in his excitement. Ethel had the other. A single pendant remained on the chain, and there were traces of two others having been taken off. Exactly alike.

"How queer! My own mother has one just like this," explained Nicholas.

"A curious relic; where did she obtain it?" The hermit's voice was suppressed.

"Oh, from her grandfather!" said Nicholas.

The old man examined the necklace closely; and for the first time since they had known him he smiled—a slow, gradual, lovely smile, which just curved the lips and lighted the whole face.

Nelson regarded him with troubled eyes.

"Who are you?"

"Do I remind you of some one? Look! Old eyes are keener than young ones. Here is a plate inscribed with English characters: 'The Rajah of Mattam to Captain Arthur Rawson.' Nicholas, it belongs to your mother."

The warm impulse of a fresh purpose strung the frame, so long inert and hopeless; the whole man rose, expanded, as the truth burst from his lips.

"Tell me about her! How have you lived? Such years of despair and suffering, and now God has sent you to me!"

He was no longer recognizable.

Nicholas, never quick-witted in emergencies, listened in bewilderment.

Nelson said:

"You are more like Ethel Hearn than any person in the world."

"Yes; I am her father."

CHAPTER XXXV.

EXPERIENCE THORNE.

THE dark house where Nelson was born stood sombre and silent in the cheerful sunshine. It was not because Experience Thorne shunned or disliked sunshine, but it did not come spontaneously to him.

The master was unchanged in habit and appearance. His only new interest was in searching the telegraphic items of the newspapers piled about him with eagerness and relief.

"After all, a soldier's life and death are noble in such a crisis as this," he soliloquized, when the door opened and Nelson entered.

The greeting between them was remarkably cordial; the usually undemonstrative father was surprised into embracing his son.

"Are you well—unhurt?" he asked, eagerly; then immediately added, with an abrupt change of tone, "You have not shirked duty, I hope. Never ran away from the enemy, or flinched under fire, eh?"

"I believe not," replied Nelson, smiling. "I tore down the colors once, when I saw that they would be taken otherwise. One does so hate to give up in battle."

Experience nodded approval. Heaven defend him from a cowardly son! Nelson was improved in appearance—more manly and self-reliant; had gained a decision of expression besides.

"So you stormed the city? Good! I like that."

Nelson described the campaign with the truthfulness of an eye-witness and the enthusiasm of a young soldier. Experience Thorne's face kindled as he listened. Indeed, so absorbed did Nelson become in the gratification of being able to tell his father any thing, and actually narrate his story well, that he nearly forgot the main object of his visit—to describe his sojourn in the old house. The remembrance now flashed back upon him, with ten-fold interest, as he sat confronting his father, the harsh features, square jaw, and keen eyes straight before him.

"There is something else, sir, that I wish to consult you about."

Experience Thorne grew thoughtful. Now the resemblance was complete to the old man, who stood on the hearth, musingly slipping the jewels through his hands.

"How extraordinary!" ejaculated the son, forgetting that his father had no possible clue to his thoughts. "Have we relatives of the name of Goffe?"

Experience Thorne sat and gazed at his interlocutor, with a slightly rigid expression of the mouth and a cold surprise—gazed so steadily and long that Nelson felt abashed from long habit of his childhood.

"Absurd! What put that into your head? Your name is Thorne." The same cold surprise, but a suppressed curiosity nevertheless.

"Of course; yet people have relatives of different names."

"True, young gentleman"—ever so slight a sarcastic emphasis on the word young. "Tell your story, and do not make it a serial, I beg, as dinner-time approaches."

"I will wait."

"No." He leaned his elbow on the table, and supported his chin in his palm, as if to hold the stern face firm.

"To abbreviate a long story, then, I have had a curious adventure. After one of our battles I found a wounded man, a foreigner, dying, and gave him water.

"He left me his pocket-book, and bade me keep it from another man who approached."

"Who was the other?" interrupted the listener.

"I do not know. A Jew, I fancy. Both were Jews. The book had neither name nor address, but contained a letter in Danish. I had to get it translated. The letter stated that the writer was searching for a chain stolen from his grandfather by an English buccaneer who boarded the vessel. He strayed, by accident, to a deserted house, where the ghost of an old man appeared to him, holding the necklace."

"Oh, an admirable serial story! Did I not tell you? Close of the number, apparition of old man to wandering Jew—for such I take your hero to be—and the reading public left with hair standing on end. Pray continue," said Experience Thorne, mockingly.

Nelson looked perplexed. "I should think so had I not seen for myself. We are apt to believe what we hear and see ourselves."

"Well, what have you seen?" asked Experience, steadily.

"Father, the man was yourself, only older and different. I went there with Nicholas Hearn, and we both saw him holding the necklace, which we afterward found behind the clock case. I forgot; the Jew wrote in his letter that he discovered a cigar-box, with the name of Frederick William Goffe inscribed on it, which aroused his scent. This would have no interest to us had the ghost not been you, and I spoke, thinking it was you."

"What did he say?" inquired the father, composedly, but with bloodless lips.

"Nothing. I cut the picture from the frame, and kept this book—the log of a pirate, I think."

He unrolled the canvas, spread it on the table; and it was as if Experience Thorne looked into his own mirrored face.

"A likeness, surely. Give me the book. You seem determined to claim relationship with a pirate."

"Heaven forbid! we spring from honest men."

"Where is the necklace?"

"Gone to the owner, Mrs. Hearn. True, I never told you. A pendant, precisely like the one you gave me, descended to her from her grandfather, a captain in the merchant service of Great Britain."

"Why did I never hear this before?" thundered the father, with an imperious gesture.

"Because the subject seemed a disagreeable one," replied the son, quietly. A more fitting response might have been that the parent, stern and self-contained, never encouraged confidence.

"And is this your story? A pretty tale, truly. The invention of fools. A pack of fools together, lured on by visions. Bah! Let us take a little solid food after so much imagination."

The difference between Nelson as a man and a boy was, that he now replied, while in childhood he would have preserved a stubborn silence.

"No, father, you are mistaken. Doubtless it seems less tangible to you than to us, and altogether borders on the marvelous; but the proof of reality is that the necklace is already restored to the rightful owner, and the husband at the same time found. He was living on the spot. It is all the providence of God."

Experience Thorne gave his son the most peculiar look, and repeated, slowly, "The providence of God!"

No further reference was made to the subject. Nelson was disappointed, until he reflected that he might have been carried away by a foolish ardor, and had best be sobered.

Was it a dream, that his father stood by his bed in the night? Did he speak, still composed, yet with the unwilling aspect of a person forced to confession?

"It is the providence of God, my son. If the secret of such a life is buried fathoms deep in death, it will appear to curse future generations. The justice of Heaven demands that such a man's children should suffer for the wrongs he has heaped on the innocent and helpless. I have kept it from you, but it is right you should know, since he would rise from the grave to tell you. My father was a buccaneer. He never revealed to me his past life, nor did his neighbors know more. I was born in a handsome house in this city, when he was a mature man. There was a certain amount of mystery about him, which he successfully lived down. During the first five years of his residence here, he was never known to have received a single letter, which marked him a stranger on the face of the earth. His increasing popularity grew out of two excellent sources: he was rich, and he gave largely to charity. I was carefully educated, but there were no bounds to the sinful extravagance of my youth. I ran completely through the gamut of pleasure; as I boastfully termed it, nor did my father severely reprimand me. He watched me with a species of morbid despair, which I can now understand, but was too heedless to note at the time. He saw in me the reproduction of his own violent youth, and was hopeless of my being better. I was afraid of my father, except when nerved to audacity by wine. He was a sinister man to dwell with;

there was something restless and stealthy about him. His moods were regular as the recurring seasons. During the autumn he was quiet, interested in the daily routine of a city's business life, projected improvements with his neighbors, sought libraries and museums. Toward spring he became irritable, and his family knew that the dark fit was coming on him, which would last the summer. He scarcely ate or drank; he paced the room all night; he seldom slept in his bed, but had an arm-chair placed where he caught a feverish doze, from which he awakened with horrors more terrible than those of Richard III. All day he walked like a man possessed, or rode miles on horseback, and never a beggar crossed his path that he did not give liberal alms. At night he would sometimes return exhausted beyond power of speech.

"Often he went on long journeys in these moods, and none ventured to question him. I was obliged to invent excuses for his prolonged absence to inquiring acquaintances. I believe that he visited some spot in the far South, which possessed a peculiar attraction to him. I have never learned where this place was; I was warned that I would do so at my peril. I grew to manhood, a striking likeness of my father; but he must have been a very old man when I reached my prime, although no one knew his exact age. With increasing years his dark fits became more firmly seated. I came to consider them periodical attacks of madness. I now believe them to have been the tortures of remorse for a monstrous deed committed at that time of year when the fresh verdure of spring brought remembrance. One year he departed and wrote me a singular, rambling letter, which showed his mind to be unhinged, and threatened vaguely suicide. He told me a hangman had tracked him for years, and he feared the pursuer was about to overtake him. He also bade me find his will in his secretary, in event of his death, and forbade my searching for him, as my own good name would suffer.

"The letter sobered me; I ceased to game and drink in the suspense of waiting. My father never returned. I opened the drawer, and found not only the will, but a letter telling me who I was. Unlimited command of the wealth foully amassed was accorded me. I was bidden to enjoy it, make the most of it; and no hope was expressed of my living other than as I had lived, or not perishing at the end, as swine perish. So little did my father value the mercy of Christ and the glories of eternity.

"This letter was like the lash of a whip across my face. I reformed. I became converted; I was received into the communion of Christian people. My desire to bear a respectable, honored name was deeply wounded by the discovery of my father's character. I firmly resolved never to marry, to let our race perish, striving to build up such a memorial as I could by real worth. I was eight-and-forty years of age when I met your mother, and one glimpse of her sweet face dispelled my wisest resolution. She consented to marry me; but, as she belonged to a very good family, I did not venture to disclose my own origin. I was afraid of losing the one pure influence my lot had known. After you were born she discovered the truth with her quick woman's instinct. I was ill, and she had access to my papers. She also found the pendant you have, which she insisted on keeping. She forgave me, but the shadow fell on her spirit. The shock of the revelation seemed not so much to wound her family pride, or mar her affection for me, as to make her watch with dread for the upspringing of a poison plant in our household, nurtured into sudden growth by some passion from the parent root—my father. She regarded me timidly, at times, as if I could have harmed a hair of her gentle head, and she guarded you with constant prayers. She implored me to give up the money, and I loved it, stained though it was with crime. I reasoned that I would do good, but I also intended to enjoy it while I lived. Your mother made me promise to place it on the altar of repentance, to build some worthy charity."

"Oh, father! Not the Orphans' Home?" said Nelson, a sudden light breaking in upon him.

"Yes. I lost my fortune in a speculation about the time the Orphans' Home was anonymously built and endowed. I, a rash speculator," said Experience Thorne, scornfully.

The sacrifice had not been made without a struggle. There was every inducement for him to retain the money. He had not sinfully acquired it, and he had a son growing up to provide for in life; yet the Orphans' Home was built, and Experience Thorne left a poor man.

"The task of educating you devolved on me after her death. I strove to eliminate all development in your youth of those traits which so nearly ruined my own, and I have endeavored to lead you to accept that anchor of faith, religion, which alone prevented my being my father over again."

"You never could have been that," said Nelson, touched by the gray face, which revealed deep lines of concentrated purpose and brooding regret in the candle-light.

"I am the same nature, curbed by society, modified by a spiritual faith. The flame is smothered, yet the volcano rages at heart. I have the periods of restlessness which in my father were remorse. And my thoughts are very dark at times. You are my son; I trust you. I would submit to the rack sooner than tell this to another. Time must develop your worth, if you have any. You are different in temperament and nature—more like your mother. That may save you. I wish you had married that girl; it would have been the making of you. If you do not prove an honest, upright man, I believe your mother will weep over your downfall, among the angels of heaven."

Experience Thorne, wrapped in his dressing-gown, tall and gaunt, went away, the candle flaring and expiring in the socket.

It was not a dream, after all.

CHAPTER XXXVI.

THE COUNTESS GUARADINI.

"IT is delightful to be home again," said the Countess Guaradini, with a sigh of satisfaction.

"And yet you went away voluntarily," observed Ethel.

"The Old World claimed her," said Mr. Raines.

Although Ethel still smiled, it just occurred to her that the Old World had not made much of a bargain, and such gallantry on her husband's part was slightly ridiculous.

"This naughty gentleman is responsible," replied the countess, extending a pretty hand, sparkling with rings, to the count.

Thus addressed, the count rose from his chair, with elaborate politeness, touched the little hand with his grizzled mustache, and murmured,

"*Mon ange.*"

Mr. Raines's lip curled slightly.

"I forget! Hester detests sentiment. It does not mean much with us, *ma chère*. I have overcome my earlier *gaucherie* by experience, and learned not to accept in sober earnest every pretty speech made by a European, as so many American girls do. There is a wide difference between courtesy and love-making."

"Are you no longer an American, that you dwell so gravely on our faults?" inquired Miss Raines.

The countess laughed, a little, rippling laugh, like the tinkle of silver bells; it brought the blood to Mr. Raines's cheek as he listened.

"My dear Hester, I scarcely know what I am, unless it is a chameleon. At Paris, I am a true Parisian; at Vienna, the most reckless pleasure-seeker; at Rome, the Holy Father's most dutiful daughter. Did you not know that I had become converted? Of course. It was Paolo's wish. We Guaradinis have been Catholic for generations. *Tiens!* All things to all men. The monkey is not more imitative than I am. I like to assume and discard a nationality like a glove."

Again the light laugh floated musically through the room, and the countess watched John Raines with half-closed eyes.

"*Qu'elle est spirituelle,*" remarked the count to Ethel. Miss Raines was unsympathetic; showed a certain degree of dislike to the guest altogether. Madame la comtesse was well aware of this aversion, but she did not permit it to disturb her. To be disliked by a woman is to be feared, was her creed.

Time, twelve o'clock in the day. Place, Mr. Raines's city house. Dramatis personæ : Count Guaradini, the Countess Guaradini, Mr. Raines, wife, and sister.

Ten years before, Hortense Raines, orphan and heiress, had become the Countess Guaradini, instead of marrying in her own country. The reason was obvious: she gained a title, position, and *éclat* by the match. Dear to our republican American heart is a position at court. Moreover, this step taken by Hortense Raines was the fruit of family doctrine, of English ancestry; the race still clung to the mother country, and Mr. Raines was more apt to boast of his English origin than his present American citizenship. This made him an echo rather than a primitive force. It is all very well to present to a young country the advancement of another older in civilization, if the comparison tends to modify a thousand crudities incident to growth; but good is seldom accomplished by passive disapproval like that of John Raines. He wished parks and entailed estates, and the difference of class more distinctly defined, in a land where nature has furnished boundless parks, and planned work for every one of her toiling sons. Mr. Raines had much leisure in which to consider these short-comings; indeed, he enjoyed that rare boon of idleness, to possess which a man inevitably deteriorates, if he does not find resource in philanthropy or study. Fortunately the instrument was not tuneless; he spent much time among his books, was an excellent linguist, sketched admirably, wrote a sonnet on occasion. And the instrument gave forth a full, rich chord of true manhood when need came: a war found him in the field of active usefulness. If it were possible for a gentleman to be out of place, John Raines seemed to have been born on the wrong shore of the ocean. He disdained to meddle with affairs, where his influence might have had weight, because he disliked publicity. He concealed vigor of mind and generosity of disposition under an habitual disguise of indifference and occasional cold sarcasm. The good his right hand did in the world, remained unknown to his left hand; his dread of ostentation and hypocrisy was morbid. Few persons really knew him, because he liked to baffle penetration; none so readily as his cousin Hortense.

A small, vivacious woman, with large, luminous black eyes, thin face, which kindled with excitement, and always in perfect taste with her surroundings. As a girl, noted for her caprices and oddity; now, graceful and well-bred, her wardrobe a marvel of French art.

The count was a very nice old gentleman indeed, having pendulous cheeks, shrewd, twinkling eyes, a portly person, and white, fat hands. What the mysteries of his toilet were his valet alone knew. There might be a suspicion of rouge beneath the eyes, there might be agonies of gout and rheumatism endured in silence, requiring prolonged sojourns at various German spas, where madame strolled, surrounded by hosts of admirers. Rumor hinted that a very different old man, in dressing-gown and smoking-cap, dwelt in the count's apartments from the gentleman who afterward issued forth, but rumor is seldom reliable. It may also have been known to the discreet valet that the count treated madame with marked respect, and never interfered with her little pleasures, but played with his pet dog in retirement, when not required to attend his sovereign, wearing many foreign orders on his breast. Nothing could have been more appropriate. The count endowed Hortense with an illustrious name, a crumbling castle, and accepted in return a youthful bride, and an ample fortune with which to render his declining years comfortable. And now the countess had returned to her native land to receive the homage due to her success.

Ethel was satisfied with her life. By nature she was receptive of surrounding influences, and there was little danger of her making blunders in her new position, with Miss Raines in the background.

"My sister is as much in love with my wife as I am," John Raines would say, and Hester would nod a gentle assent. The marriage was a nine days' wonder. Who was the bride? None of his friends had ever heard of her, and John Raines had been abandoned as a confirmed bachelor. Then Mr. Richard Hearn stepped to the front ranks, and claimed a niece in the bride, with no small satisfaction. And Hester Raines, watching it all, reflected that it was her own work. Had she desired to thwart the union, she could have done so. John should have a lovely wife, and Ethel be, also, well provided for.

"I am afraid!" the girl exclaimed, with sudden terror, clinging to her friend.

"Hush! I am here to take care of you," she returned.

Thus, in the early days of married life, Ethel depended on Miss Raines more than her husband.

John Raines was a very contented man, scarcely re-instated on his former standing of cool composure, and apt to commit extravagances over which his sister quietly smiled. The novelty of having a wife was an intoxication to which he had not yet become sedately accustomed. Ethel was an inexhaustible variety of mood and thought to his life, for she never ceased to practice the power of captivation on her husband. These very arts might be diverted into more dangerous channels later, as seeking the admiration of others; but now they sufficed to fascinate him alone.

Mrs. Raines tasted of pleasure with the zest of a novice, and became the fashion. As a married lady she received the tribute of admiration which would never have been accorded her as a young lady.

There was to be a ball in the evening, partly

in honor of the countess, and also to gratify Ethel, who had been promised such an entertainment on her birthday.

The countess swept down stairs in the most exquisite of toilets, mauve tinted, *décolleté* quite *à la mode*, and diamonds wreathed in her dark hair.

The interest manifested by Miss Raines in Ethel's appearance amounted to mania. "Thank Heaven there is such a possibility as a woman's being beautiful and modest also," she said, assisting the maid to spread Ethel's gossamer draperies.

"How much you care for my happiness!" exclaimed Ethel, kissing her impulsively.

"Am I really good to you?" questioned Miss Raines, anxiously.

"No one could be more kind."

The luxury of wearing rich dress had not lost its freshness for the young wife; she reveled in her new existence. She was always sweet-tempered from her very satisfaction in surveying her possessions. Husband, lovely baby, Miss Raines, the house, all belonged to her, and the thought brought exultation. She surveyed herself with childish satisfaction. Miss Raines had insisted on a style of costume, a shade of color which the countess would never venture to assume. Ethel, the slender, pure blonde, could robe herself in pale sea-foam green; Madame la comtesse, petite and dark, would never take such a liberty with her complexion. Miss Raines looped her own pearls in the gold hair about the white throat, and the result satisfied her.

"Go and display yourself to John."

"Oh yes, I am going. If baby was only awake! Hester, I should like him to remember me like this when I get to be old."

"Do not allow baby to usurp the father's first place."

"He receives sufficient attention," responded Ethel, merrily, and, gathering up her dainty skirts, went.

"She knows very little," sighed Miss Raines.

Ethel tripped into the library confident of praise. There stood the countess and Mr. Raines in earnest, low-toned conversation. The lady looked pensive; she was arousing her cousin's sympathy. She had unclasped a superb bracelet, gift of royalty, to show him, and was permitting him to refasten it on the delicately rounded arm.

"Gratifying as such notice is, one can only be sure of true hearts at home. John, do you remember the gold linked bracelet you gave me at sixteen? I have it still." Then almost in a whisper, with musing, downcast eyes— "What mistakes we make!"

"Good my lord, will I do?" chimed in a clear voice. Ethel had floated up in her resplendent finery.

"Well done, my beauty," Mr. Raines said, with unfeigned admiration.

A sallow tinge crept into the countess's cheek. Time had been when John Raines had no eyes for any one but herself. Was it possible that she had had her day? She had not anticipated his marrying a mere girl.

"How beautiful! such a trying color, too."

Ethel was almost melted by this ingenuous flattery, then a sharp doubt returned. What right had she to claim Mr. Raines's attention so exclusively?

"As for Prince ——," pursued the countess, resuming the thread of talk, and ignoring Ethel. The latter turned away.

"Are you going?" asked the husband.

"I do not suppose our appreciation is sufficient," said the countess, sweetly, the words conveying an indefinable sting.

Ethel roamed through the large parlors, looking at her reflection in the successive mirrors. The atmosphere was heavy with the perfume of flowers, massed in large vases, screening alcoves, waving in delicate tendrils about pictures, while a mellow light was shed from myriads of wax-candles above. The rooms seemed strangely deserted in that brilliant silence which would soon be disturbed by the hum of voices, the rustling of moving forms, the shimmer of rain-bow colors, the rich folds of velvet and satin, the transparent frost-work of lace. Ethel wished that her husband was with her. She was used to his judgment. She must peep into the library once more. What could they be talking about? The library was vacant, but the cousins were pacing the dimly lighted conservatory beyond. The sight struck Ethel like a blow. She flew up stairs, and confronted Miss Raines.

"What does it all mean? Tell me. You must know."

Miss Raines shrank from the blanched face.

"Can you not hold your own against a sly, spiteful, *passé* belle? You are young, beautiful, and his wife."

"No," said Ethel Hearn, solemnly. "I can not hold my own against a sly woman, because I would scorn to measure weapons with her. What do you all take me for? Let him go. I still have my child."

But the next moment the exquisite dress went down in a heap, and Ethel wailed:

"Oh, mother, mother, where are you?" To be again in the little house by the sea, comforted by those who loved her! Only that!

"I do not deserve this. I have tried to make you happy," said Miss Raines, in an aggrieved tone.

"So you do," assented Ethel, lifting a tear-stained face. "What do you expect of me in return? You must have some motive."

Here were the elder woman's teachings flung back at her. She was aghast. Ethel never used to question motives in her days of poverty.

"Let me hear the truth. I can bear it."

"John loved her many years ago, before she married, and she played with him. I never was able to see much in her. I hoped he had forgotten. She is worthless compared with you. Ethel, do not let her triumph. He has been kind to you, and is really fond of you."

If ever the pride of Ethel Hearn was trampled in the dust, it was when this astounding fact was presented to her. Mr. Raines was quite fond of her, then? He loved the little, sallow woman with a title. But the little woman had not always been sallow, and young men make divinities of shallow goddesses sometimes, aided by the fire of their own imagination, especially when they do not marry the divinity. Thus had Ethel built her house on the sand.

"Did you know that she was coming home?"

"Yes. You would have married him just the same, would you not?"

The girl made no reply. She arose, smoothed her dress, carefully re-arranged every leaf and flower in her hair, sought out a box of Parisian cosmetics, and deliberately tinted her pale cheeks. Miss Raines could not recognize her in this mood. Then Ethel went to the baby's cradle, a soft nest of down, where a tiny, blooming face was hidden among the coverings. She did not stoop to kiss the little sleeper, for fear that she should lose all fortitude.

"Are you ready to go down?" she inquired, calmly.

"Miss Raines, with wrath in her heart, sought the conservatory, and was provokingly obtuse to any perception of being de trop. She found her opportunity.

"If you are going to allow the woman who jilted you for a wreck of a diplomat, to ruin all our happiness, at least save appearances to-night at Ethel's ball; I can not understand it! The worse a woman is hackneyed by a thousand flirtations, the more fascinating she becomes to good men."

"You never did Hortense justice," replied Mr. Raines.

"Justice!" sneered the sister. "Blind yourself to the folly of the hour as you will."

What a stiff old maid Hester was becoming. He must be additionally attentive to their guest to cover this aversion. Mr. Raines had the largest charity for the Countess Guaradini, the spoiled child of wealth, with many caprices and follies, yet really good at heart. She always had dealt to him a subtle flattery, with some sincere affection in much alloy, and Mr. Raines was no more impervious to appreciation than most men. He laughed to scorn his sister's aspersions; his footing was secure. Poor little cousin! she fancied she had done such a brilliant thing, and this was the result, a selfish, unsympathetic husband. Tears had been shed in the conservatory, and there was no remedy now. The ball was a delightful affair, society said, and young Mrs. Raines received well. Society worshiped at the shrine of the countess, erewhile "our Hortense Raines, you know;" but, as far as beauty went, Ethel bore off the palm. Young men, slim, elegant, wearing the inevitable button-hole bouquet, each a counterpart of the other, and all with a faint Parisian flavor, flocked by dozens to her standard. Did she like the opera Thursday night? Would she summer at home or on the Continent? It was slow at our watering-places now. There was a fierce pain in Ethel's heart as she mentally questioned them, "Could you prefer that woman to me?"

The young men voted her "stunning," and she enjoyed the paltry triumph. She was studiously, coldly polite to her husband, no person could have detected a change; even the countess, watching with glistening eyes, found no flaw. But Mr. Raines was aware of a difference. Once he asked, "How have I offended you?" Ethel's heart swelled proudly. "Go away," she entreated. Her gaze had unconsciously alighted on a blonde gentleman making a passage in a leisurely fashion through the crowd, with his wife on his arm. The color glowed vividly in her cheeks, she drew herself erect, strengthened her armor for the interview. It was Captain Lacer, and Ethel had not seen him since her marriage.

Clara Hearn appeared well and happy, while the captain had acquired a wrinkle in his smooth forehead.

"Behold!" said the count to Mr. Raines, rolling up his eyes with such rapture as one would suppose only some delicate gastronomical sensation might have produced. "Such hair! Ah, *ciel!* such a skin, and the expression of a Madonna. My friend, you are indeed blessed."

The count, a great admirer of female beauty, was criticising Ethel. The countess bit her lips, with positive pain, that John Raines could thus forget her.

"Your stepbrother seems to be an old friend. How cordially she welcomes him. Ah, it is such a pleasure for us poor women to be cordially glad to meet a friend after all the mummery."

Forthwith John Raines fell to observing the interview between Captain Lacer and his wife. Aware of this fact, Ethel, possessed by some imp of perversity, sparkled into positive brilliancy.

"If I could only make her angry," murmured the countess to her fan, and the costly lace toy may have been the recipient of many similar secrets.

Mrs. Raines, the elder, greeted Ethel with the slightest possible shade of superciliousness. She wondered at John. Here was the girl who had sung in the choir, elevated above her. Mr. and Mrs. Hearn were late, but who so attentive to their niece?

"How is the darling baby? You must find time to send him around some morning. Can you lunch with us Wednesday? quite an informal family affair." This from Mrs. Hearn, in purple moire and diamonds.

"How is your mother, Ethel? Have you heard recently?" This from Richard Hearn, pink and fresh as ever. And Ethel responded in kind, because it would look strange if she did not. Her heart sickened at her uncle's amiable inquiries. Seldom would the mother's health have awakened solicitude had the daughter not have been Mrs. Raines. Then it darted through her brain like a spasm that she had not heard from home for three weeks, and had not written. The poor mother! The poor little sister! How was she treating them? They had only seen baby once. A cloud of recollections rolled over her soul, obliterating the present scene. She forgot the countess. She forgot her own fancied exaltation. The musicians were playing the same gay waltz which had floated out on the evening air to the listening sisters. She had gained what she then longed for, and how had she used her prosperity? By neglecting the mother and sister of her youth. Yes, slighting them, growing apart, ever so trifling a degree at a time, until her own conscience could measure the chasm. Could heaven or earth have believed that she would be guilty of such wrong? She was Uncle Hearn over again. A great terror of herself pressed on her brain. The remorse was so sudden and keen that she could scarcely endure it. She distinctly beheld a gaunt shape passing among her guests and gazing reproachfully at her out of Peggy's eyes. "If I am spared until to-morrow, I will make reparation," she prayed. Miss Raines touched her arm.

"Do not forget yourself," she whispered, significantly.

All this time Captain Lacer was approaching, greeting friends right and left. His wife saluted her cousin warmly; then Ethel and the captain clasped hands, and exchanged one swift glance of mutual curiosity. The meeting produced complex emotions in both. He was irritated to find Ethel in her present position, yet pleased that she did credit to his own good taste in being able to gracefully fill it. Ethel flushed and sparkled with gratified pride that he did not find her thrust aside and forgotten for a time, then waxed a trifle abstracted, Captain Lacer had so wholly passed out of her life.

"You have resigned your position in the army, then? Have you no dreams of glory as a hero?" inquired Ethel.

"I have no dreams of any kind," he replied, moodily.

Ethel trifled with the buds of her bouquet, and smiled.

"And you? Are you happy? Is existence all that it promised."

She raised her head, and calmly returned his gaze.

"I am perfectly happy, thank you. Far more so than I deserve. What a misanthropical vein for a ball, Captain Lacer!" with a playful change of tone.

"You deserve every blessing," he retorted, bowing low. "Only tell me, as an old friend, should I have retained my post? We can not live but once, you know."

Ethel thought of Nelson and Nicholas on the battle-fields, and the last fragment of regret crumbled into the dust of prosaic reality. Captain Lacer at home!

"Surely you are the best judge," she answered, coldly, slightly elevating her eyebrows.

"I am rejoiced to have found you again. The deuce!"

This remarkable change of tone was due to Ethel's sudden flight into the next room. The wrinkle deepened in Captain Lacer's forehead as he rejoined his wife.

The countess was permitting Cousin John

to fan her in a secluded corner, after the fatigue of doing her duty by her old friends.

"If you could appreciate the relief it is to chat quietly with you, John," she said, softly. Mr. Raines's jesting response was never uttered.

"Take me home. Pray take me home," implored Ethel.

"Have you seen a ghost? Your eyes are quite bloodshot," said the countess, gravely. She had far too much tact to ridicule her cousin's wife just then.

Mr. Raines was touched and alarmed. He took Ethel's hand.

"What has frightened you? Have you bad news?"

"I am sure I must go. How can we get there?"

"To-night, Ethel! You are mad. It is impossible. To-morrow we can go, if you like," said Mr. Raines.

Ethel sighed with relief, but still clung to him. She could not have done better. In her right mind, pride would have kept her at the farthest limit of the room, and, like most efforts of pride, would have been entirely unperceived by her husband. In her fear she sought him, and John-Raines was vain of this proof of confidence in his young wife. The countess sipped her Champagne, and ate her salad with the good digestion a clear conscience is supposed to give. Ethel, seated beside her child, waited for the dawn with sleepless eyes.

Next morning the coupé drove up to the door, and the countess appeared dressed in black, with a heavy lace veil over her face. She was equipped for an early drive; and, while she awaited a companion, a small boy hurried up the steps with an ominous yellow envelope. The countess received it, signed the book, and poised the envelope between her fingers, while these thoughts coursed rapidly through her mind. "I shall not read it, and am therefore ignorant of its importance. No one has seen me receive it except the coachman. If I deliver it, all will be over; if not—" She tore the envelope into bits, and showered it into a tall vase just as Mr. Raines appeared.

"I hope your wife does not object?"

"I shall have time to return before the boat leaves," he replied, evasively. Mr. Raines was ruffled. His sister had flatly rebelled against the course of events; his wife had been a spectator, but one with resolute look and clasped hands. He had promised to take his cousin to the grave of her parents.

"She does it to show her power. The coupé, forsooth!"

"Do not forget that you are a lady, my dear. I have promised."

But Miss Raines found it exceedingly difficult not to forget that she was a lady in these days. Could she not see the mischief brewing? Could she preach patience to Ethel forever, and hope that all her cherished plans would not be frustrated?

"Will you take me to-day?" asked Ethel, almost humbly.

"Without fail," he responded, framing the pale face caressingly between his hands a moment.

He kept his word, and took Countess Hortense to the cemetery, surely on a melancholy errand enough, but he was ill at ease. Hester had never been so unreasonable, and he dreaded rudeness to their guest. At three o'clock nurse stood dandling the baby at the nursery window. The carriage had not returned.

"It will be too late. I do not know how he could be so unkind," burst forth Ethel, tossing aside her hat.

"I will go with you," said Miss Raines, earnestly.

"No; wait!" returned Ethel, with sudden quiet.

Miss Raines went away, nurse was dispatched on an errand. The carriage dashed up, and Mr. Raines assisted his cousin to alight. The count had not yet arisen. Miss Raines met them in the hall.

"Hortense got lost in the by-ways of the cemetery."

"Yes, we were actually going farther away from each other for a long time. It was odd," explained the lady.

"Very," assented Miss Raines, with peculiar emphasis.

"Am I too late? Where is Ethel?" inquired Mr. Raines, with real concern.

Nurse was seated beside the empty cradle wringing her hands and weeping vaguely, after the manner of her class. Ethel and the child were gone. That same morning, Richard Hearn received a letter from his brother, containing this astounding information: "Our debt is paid, principal and interest."

CHAPTER XXXVII

TOO LATE.

CLASPING her baby to her heart, Ethel felt almost happy in her freedom. Last night she was rich, surrounded by friends, to-day a fugitive. Her child was wholly dependent on her to fondle and dress. Ethel gained a new self-reliance and courage from this dignity of motherhood. She must learn to think and act wisely alone. She had no plan for the future; she discarded the bare thought of it. She was going home to make reparation for her past neglect, and no human agency should delay her longer.

A great dread oppressed her, yet urged her on. It was sickening fear in some indefinable shape. If her husband would not accompany her, she must go unattended.

Ethel's anger was very bitter when she thought of his absence, but for the most part her resentment was ingulfed in another anxiety. For the time, she shut out her present life and returned to her girlhood. She had left nothing behind, the baby was her own. The countess could not rob her of that. Thus she retraced her steps, memory busy with every trifle, over the pathway she had hastened along so eagerly a year before.

Innocence slept on her bosom, tenderly guarded, or, waking, gurgled with laughter from rosy lips, and plucked at the mother's golden tresses with daring little fingers.

Press on, Ethel, through the silent night, your impatience urging the lagging movements of the steamboat to rapid progress. Hasten along the beach, the sad music of the waves accompanying your footsteps, familiar Shellport, dim, and ghostly, and chill in the early morning. The little cottage at last meets her eager gaze, and the Rev. Hexham White, with grave demeanor, is coming out the door. Ethel does not dare to question him; the landscape is reeling around her, but she enters the house.

The lower story is deserted; the windows open as if there was no fear of intruders. A large, rough dog, of sagacious aspect, is stationed at the foot of the stairs, and sniffs at Ethel, keeping a doubtful eye on her movements afterward.

Baby, influenced by the mother's silent terror, perhaps, gives a fretful wail; Ethel does not hear it as she ascends the stairway, trembling in every limb. Now she approaches the mother's chamber. There is a sound of suppressed weeping within. The mother lies on her bed; an old man with snowy hair and beard clasps her hand; Nicholas crouches on the ground in an agony of grief, burying his head in the coverlet; the little sister stands where the last recognition of the dying may reach her; Peggy's fingers touch the silvered hair of her mistress with a groping instinct of affection. Ethel pushes aside the old man—she does not know him—and kneels.

" Mother, speak to me, once!"

Does the failing ear catch the words? Do the failing eyes behold the missing daughter? Surely there is a quiver of remembrance, a breath. "At last!" and all was still.

To Ethel her mother is lost, dropped shudderingly into an abyss of the unknown. To Olive that mother has cast the shackles of a wearisome life, cramped within narrow limits so long, and gone before to a glorious heaven. To Ethel the poor mother she has wounded will be hidden away in the fearful grave, a mute reproach forever. To Olive the mother has merely laid that worn, frayed garment, the body, in the sheltering earth, and risen, on angel's pinions, to the presence of the Redeemer.

Nicholas Hearn has lost his tender comforter. And the old man, who has made way for passionate Ethel, gazes at her and at the child without venturing to touch either. Thus has Albert Hearn returned to his family after many years, and his youngest daughter does not recognize him.

Outside the tide is ebbing gently, perhaps bearing a soul out to the golden gates of day, and a gilded arrow of the rising sun, the last of a life, falls on the marble face of the dead.

"When we reach the shore at last,
Who will count the billows past?"

CHAPTER XXXVIII.

CONFESSION.

THE child was asleep in the cradle; the two women conversed in a low tone. If ever they resembled one another, it was now. Both wore black dresses; and Ethel's face, sharpened by the illness of grief, had lost something of its rounded bloom.

Miss Raines held a newspaper, in which the Countess Guaradini was described at a court ball, resplendent in amethyst velvet. The name revived the memory of a mystery.

"Surely sufficient time has elapsed, Hester, and I may know," coaxed Ethel, with unusual animation.

"The telegram was received by Hortense," replied the elder lady. "James saw her take it, and tear it up in a vase afterward. He supposed it was her own. I traced it from the office while you were absent, and found the fragments in the vase. The honor of the telegraph was at stake. Methinks our own family honor was, as well. One must make compromises. The boy was discharged unjustly. I have taken care of his family since. I pieced the bits of paper together on a whole sheet, like the mosaic workers, and showed them to John. That is all."

"It might have made so much difference," said Ethel, with quivering lips. "I do not envy the countess."

Best not, Ethel. Who is worth envying in this world? She went down stairs to her husband's library, and, entering the room, found it untenanted. For a moment she hesitated, then took her place in the window, dropping the lace curtain behind her, to await his return. The flower-clock grew in the semi-darkness, with alternate closed petals and brilliant blossoms expanded to welcome night.

Lessons like that learned by Ethel Hearn at her mother's grave leave an impress on after-years. In her first agony of remorse, she did not believe that a whole lifetime could expiate her sins of omission. She had no anger to expend on her husband when he came to her; she was too much in need of warm, human sympathy. He was very tender and good to her; yet before the cloud wholly passed away a fresh doubt weighed on her mind. They were bound together for life. Why was it more culpable in John Raines not to have unveiled his previous life than for Ethel, his wife, to have once loved Nelson Thorne? Yes, once; for those elements were fading from her existence. Ethel had the gift, blessed in one sense, of forgetfulness. It was painful, even humiliating; but she believed it was her duty to tell her husband all, and now sought him for the purpose. In entire security Mr. Raines entered the library, seated himself, and beheld Ethel emerge from the window. The visit of Countess Hortense had been productive of good; it had swept away the last remnant of softened regret in which her memory had been enshrined.

Ethel paused, with clasped hands and drooping head, a moment, then advanced swiftly to his side. She avoided his kiss of welcome.

"Not yet. I have something to tell you which you should have known sooner. I—I could not bear to speak!"

"A milliner's bill of unusual length? Oh, I am very angry in advance, depend upon it."

"Nothing very serious, you may think," said Ethel, laughing nervously, and trifling with her rings. "Do you remember the day when you found my sister on the beach? No, no; let me kneel beside your chair if I will. It is my proper place, for I am making a confession."

"I remember it very well," replied Mr. Raines, uneasily. "My dear, a woman should never kneel to a man."

"Listen! She had fainted because she then discovered that her lover, Nelson Thorne, was unfaithful. I told you that much on the steamboat, did I not?"

"You certainly did."

"But I did not reveal *all*," pursued Ethel, in a lower tone, hiding her face against the arm of the chair. "I never said that I loved him also."

There was a silence. The blow had fallen, and John Raines received it without comment. No matter how many ideal fancies he might have cherished since boyhood, the shock was severe to find that his wife had ever loved another man. What she should be amounted to a fastidious delicacy in his estimation. He was, by virtue of his masculine fibre, the rough ware, capable of resisting blows; she was the fragile vase that should never be carried to the public fountain. His was the strength and sap of the branch, hers the delicate bloom of the fruit.

"Do you love this man still?"

"No;" raising her face to look at him.

"Who, then?" keeping his eyes steadily averted.

"You."

"When did I succeed him?" with curling lip.

"A long time ago," said Ethel, drearily, with unconscious pathos. "John, do you forgive me?"

"Yes;" reluctantly, and after a pause.

"Will you try to forget what I have said to-night?"

"That is not expected of me," said Mr. Raines, harshly.

"I suppose this is to be my punishment," said Ethel, rising. A moment before she was a penitent child; now she was a dignified woman.

The husband made no effort to detain her. She sought a small dressing-room sacred to herself, and locked the door. On the wall was a picture of Christ crowned with thorns, the splendor of immortality in the far-seeing gaze. Below the picture was a wreath of immortelles fresh from the mother's tomb.

CHAPTER XXXIX.

A NEW YEAR.

"STAND back, little man! It may prove an infernal machine," said Miss Raines, holding up a package which had evidently excited her curiosity.

She addressed her nephew, who had toddled forward to receive a gift when his name was mentioned, and stood regarding her with that irresolute expression on the little face which foreboded tears or smiles.

"Wait until mamma opens it," advised Ethel, re-assuringly.

The parcel was addressed to Francis Raines, and, with some wonder, Ethel proceeded to reveal the contents. A letter, and the sum of five thousand dollars. She read :

"I devoted the first-fruits of my earnings to my nephew, Francis Raines, in payment of a debt contracted long ago. When I was a poor lad, and desired to go to college, I applied to his father, then in Europe, and he responded most generously to my appeal. He knew nothing of my claims to his consideration, yet extended the helping hand which was to mold my whole career. God bless him for it! He has twice refused to receive the sum then expended, but I feel convinced that he will not reject it in this form, as it will render me a free man, besides possessing to me the value of having been self-earned. My uncle, Jared Hearn, was benefited, by a suggestion of mine, in the economy of labor, and has, most unexpectedly, transmitted to me this amount as my share. If my nephew ever needs a friend in early youth, may he find such a one as I did in his father!   NICHOLAS HEARN."

Ethel folded the letter mechanically. Her husband had sent Nicholas to college. Incredible fact, of which she had never dreamed. How good he had been to them!

The little man turned away to his play, disappointed that the gift did not prove a hobbyhorse, and all day his mother pondered on the matter.

Husband and wife were estranged, and Ethel almost repented of her frankness in making the confession. This circumstance of Nelson Thorne had not the importance in the wife's eyes which it possessed to the husband. It was all of the past.

Young Mrs. Raines became, in the estimation of society, very religious. Wherever she went, she was haunted by the remembrance of a wrong. Often, in the quiet night, she seemed to see the moonlight falling on her mother's grave, until the picture dissolved in tears. Miss Raines never alluded to the proud reserve maintained between them.

With the reception of her brother's present, it smote on Ethel's heart that it was the close of the year. What was the future to be? Life was brief at the best. Foolish to spend it quarreling. Ah! the beck is only a step across at first, but it widens as it reaches the sea. A whole year of cold restraint had elapsed. What if one or the other had died? Was the Countess Guaradini responsible for all? How vividly she stood before Ethel, in her mauve draperies, as on the night of the ball—a time which was the beginning of evil that had strengthened into a stern barrier since!

Softer influences stole over her unawares; she could not have fortified her better nature against them if she would. She must make one more effort at reconciliation before yielding to this tacit separation as inevitable. Ethel went slowly to the library door, and paused. It is very hard to break down the obstacle after long silence, and say you are sorry.

"Come in." The master's voice was dis-

couraging. How could she do it? Ethel turned and glided away. Mr. Raines opened the
door and closed it again, with marked emphasis and a discontented sigh, although this last
was inaudible outside.

Ethel sought her chamber, laid her head on
her arms, and wept passionately. What a
wretched waste her life was! And she so richly deserved it all. When her son grew to manhood, he would treat her just as she had be-
haved to her own mother. Measure for measure. Even in the abandon of despair her brain
was busy with expedients. Suddenly she dried
her tears and went to a wardrobe.

John Raines sat at his desk writing. He,
too, had been thinking gloomily of the dawning year, and of his disappointment, for he was
grievously disappointed in his wife. Then the
child—the son who was to succeed him and
keep his name a little longer on the earth—
what glorious dreams he had indulged in concerning the boy! A child can do much, but
can he bridge an ever-widening gulf between
parents? "*Mira que ates, que desates,*" he said,
regretfully.

A light step caused him to turn. There
stood a girl in a plain gown, cloak, and hat,
with veil thrown back, holding a little traveling-bag. It was Ethel Hearn of the steamboat,
when he had rescued and protected her. It
was the girl who had wandered through the
city when mob rule prevailed, and kept up her
courage to the last. It was the wife who had
sung to him in the twilight, the mother of his
child. After all, what had she done? Loved
her sister's lover, and run away from temptation.

Ethel, standing before him as Queen Esther
did in the presence of Ahasuerus, saw him
smile.

"Have you come to visit me in masquer-
ade? Welcome."

"Am I welcome?"

"Assuredly. I am writing—"

"So I perceive. Do not allow me to interrupt;" proudly, and on the verge of freezing
again.

"It is a pleasant interruption. Tell me
why you assumed the dress, and I will read
you what I have written."

"I wear it because I think we both need it
as a reminder," said Ethel, half timidly.

Mr. Raines adjusted his papers, and played
with his pen a moment, before replying:

"Good. I have written with the same motive. Will you oblige me by listening? Pray
remove your hat; it may require a long time."

Instead of resuming his arm-chair, he seated
himself on a sofa, thus seriously endangering
his eye-sight, and motioned Ethel to a place
beside him. She obeyed demurely, while he
read aloud:

"In a Devonshire lane, as I trotted along
T'other day, much in want of a subject for song,
Thinks I to myself, I have hit on a strain—
Sure marriage is much like a Devonshire lane!

"In the first place, 'tis long; and when once you are
   in it,
It holds you on as fast as the cage holds the linnet:
For howe'er rough and dirty the road may be found,
Drive forward you must, since there's no turning
   round.

"But though 'tis so long, it is not very wide,
For two are the most that together can ride;
And even there 'tis a chance but they get in a poth-
   er,
And jostle and cross, and run foul of each other.

"Oft Poverty greets them with mendicant looks,
And Care pushes by them, o'erladen with crooks,
And Strife's grating wheels try between them to
   pass,
Or Stubbornness blocks up the way on her ass."

Here Mr. Raines's disengaged hand strayed
over the boundary of his wife's gown, without
his raising his eyes from the paper. Ethel
dimpled, looked at the hand askance, then slid
her own, warm and clinging, within that sheltering clasp.

"But thinks I too, these banks within which we are
   pent,
With bud, blossom, and berry, are richly besprent;
And the conjugal fence which forbids us to roam,
Looks lovely when decked with the comforts of
   home.

"In the rock's gloomy crevice the bright holly grows,
The ivy waves fresh o'er the withering rose,
And the ever-green love of a virtuous wife
Smooths the roughness of care, cheers the winter
   of life."

A pretty face, merry once more, interposed
between reader and page, and, finding in that
a good excuse, John Raines clasped her in his
arms. The ardor of love dwelt in the soft thrill
of kisses showered on cheek and brow, lingering in the sweet union of lips. Strong, pure
love at last! Ethel's first coherent words were:
"You have been dreadfully ugly; you can
have no idea how disagreeable you have made
yourself."

"So have you," he replied, his fingers wandering caressingly over the waving hair.

"I?" laughed Ethel. "I have been a martyr."

But suddenly her mood changed; her eyes
dimmed; she hid her face on her husband's
shoulder in convulsive weeping; for the chimes
of a neighboring church rang out on the frosty
air their peals of airy music. The bells sang

with their silvery voices, of the happiness coming, yet they also had a sad minor strain of the past, which was gone, and never could be recalled. Mr. Raines thought, as he tenderly soothed her, that he had been a brute to nurse his own wrath so long, and repulse her in her affliction. She would have been a million times better off had she lived with Hester alone instead of marrying him.

Then they opened the window, and stood listening to the chimes. Far above glittered the other worlds, remote, vast, inaccessible; below lay the city, hushed to the quiet of midnight.

"How we play with destiny, and fill up our life measure with petty spites and evils! Sometimes all these works of ours, seemingly so durable, may vanish beneath the waves, and these very bells we hear ring faintly to those in the upper world, even as Iduna murmurs in fathomless depths. Let us look a little higher, my love," said John Raines.

The past rolled away like a scroll, and the night ushered in an undivided future.

The metal, silvery bright, which dances and floats on the water surface, a tiny globe, and the imponderable vapor seek each other through all nature; embrace, and their individuality perishes in the formation of a crystal. May not two souls blend, and, never the same again, form, in union, the crystallization of a better life?

CHAPTER XL.

A SHIP COMES IN.

A RUDDY glow is shed through the little house from the crackling logs on the hearth.

Albert Hearn is asleep in his arm-chair, and the light flickers over his worn face. The little sister is seated opposite, with hands clasped on her knee, gazing at the fire and thinking. On the rug lies a dog of venerable aspect, with gray hair growing on his face, and a care-worn expression. The dog appears to be indulging in reflection, as well as his mistress. One can not but wonder if his reverie leads him down to the south where the old Indian dwelt, and the probability of an alligator having got her by this time.

The little sister is thinking, with a heartache, of the silent chamber up stairs, where she never finds occupation now, but she resolutely checks the falling tears as she looks at the sleeping face opposite. Her father is the charge intrusted to her by the dying mother, and sorely needs tender care.

Albert Hearn is a man wounded in the battle; he has come home too late to atone for the sin of his youth. The death of his wife has left him without courage. The longing of weary years is indeed at last realized. He has returned to his family; the debt of his disgrace is paid. But Albert Hearn shrinks from contact with his former world, as the restored blind avoid the dazzling noonday. · He does not wish to see his brothers; he has never visited the scene of his former life. He can not be induced to leave the little house, except to wander listlessly on the strand or visit his wife's grave. He believes in the fatality of his career's being a total failure, and does not strive to rally. As the youth of Albert Hearn yielded to the stress of a great temptation, so his maturity lacks fortitude in endurance. What is he to do? The tree rudely uprooted, and lying prone on the ground for a season, can not regain its hold in the soil with the elasticity of a slender sapling. He studies his children with interest and affection, yet can never forget that he was no assistance to their growing years—even returns at last a stranger. He has many secret projects for the happiness of his eldest daughter of which she is ignorant. Ethel is the pride of his heart, even as she was in the days of ringlets and pink boots, before trouble came. Ethel is very attentive to her father; surrounds him with many luxuries, the fruit of constant thoughtfulness. She has all the more anxiety to be filial in her respect, from the fact that his first arrival was kept a secret from her, lest Mrs. Raines might consider him a disgrace. Albert Hearn is always delighted to see her, welcomes her husband courteously, but never has or will visit her home in return. Ethel may come to him, but he may never cross her threshold. He takes refuge in any commonplace excuse of being a nervous old man, not fond of society, and Ethel must be satisfied. "Let her take her own stand without me," he reflects.

Nicholas Hearn also dwells at Shellport, and treats his father with careful tenderness; still his train of thought frequently bewilders the parent. The patent adjustable lock has proved a success in a small way. The invention is not exalted, but satisfactory, on the principle of making a better pin-head, a more perfect button, than the rest of mankind. Nicholas has a large, rambling loft, full of heterogeneous materials, half workshop, half laboratory, where he delves early and late. It is doubtful if he will ever be a rich man, for he converts ready money into the solution of fresh problems, and looks ever to the future.

Nicholas has not married; the most skillful match-maker would find in him a dry subject. "The idea! With my brain so full of things," he says, contemptuously, "if the subject is broached. "We have paid our debts, and let us begin the world. Then a shade of sadness steals over the rugged face: "I wish mother could have lived to see my lock accepted, and known something of my project for utilizing the sun's rays."

Perhaps the best friend Nicholas finds, in these days, is Mr. John Raines, who likes nothing better than to spend hours in the dusty work-room, making suggestions, discussing discoveries. Nicholas never visits the great house either; he has no time, he says decisively. The little sister has not that faith in her erratic brother which he actually deserves. He has always seemed so out of place in her small life.

A blooming young woman, much interested in the condition of her back hair, reigns in the kitchen. Where is Peggy? A year before Olive found the old woman, in the act of leaving her room to perform her daily duties, stiffened into the rigidity of paralysis. Chained in every limb, dumb, motionless, Peggy fixed her eyes on the girl with a passionate entreaty. All day Olive tried to fathom the look. She brought her father and Nicholas; the look never swerved from herself. She tried food, drink, reading in the worn Bible—even held up the dearest companion and solace of a lifetime, the snuff-box. The living eyes in the frozen face gathered anger rather than relief. Olive was haunted by the expression. Peggy dumb, and striving to utter a word. Finally she approached the bed. "You wish me to do something. Close your eyes if I guess aright." Even at that grave moment, so oddly do inopportune ideas flash into our minds, Olive could not help thinking of the game of twenty ques-

tions, and the inquiry, "Is it animal, mineral, or vegetable?" Peggy evidently waited, with intense eagerness, for her first suggestion.

"Is it about me?" The eyelids quivered assent.

"To be done for you?"

"Yes."

"About your illness?"

"Yes."

"The doctor? A medicine?"

"No."

"Give you something in this house?"

"Yes;" the eyes brightening hopefully.

"In this room?"

"Yes, yes!"

"Your own property?"

"Yes."

Olive made a tour of the room, touching each article of furniture, and looking at Peggy interrogatively. When she reached a chest of drawers, the eyelids signified that she was to open the upper one. Inside was a box, which Olive brought to the bedside. The box contained a small business card, with the name of "L. Andrews, attorney-at-law, Concord, New Hampshire."

"Am I to keep this?"

"Yes."

"Is that all?"

"No."

"Send for this man? Very well. You must rest now."

And Peggy, listening to the grand words of Job, "I know that my Redeemer liveth," read from the worn Bible, sank into the long rest which knows no waking.

Afterward L. Andrews, attorney-at-law, presented himself to Olive Hearn, in reply to her letter. The prime little man was in possession of Peggy's will, made several years before, in which she left the house beyond the beach to her dear girl, Olive, forever. The much-maligned brother had bequeathed her the money, and she had purchased the home which sheltered the Hearn family so long. This truth was never known until the faithful nurse had gone to her reward.

Olive reflects on these events, sitting by the fire, with her father calmly sleeping opposite, and the dog of large experience between. She is happy in her life, capable of a full, rounded womanhood, without the sharp angularity of peculiarities or the restless aims of ambition. Where is Nelson Thorne, in all the wide universe? She forgave him long ago, and she has become used to thinking Ethel more contented, married as she is. Ethel enjoys much, in her present condition, which might not have been her portion as Nelson's wife. Where is he wandering at the close of this year? She thinks, with a thrill of alarm, that he may be dead, and she would never know. Or he may have home, wife, and children.

The night without is black and cold. Icicles fringe the eaves, and suspend diamonds on every pendent twig of the shrubbery. Snow mantles the earth, and yields reluctantly to the dark waves, which, moaning of tempests abroad, toss their spray high on the shore in congealed masses.

The little sister's ship, through storm and darkness, is coming into port. The fairy craft is fashioned of pearl and gold; gossamer sails are spread, and reflect rainbow hues of joy; the sullen waters are furrowed into a sparkling track of light by the slender prow; a tiny god holds the helm.

Hark! The keel grates on the strand. There are footsteps on the beach at the gate. She rises to her feet, swayed by some powerful impulse; the door-bell rings on her startled, expectant senses; the room circles around.

Albert Hearn opens his eyes in glad surprise; the dog is wagging his tail amicably; and penitent, humbled Nelson, stands on the hearth, with Olive's hand clasped firmly in his own. Even while he returns the father's cordial greeting, he searches the daughter's serene eyes for his answer. She knows what he has come to ask long before he finds an opportunity to speak. The years have brought trouble, sorrow, repentance—above all, need of her.

To the little sister the gift has been so long coming, had seemed a moment before so hopeless of fulfillment, that she turns it on her palm, wondering if it be worth the pain, the tears, the golden expectation. Purified and ennobled, the first love of Nelson Thorne is well worth acceptance. The boon is very sweet to the little sister. Experience Thorne's prayer is answered.

Oublier, c'est le grand secret des natures fortes.

The rajah's chain, dismantled of jewels, lies in the case, having interwoven the lives of the descendants, even as it had originally linked together those of the grandparents. The diamond-brokers might never know, but Joseph the Jew has fulfilled his allotted task.